Mathematics for
Mechanical Technicians

Book 1

With the introduction of the new City and Guilds scheme for Mechanical Engineering Technicians it has become necessary to bring together those essential elements which would other-wise have to be sought from a variety of more comprehensive volumes of mathematics and science. Mr. Page has done this in *Mathematics for Mechanical Technicians* and its companion volume, *Science for Mechanical Technicians*.

The mathematical tools of the science are provided in the five chapters of this present work. The titles of these are: Calculations; Algebra; Graphs; Geometry and Trigonometry; and Mensuration.

Mr Page, Head of the Dept. of Production Engineering at the Polytechnic, Wolverhampton, was a member of the syllabus-drafting panel for the new course, and is the Chief Examiner in Mathematics and Science for examinations conducted for the course by the City and Guilds of London Institute.

Mathematics for Mechanical Technicians

BOOK 1
SI METRIC EDITION

by M. G. PAGE

B.Sc. (Hons.) (Eng.), C. Eng., F.I.Mech.E., F.I.Prod.E., M.B.I.M., F.S.S.

Head of the Department of Production Engineering at The Polytechnic Wolverhampton

CASSELL · LONDON

CASSELL & COMPANY LTD
35 Red Lion Square, London, WC1R 4SG
Sydney, Auckland
Toronto, Johannesburg

First edition September 1963
Second edition November 1964
Third edition June 1965
Fourth (revised) edition October 1970
Fourth edition, second impression July 1971
Fourth edition, third impression February 1972
Fourth edition, fourth impression August 1973

I.S.B.N. 0 304 93579 4

To all those who have contributed,
and are contributing,
to the education of the author

Typeset by Gloucester Typesetting Co. Ltd., Gloucester
and printed in Great Britain by the Camelot Press Ltd.,
London and Southampton

Preface to the Fourth Edition

Since the publication of the first edition of this book, two significant changes have occurred in the course for Mechanical Engineering Technicians. The first is the introduction of metric units, with SI units as a first order of preference. The second is the increasing movement away from part-time courses toward block release and full-time courses, the latter being mainly of the sandwich type. This new edition reflects these changes. It has been rewritten in metric units, with SI units as a first order of preference. It conforms, except for very minor instances as indicated in the text, to recommendations in.

BS 3763: *The International System (SI) Units,*
BS 1957: *The Presentation of Numerical Values,* and
BS 1991: *Letter Symbols, Signs and Abbreviations.*

The trend away from part-time studies has shown that the original decision to publish one volume for the Part I portion of the course was correct. The transfer of students from stages such as T1 to T2 should be placed where it rightly belongs, in the hands of the educational establishment. Part I work is examined at the end of the T2 stage and examiners are not restricted to T1 studies. The breakdown suggested by examining bodies between T1 and T2 is not necessarily the best division, especially with block release and sandwich studies. It is far better to consider the Part I work to be a complete entity, leaving the course arrangement to the educational establishment. If examinations are required at the end of the T1 stage (and with continuous assessment this is becoming less critical), it is preferable for such examinations to be conducted by a college to suit its own particular division of the syllabus.

As experience has been gained since the course was introduced, it is no longer necessary for the author, in his capacity as Chief Examiner in Mathematics and Science for Course 293 of the City and Guilds of London Institute, to give his opinion of the type of question to be expected in examination papers. Consequently, problems now appear at the end of each article instead of each chapter, and their number has been considerably increased. Certain of these problems are metric versions of questions the author has set for the City and Guilds of London Institute, and he wishes to record his appreciation of the kind permission so readily granted by that body to use such questions as bases for the metric ones. Finally, the author wishes to acknowledge the help of his colleagues in producing this improved version of the original publication, and especially of Miss Ann Crick, who rendered valuable assistance in typing the for the metric edition.

M.G.P., Wolverhampton, 1970

Contents

Chapter One

Calculations

1.1 The Presentation of Numerical Values and Units

1.1.1 THE DENARY SYSTEM OF NUMBERS

The number we normally write as 823 is the sum of eight hundreds, two tens and three units. Ten can be indicated as 10^1 and unity as 10^0. Hence:

$$823 = 8(10^2) + 2(10^1) + 3(10^0)$$

The powers of ten are in descending magnitude, and any positive whole number can be written by stating the coefficients of the powers of ten in descending order, terminating with the coefficient of 10^0. For example:

$$82 = 8(10^1) + 2(10^0)$$
and
$$40 = 4(10^1) + 0(10^0)$$
while
$$7 = 7(10^0)$$

A number expressed in the ordinary way, i.e. as 82, 40, 7, etc. is said to be expressed in *denary* form.

If we wish to add on to a positive whole number a positive quantity of less than unity, we can still continue with the powers of ten. The powers now become negative and in denary notation we show the change from whole numbers to a part of a number by a decimal point. As we proceed along a denary number, at the decimal point the power of 10 becomes negative. Thus:

$$75{\cdot}42 = 7(10^1) + 5(10^0) + \text{decimal point} + 4(10^{-1}) + 2(10^{-2})$$

and 75·42 is the sum of seven tens, five units, four tenths and two hundredths.

Let us now consider the significance of a negative sign when it is attached to a numerical value. We have to consider most things with reference to some datum. With geographical heights, a convenient datum is sea-level, as when stating that a particular situation is 450 metres above sea-level. Having fixed a convenient datum, there may be occasions when we require to reckon on the other side of the datum in the opposite direction. The foot of a mine shaft may be 200 metres below sea-level, and we could, if we so wished, ascribe to it the level of −200 metres. In our series of numbers, our arbitrary datum is zero. Most of our quantities are reckoned in excess of zero, and it is convenient to designate them as positive. We could put a positive sign in front, but it is simpler if we agree to recognize that if no sign is given, a positive sign is to be inferred. A negative sign therefore indicates reckoning on the other side of datum, in the opposite direction to the usual one.

Returning to our denary notation, let us recapitulate that we can indicate a fraction by a decimal point and figures. A fraction in this form is commonly termed a *decimal fraction*. On the Continent, a comma is used where we in this country use a decimal point. The continental engineer would indicate 8·456 as 8,456. Unless we were aware of continental practice we would normally regard 8,456 as eight thousand, four hundred and fifty-six. To avoid confusion it is recommended that the comma should not be used when grouping numbers, but that figures should be grouped in threes either side of the decimal point, with a space between each group. For decimal quantities less than unity, a cypher (i.e., a nought or a zero) should precede the decimal point. As examples:

$$
\begin{array}{rcl}
87\ 604 & \text{and not} & 87,604 \\
5\ 732 & ,, \quad ,, & 5,732 \\
0\cdot5 & ,, \quad ,, & \cdot5 \\
0\cdot007\ 173 & ,, \quad ,, & \cdot007173
\end{array}
$$

In the denary system, numbers are expressed as powers of 10, 10 being known as the *base* of the denary system. It is interesting to note that we can invent other series of numbers by changing the base. If the base is 2, we have what is known as a *binary* system. Returning to our denary number 823, we note:

$$823 = 1(2^9) + 1(2^8) + 0(2^7) + 0(2^6) + 1(2^5) + 1(2^4)$$
$$+ 0(2^3) + 1(2^2) + 1(2^1) + 1(2^0)$$

and the denary number 823 can be expressed as 1100110111 as a binary number. We can see that it takes a lot of figures (*digits* is the mathematical term) to indicate a number of quite small magnitude. On the other hand, the digits are either zeros or ones. We might speculate that if man had evolved with two digits on each hand, our system of counting might well have taken the form of binary numbers.

1.1.2 NUMBERS IN STANDARD FORM

Any positive number can be expressed as a product of:

(*a*) a coefficient, which is unity or greater, but is less than 10;
(*b*) 10 raised to an appropriate power.

A number quoted in this manner is said to be expressed in *standard form*. The coefficient is determined by moving the decimal point to leave a number which is unity or greater, but is less than ten. Thus for 0·004 16 we move the decimal point three places to the right to obtain 4·16. For the number 31 764 we move the decimal point (not indicated, but implied after the figure 4) four places to the left to obtain 3·176 4. The power of 10 is determined by the number of places we move the decimal point. Its arithmetical sign depends upon whether the decimal point is moved to the left or to the right. If it is moved to the left, the sign is positive. If it is moved to the right, the sign is negative. For example:

$$4\,765\cdot4 = 4\cdot765\,4 \times 10^3$$
(decimal point moved three places to the left)
$$0\cdot071\,3 = 7\cdot13 \times 10^{-2}$$
(decimal point moved two places to the right)

For reasons which will be apparent as our studies develop, we shall find that on many occasions our working can be eased by using only certain powers of 10. We call this usage *preferred standard form* because we prefer to use it instead of other available methods. When numbers are expressed in preferred standard form, we use only those powers of 10 which conform to the pattern of $10^{\pm 3n}$, where n is a whole number. We also find it convenient for the multiplier of our power of 10 to range from 0·1 to 1 000.

Let us take, for instance, the number 101 325. In standard form it is:

$$1\cdot013\,25 \times 10^5$$

because the implied decimal point was moved five places to the left. In preferred standard form, the number is either:

$$101\cdot325 \times 10^3 \quad\text{or}\quad 0\cdot101\,325 \times 10^6$$

We must emphasize that preferred standard form can, on certain occasions, be unrealistic. With areas, powers of 10 restricted to $10^{\pm 2n}$ will be found far more logical. When we go on to consider units, we shall see the delightful connection between grouping our digits in groups of three and the preferred standard form of numbers.

Symbolically:

$$(a \times x^m) \times (b \times x^n) = (a \times b)(x^{m+n})$$

and

$$(a \times x^m) \div (b \times x^n) = \left(\frac{a}{b}\right)(x^{m-n})$$

Example

Give the exact values of the following:

(a) $0{\cdot}000\,461 \times 1{\cdot}2 \times 10^3$
(b) $0{\cdot}006\,858 \div 9 \times 10^{-4}$

(a)

$$0{\cdot}000\,461 = 4{\cdot}61 \times 10^{-4}$$

$$\begin{aligned}
0{\cdot}000\,461 \times 1{\cdot}2 \times 10^3 &= (4{\cdot}61 \times 10^{-4})(1{\cdot}2 \times 10^3) \\
&= (4{\cdot}61 \times 1{\cdot}2)(10^{-4} \times 10^3) \\
&= (5{\cdot}532)(10^{-4+3}) \\
&= 5{\cdot}532 \times 10^{-1} \\
&= 0{\cdot}553\,2
\end{aligned}$$

(b)

$$0{\cdot}006\,858 = 6{\cdot}858 \times 10^{-3}$$

$$\begin{aligned}
0{\cdot}006\,858 \div 9 \times 10^{-4} &= \frac{6{\cdot}858 \times 10^{-3}}{9 \times 10^{-4}} \\
&= \frac{6{\cdot}858}{9} \times 10^{\{-3-(-4)\}} \\
&= 0{\cdot}762 \times 10^{\{-3+4\}} \\
&= 0{\cdot}762 \times 10^1 \\
&= 7{\cdot}62
\end{aligned}$$

Answers: (a) $0{\cdot}553\,2$
(b) $7{\cdot}62$

The reader should note carefully the manner in which minus 4 was subtracted from minus 3. He may be accustomed to the rule which says, 'To subtract, change the sign and add.' The above example is used to introduce the use of differently shaped brackets; it should be observed that the 'inner bracket' is operated upon first.

1.1.3. METRIC UNITS

A *denary* (sometimes called 'decimal') system of numbers should not be confused with a so-called metric system. A *metric* system is a system of dimensions, not numbers, associated with the metre as a measurement of length. In engineering we are concerned not only with magnitude, but also with what that magnitude describes, i.e. its *unit*. There is a considerable difference between 3 millimetres and 3 metres. The unit of a quantity has just as much importance as the number.

The fundamental units of engineering are those of length, mass and time. If we use as basic units the metre, the kilogramme and the second, we have a metric system of units. If we use the centimetre, the gramme and the second as our basic units, we can form a different metric system of units. Of all the metric systems which are available or could be formed, it has been internationally agreed that the preferred system will be the Système International des Unités, or *SI system of units*. In the SI system, the fundamental units of length, mass and time are the metre, the kilogramme and the second respectively. As our scientific knowledge extends, we may conveniently add to what we can call the three primary fundamental units certain supplementary secondary fundamental units. At present there are three: the ampere for electricity, the candela for light, and the kelvin for heat. Others may be added in the future. Just out of interest, the degree celsius can be regarded as a unit 'associated with the SI system'.

Although the basic SI unit of length is the metre, it is absurd to presume that all lengths must be expressed in metres. Similarly, it would be completely unrealistic to express a person's age in seconds. Common sense dictates that we shall use multiples and sub-multiples of our basic units. It is extremely convenient to associate a denary system of numbers with a metric system of units, and an elegant way of doing this is to use a prefix with the basic unit to indicate the multiplier of that unit. The reader is probably aware of the prefixes kilo (meaning one thousand) and milli (meaning one thousandth) in such units as a kilogramme and a millimetre. A list of multipliers is given in the following table:

Multiplier	Standard form	Name	Symbol
Million million	10^{12}	tera	T
Thousand million	10^{9}	giga	G
Million	10^{6}	mega	M
Thousand	10^{3}	kilo	k
Hundred	10^{2}	hecto	h
Ten	10^{1}	deca	da
Tenth	10^{-1}	deci	d
Hundredth	10^{-2}	centi	c
Thousandth	10^{-3}	milli	m
Millionth	10^{-6}	micro	μ
Thousand millionth	10^{-9}	nano	n
Million millionth	10^{-12}	pico	p
Thousand million millionth	10^{-15}	femto	f
Million million millionth	10^{-18}	atto	a

It will be observed that there are only four multipliers which do not conform to preferred standard form; these are hecto, deca, deci and centi. While it can be expected that they will be used somewhat less frequently than the others, to presume they will be completely eliminated is erroneous. The attitude that the centimetre is not a recommended SI unit and should never be used is taking purity to a ridiculous extreme. We must use those units which are suitable for a particular situation.

Just as our conventional method of indicating the number twenty-five thousand four hundred and fifty-three is

$$25\ 453 \qquad \text{in denary form,}$$
$$2{\cdot}545\ 3 \times 10^4 \text{ in standard form, and}$$
$$25{\cdot}453 \times 10^3 \text{ in preferred standard form,}$$

so we can adopt a similar convention with the presentation of units by using abbreviations. The conventions recommended by BS 1991 are our first order of preference, but if an abbreviation could lead to misinterpretation, the unit should be written out in full. The basic derived SI unit of capacity is the cubic metre. A far more practical unit is one thousandth of a cubic metre, which is a cubic decimetre. This particular unit is familiarly known all over the world as the *litre*. The litre is not an SI unit, but to presume it will not be a commonly used unit of capacity is closing one's eyes to reality. It is unfortunate that the recommended abbreviation for litre is the small letter 'el', and since this could easily be confused with the number representing unity, on occasions the unit may have to be written out in full. *Through out this book, to avoid confusion with unity, the small 'el' will not be used as a symbol or an abbreviation.* In abbreviations, any prefix used as a multiplier adjoins the unit without a space between them, and the abbreviation is the same for the singular and plural. For example:

$$\begin{array}{llll}
5 \text{ kilometres} & \text{is abbreviated to} & 5 \text{ km} \\
36 \text{ millimetres} & ,, & ,, & ,, \ 36 \text{ mm} \\
53 \text{ microseconds} & ,, & ,, & ,, \ 53 \ \mu\text{s}
\end{array}$$

Multiplication and division of units follow the normal rules of algebra, except that we use a small but distinct space (not a hyphen) when units are multiplied, whilst for convenience in typesetting, division may be indicated by an oblique stroke. Thus:

$$5 \text{ m} \times 5 \text{ m} \times 2 \text{ m} = 50 \text{ m}^3$$
$$25 \text{ kg} \times 3 \text{ s} = 75 \text{ kg s}$$
$$6 \text{ km} \div 5 \text{ s} = \frac{6 \text{ km}}{5 \text{ s}} = 1{\cdot}2 \ \frac{\text{km}}{\text{s}} = 1{\cdot}2 \text{ km/s}$$

Presentation of units is given more detailed consideration in the companion volume *Science for Mechanical Technicians*, Book 1, to which the reader is referred. At this point it should be emphasized that while a multiplier should ideally be used in the numerator rather than the denominator, to adhere strictly to such a rule is, on certain occasions, unwarranted. For instance, although $5 \text{ MN/m}^2 = 5 \text{ N/mm}^2$ and the first presentation is normally preferred, to say that the second presentation must never be used is again taking purity too far. This will soon become obvious when dealing with stresses and deformations.

The SI system must be applied with common sense rather than used blindly in any circumstances. Recommendations and preferences mean only what they say. If they can be used naturally, they are the logical first choice. The intelligent person will depart from them when good and sufficient reasons prevail.

1.1.4 SIGNIFICANCE OF NUMBERS, DECIMAL PLACES AND ROUNDING OFF

Let us suppose that a coil of copper wire in a factory had to be lifted by a crane, and that the cranes available had lifting capacities of 100 kg, 500 kg and 1 000 kg. To ensure safety, the coil was weighed, and the weighbridge operator said it was 'between six and seven hundred kilogrammes'. This information is sufficient to decide which of the cranes to use: it would be dangerous to use either of the two cranes of lowest capacity. If someone now came along to decide the monetary value of the coil of copper wire, the difference in the value of 600 and 700 kilogrammes of copper would be quite appreciable. He would probably ask for the weight to be given to the nearest kilogramme. Depending upon the use to which information is put, different circumstances require different degrees of accuracy, or *significance*.

Note: To the purist, the previous statements are probably disturbing. He will aver that weight is a force, and the unit of force is the newton, not the kilogramme. Of course he is right. What the weighbridge operator has quoted is a mass. Nevertheless, everyday non-technical usage will still refer to 'weights' in kilogrammes instead of newtons, and the introduction of SI units will not immediately lead to changes. Let us exercise a little sympathetic patience.

For the purpose of mathematics, the number of significant figures is the number of figures obtained by counting rightward from the leftmost non-zero figure inclusive. The position of a decimal point is not considered when determining the number of significant figures.

Thus:

> 72 has two significant figures
> 72·0 ,, three ,, ,,
> 0·7 ,, one significant figure
> 0·005 7 ,, two significant figures
> 0·001 070 ,, four ,, ,,
> 1·005 ,, four ,, ,,

It should be carefully noted that only the zeros prior to the first non-zero figure are discarded. Any zeros after the first non-zero figure must be included.

The number of decimal places is the number of places traversed rightward in moving from the decimal point to immediately beyond the last figure. Thus:

> 5·7 has one decimal place
> 5·75 ,, two decimal places
> 5·70 ,, two ,, ,,
> 0·005 85 ,, five ,, ,,
> 0·005 850 ,, six ,, ,,

The number of decimal places is no real indication of accuracy. However many decimal places are used, the answer obtained in the form of a decimal fraction for the value of $2 \div 7$ will never be as accurate as the vulgar fraction $\frac{2}{7}$. Consequently, a student should never be afraid of expressing an answer in the form of a vulgar fraction. It can often be more accurate than one using a multiplicity of decimal places. Degrees of accuracy are indicated by significant figures, not by places of decimals. Answers are sometimes requested to a particular number of decimal places for convenience, not as a general indication of accuracy.

The answer to any problem should be given to an appropriate number of significant figures. The items which are considered when deciding on appropriate number of significant figures are:

(*a*) the degree of accuracy of the data supplied;
(*b*) the accuracy of the processing method;
(*c*) the use to which the answer is to be put.

The reader cannot be given any real guidance, since all these considerations may not be known. An answer should be given precisely if possible. Furthermore, no more significant figures should be used than is necessary. If the answer to a question is *exactly* 37, the answer should be given as 37 and not 37·0 or 37·00.

If the degree of accuracy of the data supplied and the use to which the answer is put are not known, the remaining consideration is the accuracy of the processing method. A good principle to adopt is to carry out all processes as accurately as the tools allow, and only to make an approximation as the final step. For a considerable proportion of the calculations made at our present stage of studies, we use four-figure tables. We shall see in a little while that the last figure is suspect, and consequently *if four-figure tables are used, as a final step we should always round off the answer to three significant figures.* As a general guide:

(a) An answer should be quoted accurately if possible.
(b) If four-figure tables have been used the answer should be finally expressed to three significant figures.

As this juncture, it is appropriate to consider that very important quantity which we indicate by π. This quantity cannot be expressed precisely, either as a decimal or as a vulgar fraction. If we take π as $\frac{22}{7}$, the proportionate error is about one part in 2 500. If we take π as 3·142, the proportionate error is about one part in 7 500. For the accuracy required in problems at our present stage of studies, if we are not instructed specifically to the contrary and have a free choice, there is no valid objection to the use of the very simple approximation $\frac{22}{7}$, provided that we express a final answer in vulgar fractional form or to no more than three significant figures.

Our working may produce an answer to more than three significant figures, and to present our final result we have to round off to three significant figures. The rounding off should be accomplished in a single step, never one step at a time. We should choose whichever rounding off is the nearer, up or down. In most cases this is self-evident.

Example

Round off to three significant figures:

(a) 7·857　　(b) 0·017 62
(c) 234 565　　(d) 0·018 437

(a) 7·857 is nearer to 7·86 than it is to 7·85.
(b) 0·017 62 is nearer to 0·017 6 than it is to 0·017 7.
(c) 234 565 is nearer to 235 000 than it is to 234 000.
(d) 0·018 437 is nearer to 0·018 4 than it is to 0·018 5.

Answers: (a) 7·86　　(b) 0·017 6
(c) 235 000　　(d) 0·018 4

In certain cases, the value may fall midway, and rounding off could be in either direction. Suppose we had to round off 7·45 to two significant figures. 7·45 is just as near to 7·4 as it is to 7·5. In such cases, we round off to the even value. 7·45 rounded off to two significant figures is the even value of 7·4 and not the odd value of 7·5. By similar reasoning, 7·55 to two significant figures is 7·6. This rule (which is included in BS 1957) may seem peculiar to a student who has previously been instructed, 'If the last figure is 5, round it upwards'.

If we use the rounding off rule recommended by BS 1957, as many mid-values are rounded up as are rounded down, so that when we total rounded off values we do not introduce a significant amount of bias. Rounding by rule:

$$0·25 \text{ to one significant figure is } 0·2$$
$$0·435 \text{ ,, two significant figures ,, } 0·44$$
$$7·355 \text{ ,, three ,, ,, ,, } 7·36$$
$$7·245 \text{ ,, three ,, ,, ,, } 7·24$$

The procedure of rounding off a value to a lower number of significant figures is:

(*a*) Perform the rounding off in a single step.
(*b*) Round off to the nearer value, but if the number is midway, round off to the even value.

Problems 1.1

1. Express the following quantities in standard form, by quoting the product of a coefficient and ten raised to an appropriate power:

(*a*) 4 632   (*b*) One thousand
(*c*) 0·762   (*d*) 0·800
(*e*) Minus one-half   (*f*) Thirty million
(*g*) Five and a half thousandths

2. Express the following standard numbers in denary form:

(*a*) $6·4 \times 10^{-3}$ (*b*) $8·431 \times 10^{2}$
(*c*) 8×10^{-2} (*d*) $3·146 \times 10^{-1}$
(*e*) $3·474 \times 10^{4}$ (*f*) $1·87 \times 10^{-4}$

3. Without the use of mathematical tables, give the exact values of the following, expressing answers both in standard and denary form:

(*a*) $(4·2 \times 10^{2}) \times (1·3 \times 10^{2})$
(*b*) $(45 \times 10^{5}) \div (9 \times 10^{3})$

    (*c*) 0·000 082 3 × (1·1 × 10⁵)
    (*d*) 8 263·5 ÷ (7 × 10⁴)
    (*e*) (3 × 10⁷) ÷ (8 × 10⁸)

4. How many significant figures has each of the following?
    (*a*) 437   (*b*) 45·42   (*c*) 1·730
    (*d*) 45·054 00   (*e*) 23·700   (*f*) 0·5
    (*g*) 0·050   (*h*) 0·007 010   (*j*) 0·007 01

5. How many places of decimals has each of the following?
    (*a*) 6·02   (*b*) 10·030   (*c*) 0·03
    (*d*) 0·007 04   (*e*) 500·007 040   (*f*) 200·5

6. Using the recommendations of BS 1957, round off the following values to three significant figures:
    (*a*) 437·4   (*b*) 5 376·41   (*c*) 9·235
    (*d*) 9·225   (*e*) 53·94 × 10⁴   (*f*) 0·004 125

7. How many millimetres are there in a kilometre? Give the answer in both standard and denary form.

8. What number, in standard form, can replace the multiplier milli/micro?

Answers to Problems 1.1

1. (*a*) 4·632 × 10³   (*b*) 1 × 10³ (or 10³)
    (*c*) 7·62 × 10⁻¹   (*d*) 8·00 × 10⁻¹
    (*e*) −5 × 10⁻¹   (*f*) 3 × 10⁷
    (*g*) 5·5 × 10⁻³

2. (*a*) 0·006 4   (*b*) 843·1
    (*c*) 0·08   (*d*) 0·314 6
    (*e*) 34 740   (*f*) 0·000 187

3. (*a*) 5·46 × 10⁴ = 54 600
    (*b*) 5 × 10² = 500
    (*c*) 9·053 × 10⁰ = 9·053
    (*d*) 1·180 5 × 10⁻¹ = 0·118 05
    (*e*) 3·75 × 10⁻² = 0·037 5

4. (*a*) 3   (*b*) 4   (*c*) 4
   (*d*) 7   (*e*) 5   (*f*) 1
   (*g*) 2   (*h*) 4   (*j*) 3

5. (*a*) 2   (*b*) 3   (*c*) 2
   (*d*) 5   (*e*) 6   (*f*) 1

6. (*a*) 437   (*b*) 5 380   (*c*) 9·24
   (*d*) 9·22   (*e*) 53·9 × 10⁴   (*f*) 0·004 12

7. $10^6 = 1\,000\,000$

8. 10^3

1.2 Logarithms

1.2.1 LOGARITHMS IN GENERAL

Numbers can be indicated in various forms. The number which in usual practice is written as 8 000 (the denary form) can also be written as:

$$8 \times 10^3 \quad \text{or} \quad 20^3 \quad \text{or} \quad 10^{3·903\ 1}$$

The first number is written in standard form, while the latter two are written in *indicial forms*. Using symbolic notation, the general case of a number in indicial form is that:

$$N = b^x$$

If two of the values of *N*, *b* and *x* are known, the third is automatically fixed. We say that *x* is the logarithm of *N* to the base *b*. *The logarithm of a number to a given base is therefore the power to which the base has to be raised to give that number.* The word logarithm is conveniently abbreviated to 'log', and the base is indicated in the following manner:

If $N = b^x$
then $\log_b N = x$

As examples:
since $8 = 2^3,$ $\log_2 8 = 3$
similarly $25 = 5^2,$ $\log_5 25 = 2$
                  $4 = 16^{\frac{1}{2}},$ $\log_{16} 4 = 0·5$
and finally $0·1 = 10^{-1},$ $\log_{10} 0·1 = -1$

Logarithms with a base of 10 are the most commonly used and are referred to as *common logarithms*. If the base is 10, it is not usual to indicate the base. For instance, since $1\,000 = 10^3$ we simply write $\log 1\,000 = 3$. The base is only indicated if it is a base other than 10.

The rules for logarithmic computation follow from the rules for indices.

Let M and N be two numbers and b be the base of their logarithms, so that $M = b^x$ and $N = b^y$; then $\log_b M = x$ and $\log_b N = y$.

(a) Multiplication
$$MN = b^x \times b^y = b^{x+y}$$
hence
$$\log_b MN = x + y$$
$$\log_b MN = \log_b M + \log_b N$$
and generally
$$\log MN = \log M + \log N$$

(b) Division
$$\frac{M}{N} = \frac{b^x}{b^y} = b^{x-y}$$
hence
$$\log_b \frac{M}{N} = x - y$$

$$\log_b \frac{M}{N} = \log_b M - \log_b N$$

and generally
$$\log \frac{M}{N} = \log M - \log N$$

(c) Powers
$$M^n = (b^x)^n = b^{nx}$$
hence
$$\log_b M^n = nx$$
$$\log_b M^n = n \log_b M$$
and generally
$$\log M^n = n \log M$$

(d) Roots
$$\sqrt[n]{M} = \sqrt[n]{b^x} = b^{x/n}$$
hence
$$\log_b \sqrt[n]{M} = \frac{x}{n}$$

$$\log_b \sqrt[n]{M} = \frac{\log_b M}{n}$$

and generally
$$\log \sqrt[n]{M} = \frac{\log M}{n}$$

Example

If log $x = a$, write down the expressions for:

(i) log $(10x)$;   (ii) log $\left(\dfrac{x}{10}\right)$;   (iii) log (x^2);

(iv) log $(1\ 000x)$

assuming all logarithms are to the base 10.   (C.G.L.I.)

Answers: (i) $1 + a$ (ii) $a - 1$
                  (iii) $2a$ (iv) $3 + a$

Note: The problem said 'write down' the answers, and this means what it says. The examiner expects no working, but to show how the answers were obtained, the following are the thought processes which resulted in the answers.

$$\log 10x = \log (10 \times x) = \log 10^1 + \log x = 1 + a$$
$$\log \frac{x}{10} = \log x - \log 10^1 = a - 1$$
$$\log x^2 = 2 \log x = 2a$$
$$\log 1\ 000x = \log (1\ 000 \times x) = \log 1\ 000 + \log x$$
$$= \log 10^3 + \log x = 3 + a$$

Example

If log $(xy) = a + b$ and log $x = a$, explain why log y $= b$. Find in terms of a and b:

(i) log $\left(\dfrac{x}{y}\right)$;   (ii) log (x^2);   (iii) log (xy^2);

(iv) log $\sqrt{xy}$ (C.G.L.I.)

The log of a product is the sum of the separate logs.
Hence $\log (xy) = \log x + \log y$
We are told $\log (xy) = a + b$
                         $\therefore \log x + \log y = a + b$
and since $\log x = a$
by subtracting these equations $\log y = b$

(i) $\log \dfrac{x}{y} = \log x - \log y = a - b$

(ii) $\log x^2 = 2 \log x = 2a$

(iii) $\log xy^2 = \log x + \log y^2 = \log x + 2 \log y$
              $= a + 2b$

(iv) $\log (\sqrt{xy}) = \dfrac{\log x + \log y}{2} = \dfrac{a + b}{2}$

Answers: (i) $a - b$ (iv) $\dfrac{a + b}{2}$
        (ii) $2a$
        (iii) $a + 2b$

1.2.2. LOGARITHM TABLES

If formal arithmetic were used, the calculations necessary to obtain a single value for:

$$\frac{453 \cdot 7 \times 10 \cdot 14^2}{(\sqrt[3]{141}) \times 0 \cdot 08}$$

would be extremely tedious. If, however, we recall the rules for logarithmic computation from the previous article, the log of the answer to the above problem would be:

$$\{\log 453 \cdot 7 + 2(\log 10 \cdot 14)\} - \left(\frac{\log 141}{3} + \log 0 \cdot 08\right)$$

If we can find the log of any number, and also a number corresponding to a log, then the tedious processes of multiplication, division, the determination of powers and the extraction of roots can be replaced by simple addition and subtraction together with multiplication and division by very simple numbers.

We know that we can express any number in standard form by stating a coefficient between unity and ten, together with 10 raised to a power. For revision:

$$65 = 6 \cdot 5 \times 10^1$$
$$6\,500 = 6 \cdot 5 \times 10^3$$
$$0 \cdot 065 = 6 \cdot 5 \times 10^{-2}$$
$$0 \cdot 000\,065 = 6 \cdot 5 \times 10^{-5}$$

Applying the rules of logarithms, and using common logarithms (i.e. logs to the base 10):

$\log 10^1 = 1$, $\log 10^3 = 3$, $\log 10^{-2} = -2$ and $\log 10^{-5} = -5$
and since $\log (ab) = \log a + \log b$
then $\log 65 = (\log 6 \cdot 5) + 1$
                $\log 6\,500 = (\log 6 \cdot 5) + 3$
                $\log 0 \cdot 065 = (\log 6 \cdot 5) - 2$
        $\log 0 \cdot 000\,065 = (\log 6 \cdot 5) - 5$

Hence the common logarithm of any number which consists of 65 followed by zeros, or 65 preceded by a decimal point and zeros, can be determined if we can find the common logarithm of 6·5. It follows that we can find the common logarithm of any positive number, no matter how large or how small, if we can find the common logarithm of any number between unity and 10. (The common logarithm of unity is zero.) It is for this reason that common logarithms are so convenient. In future we shall not use the full expression 'common logarithm' but the conventional abbreviation 'log'.

With the aid of a series it is possible to calculate the log of any number between 1 and 10. This has been done for us, and the information has been collected in tables. Many tables of logs have been published. Those recommended by the author for use in the initial studies of technician mathematics are *Four-figure Mathematical Tables* by Frank Castle, published by Macmillan. The title should be carefully noted, as Mr Castle has compiled several books of mathematical tables. As the title indicates, the values are given to a significance of four figures. The last figure is therefore suspect, particularly if several values are added and/or subtracted. In general, the use of four-figure tables produces reliable answers to three significant figures. If a greater degree of accuracy is required, tables with more than four figures should be used. In engineering manufacture, the accurate location of holes often necessitates the use of seven-figure tables. For the degree of accuracy we require at present, four-figure tables will suffice. Castle's *Four-figure Mathematical Tables* are recommended because, in addition to tables of logs, they contain many other tables which we shall eventually find extremely useful.

The reader should now open the tables at the pages headed 'logarithms'. He will observe that there are no decimal points, since all we need from the tables are significant figures. The first two significant figures of the number whose log is required are given in the extreme left-hand column. There are ten columns of four-figure numbers corresponding to the third significant figure of the number, and finally nine vertical columns of small additions for the fourth significant figure of the number. The tables produce the decimal portion of a logarithm; since the logs of numbers between unity and ten lie between zero and unity, and noting that a decimal point is implied previous to every set of four figures:

$$\log 3{\cdot}000 = 0{\cdot}477\ 1$$
$$\log 3{\cdot}100 = 0{\cdot}491\ 4$$
$$\log 3{\cdot}170 = 0{\cdot}501\ 1$$
$$\log 3{\cdot}174 = 0{\cdot}501\ 7 \text{ (obtained from } 5\ 011 + 6)$$

This decimal portion is called the *mantissa* of the log, and since the log of any number between unity and ten lies between zero and unity, *the mantissa is always positive*.

16

Using our rules for logarithmic computation, and the mantissas given above:

$$\begin{aligned}
\log 30 &= \log(3 \times 10) &&= \log 3 + \log 10 \\
&= 0{\cdot}477\,1 + 1 &&= 1{\cdot}477\,1
\end{aligned}$$

$$\begin{aligned}
\log 3\,100 &= \log(3{\cdot}1 \times 10^3) &&= \log 3{\cdot}1 + \log 10^3 \\
&= 0{\cdot}491\,4 + 3 &&= 3{\cdot}491\,4
\end{aligned}$$

$$\begin{aligned}
\log 317 &= \log(3{\cdot}17 \times 10^2) &&= \log 3{\cdot}17 + \log 10^2 \\
&= 0{\cdot}501\,1 + 2 &&= 2{\cdot}501\,1
\end{aligned}$$

$$\begin{aligned}
\log 31{\cdot}74 &= \log(3{\cdot}174 \times 10) &&= \log 3{\cdot}174 + \log 10 \\
&= 0{\cdot}501\,7 + 1 &&= 1{\cdot}501\,7
\end{aligned}$$

Suppose we had to obtain $\log 0{\cdot}03$:

$$\log 0{\cdot}03 = \log(3 \div 100) = \log 3 - \log 100 = 0{\cdot}477\,1 - 2$$

We will now pause a moment and remember that the mantissa is positive. The whole number portion of a logarithm is called the *characteristic*, and here we have the combination of a negative characteristic and a positive mantissa. *We show that only the characteristic is negative by placing the negative sign above the characteristic*, referring to it as a bar, $\bar{2}$ being read as 'bar two'. Thus:

$$\log 0{\cdot}03 = \bar{2}{\cdot}477\,1, \text{ implying } -2 + 0{\cdot}477\,1$$

similarly:

$$\begin{aligned}
\log 0{\cdot}003\,17 &= \log(3{\cdot}17 \times 10^{-3}) = \log 3{\cdot}17 + \log 10^{-3} \\
&= 0{\cdot}501\,1 + (-3) = \bar{3}{\cdot}501\,1
\end{aligned}$$

The characteristic of a log is the power of 10 when the number is expressed in standard form. It is the number of decimal places we have to traverse to produce a number between unity and ten. If we move to the right it is negative, while if we move to the left it is positive. If we try this out we shall find the following simple methods of determining characteristics:

(a) If the number is greater than unity, the characteristic is positive and one less than the number of figures to the left of the decimal point.

(b) If the number lies between unity and zero, the characteristic is negative and one more than the number of zeros immediately after the decimal point.

Hence   the characteristic for $3{\cdot}142$ is 0

        ,, $31{\cdot}42$,, 1

        ,, $0{\cdot}031\,42$,, $\bar{2}$

        ,, $0{\cdot}314\,2$,, $\bar{1}$

        ,, $0{\cdot}000\,314\,2$,, $\bar{4}$

The logs of 3·142, 31·42, 0·031 42, etc. all have the same positive mantissa of 0·497 2.

If the first two significant figures of the number lie between 10 and 20, the differences in the final columns of log tables are appreciable. In order to obtain as accurate a mantissa as possible, we use two different sets of small differences for the last significant figure. The set we use depends upon whether the line of four figures in the log tables is the upper row or the lower row. For example:

$$\log 1·236 = 0·092\ 0 \text{ (obtained from } 0899 + 21)$$
but $$\quad\log 1·276 = 0·105\ 8 \text{ (obtained from } 1038 + 20)$$

If we require to find the log of a number which has more than four significant figures, it would be most unwise to jump to the conclusion that we should round off the number to four figures and then look up its logarithm. We should work as accurately as the tables allow, and our procedure should be decided by the steps in the small differences columns. For example:

$$\log 3·095 = 0·490\ 7$$
and $$\quad\log 3·096 = 0·490\ 9$$

in which case log 3·095 5 could be reasoned as 0·490 8.

Our best course is to find the logs of the nearset four significant figures above and below and allocate the mantissa by proportion.

Example

Find log 904·457.
The characteristic is 2:

$$\log 904·5 = 2·956\ 4$$
$$\log 904·4 = 2·956\ 4$$

Hence, since the logs are the same:

$$\log 904·457 = 2·956\ 4$$

Example

Find log 14·733 2.
The characteristic is 1:

$$\log 14·74 = 1·168\ 5$$
$$\log 14·73 = 1·168\ 2$$

14·733 2 is about one-third of the way from 14·73 to 14·74.

Hence we take $$\quad\log 14·733\ 2 = 1·168\ 3$$

18

1.2.3 ANTILOGARITHMS

By adopting the rules of logarithmic computation to obtain the value of:

$$45 \cdot 26 \times 0 \cdot 407\,2 \times 317 \cdot 4$$

our first step is to find the logarithms of each of these numbers and add them together. We then have the logarithm of the answer. As a final step, we have to convert this logarithm to the number which is the answer. We shall be reversing the process of finding the logarithm of a number; consequently the operation is called finding an *antilogarithm*, colloquially known as an 'antilog'.

Returning for a moment to common logarithms, the common logarithm of a number consists of two parts:

(*a*) a mantissa, in the form of a positive decimal fraction between zero and unity;

(*b*) a characteristic, in the form of a positive or negative whole number, or occasionally zero.

If, in finding a common logarithm, the significant figures of a number are used to decide the mantissa, then conversely, when finding an antilog, the mantissa is used to decide the significant figures of the number. The characteristic is then used to fix the position of the decimal point. In finding the significant figures corresponding to a mantissa, we could use the logarithm tables in reverse. For convenience we use a separate set of tables, so that in looking up an antilog we follow the same general method as looking up a log. This convenience is adversely balanced by the possibility of using the wrong set of tables. The reader is now advised to open Castle's *Four-figure Tables* to the antilogarithm tables and to write in very large capitals in red, across the top of each page, ANTILOGS.

As already indicated, the reading of antilog tables follows the same general principle as reading log tables. The reader should now check the following sets of significant figures obtained from the mantissas quoted:

0·100 0	1 259
0·180 0	1 514
0·186 0	1 535
0·187 4	1 539 (obtained from 1 538 + 1)

Having obtained the significant figures, the decimal point has to be positioned according to the characteristic. Reversing the rules used to obtain characteristics, we reason:

    (*a*) If the characteristic is positive, the antilog is greater than unity, while the number of the figures to the left of the decimal point is one more than the magnitude of the characteristic.

    (*b*) If the characteristic is negative, the antilog lies between zero and unity, and the number of zeros immediately after the decimal point is one less than the magnitude of the characteristic (after the negative sign has been discarded).

Example

Find the antilogs of:

    (*a*) 2·517 6   (*b*) $\bar{3}$·098 5

(*a*) From the antilog tables, the significant figures of the number are 3 289 + 5 = 3 294. The positive characteristic tells us the antilog exceeds unity, and that there are three figures to the left of the decimal point. Hence the value required is 329·4.

(*b*) From antilog tables, the significant figures of the answer are 1 253 + 1 = 1 254. The negative characteristic tells us the answer lies between zero and unity, and there are two zeros after the decimal point. Hence the value required is 0·001 254.

        Answers: (*a*) 329·4   (*b*) 0·001 254

1.2.4   MANIPULATION OF LOGARITHMS

The basic rules of logarithmic computation are:

$$\log abc = \log a + \log b + \log c$$

$$\log \frac{a}{b} = \log a - \log b$$

$$\log a^n = n \log a$$

$$\log \sqrt[n]{a} = \frac{\log a}{n}$$

$$\log \sqrt[n]{a^m} = \frac{m \log a}{n}$$

The manipulation of logarithms follows the same rules as ordinary arithmetic, but especial care must be taken if a logarithm has a negative characteristic and positive mantissa. Let us illustrate the processes with examples.

Example

Add 2·079 2 and $\bar{1}$·437 2.

$$
\begin{array}{r}
2 \cdot 079\ 2 \\
\bar{1} \cdot 437\ 2 \\
\hline
1 \cdot 516\ 4 \\
\hline
\end{array}
$$

The formal method is followed for the mantissa, and since nothing is carried forward from the mantissa, adding 2 to -1 produces 1 for the characteristic.

Example

Add $\bar{2}$·817 6, $\bar{1}$·417 8 and 3·007 4.

$$
\begin{array}{r}
\bar{2} \cdot 817\ 6 \\
\bar{1} \cdot 417\ 8 \\
3 \cdot 007\ 4 \\
\hline
1 \cdot 242\ 8 \\
\hline
\end{array}
$$

Once more we commence with adding mantissas, but in this case we have to 'carry 1'. The characteristic is the addition of 1, 3, -1 and -2, which equals 1.

Example

Subtract $\bar{2}$·509 7 from 4·959 9.

$$
\begin{array}{r}
4 \cdot 959\ 9 \\
\bar{2} \cdot 509\ 7 \\
\hline
6 \cdot 450\ 2 \\
\hline
\end{array}
$$

Here there are no differences from ordinary arithmetic until we come to the subtraction of characteristics, when we obey the rule 'change the sign of the bottom line and add'. $4 - (-2)$ is equal to $4 + 2$, or 6.

Example

Subtract $\bar{3}$·470 2 from $\bar{4}$·395 7.

$$
\begin{array}{r}
\bar{4} \cdot 395\ 7 \\
\bar{3} \cdot 470\ 2 \\
\hline
\bar{2} \cdot 925\ 5 \\
\hline
\end{array}
$$

Commencing at the mantissas, we proceed according to formal artithmetic until we come to the point of 'borrowing one' from the top characteristic. This makes it -5, and then:

$$-5 - (-3) = -5 + 3 = -2$$

which in logarithmic notation is written $\bar{2}$.

Example

Multiply $\bar{1}\cdot307\,6$ by 3.

$$\bar{1}\cdot307\,6 \times 3 = \bar{3}\cdot922\,8$$

Here there is no 'carrying forward' and we simply multiply both the mantissa and characteristic by 3.

Example

Multiply $\bar{1}\cdot407\,8$ by 4.

$$\bar{1}\cdot407\,8 \times 4 = \bar{3}\cdot631\,2$$

We proceed along the mantissa until the stage '4 × 4 = 16, put down 6 and carry 1'. Thence $(4 \times -1) = -4$, and since there is 1 to carry, $-4 + 1 = -3$, which is written $\bar{3}$.

Example

Divide $\bar{3}\cdot507\,2$ by 3.

$$\frac{\bar{3}\cdot507\,2}{3} = \frac{\bar{3} + 0\cdot507\,2}{3}$$
$$= \bar{1} + 0\cdot169\,1 \text{ (rounding off)}$$
$$= \bar{1}\cdot169\,1$$

The characteristic was exactly divisible by three, and we simply divided the characteristic and the mantissa by 3.

Example

Divide $\bar{3}\cdot649\,2$ by 5.

Here we have to obtain $\dfrac{\bar{3}\cdot649\,2}{5}$ which can be written:

$$\frac{-3 + 0\cdot649\,2}{5}$$

We want to make the characteristic divisible by 5, without altering the magnitude of $(-3 + 0\cdot649\,2)$. This we can accomplish by subtracting 2 from the characteristic and adding it to the mantissa:

$$\frac{-3 + 0\cdot649\,2}{5} = \frac{-5 + 2\cdot649\,2}{5} = -1 + 0\cdot529\,8 \text{ (rounding off)}$$

which we write as $\bar{1}\cdot529\,8$.

Problems 1.2

1. P, Q, R, S are numbers whose common logarithms (i.e. logs to the base 10) are a, b, c and d respectively. Obtain in terms of a, b, c and d expressions for the common logarithms of:

(a) PQ (b) PR (c) QS

(d) $PQRS$ (e) PQS (f) $\dfrac{P}{Q}$

(g) $\dfrac{R}{S}$ (h) $\dfrac{PQ}{RS}$ (j) $\dfrac{PQR}{S}$

(k) P^2 (l) P^2Q (m) P^2Q^2

(n) P^2QR^2S (o) $\sqrt{P}$ (p) $\sqrt[u]{P}$

(q) $\sqrt[2]{(PQ)}$ (r) $\sqrt[3]{(P^2Q)}$ (s) $\sqrt[3]{(P^3QR^2)}$

(t) $\dfrac{PQR^2}{\sqrt{S}}$ (u) $\dfrac{\sqrt{P} \times (QS)}{\sqrt[3]{R}}$ (v) $\dfrac{P^4Q}{\sqrt[5]{S^2}}$

(w) $10P$ (x) $100S$ (y) $\dfrac{PQ}{100}$

(z) $\dfrac{100PQ}{\sqrt{R^3}}$ (aa) $\dfrac{R^2}{\sqrt{(100P)}}$ (ab) $\dfrac{P^3}{\sqrt[3]{(1\,000RS^2)}}$

2. Find the logs of the following numbers:

(a) 82   (b) 95   (c) 7
(d) 435   (e) 174   (f) 1 143
(g) 1 183   (h) 4·9   (j) 0·004 9
(k) 0·000 9   (l) 0·053 2   (m) 0·021 32
(n) 213·2   (o) 1·175   (p) 10^4
(q) 10^{-2} (r) $5·372 \times 10^4$ (s) $8·168 \times 10^{-5}$
(t) 704·138   (u) 80 873   (v) 1·027 5
(w) 16·965   (x) 1·066 25   (y) 15·833 7

3. Find antilogarithms of:

(a) 0·387 2   (b) 4·387 2   (c) 3·387 2
(d) $\bar{1}$·387 2   (e) 0·000 0   (f) $\bar{2}$·400 0
(g) 1·355 0   (h) 0·301 0   (j) $\bar{1}$·687 1
(k) 2·531 1   (l) 0·137 1   (m) $\bar{4}$·590 2

The answers to the problems 4, 5, 6, 7 should be left in logarithm form. There is no need to look up antilogarithms as a final step.

4. Perform the following additions:

(a) $2 \cdot 170\ 9$
$\overline{1} \cdot 307\ 2$
$3 \cdot 145\ 8$

(b) $\overline{1} \cdot 380\ 6$
$\overline{1} \cdot 070\ 4$
$\overline{2} \cdot 691\ 5$

(c) $\overline{1} \cdot 306\ 4$
$\overline{2} \cdot 517\ 8$
$3 \cdot 508\ 1$
$1 \cdot 001\ 7$

(d) $0 \cdot 101\ 5$
$\overline{1} \cdot 170\ 6$
$2 \cdot 938\ 4$
$\overline{4} \cdot 497\ 2$

5. In the following, subtract the lower logarithm from the one above:

(a) $3 \cdot 176\ 2$
$2 \cdot 548\ 1$

(b) $2 \cdot 760\ 9$
$3 \cdot 428\ 1$

(c) $1 \cdot 846\ 1$
$\overline{1} \cdot 475\ 4$

(d) $\overline{2} \cdot 381\ 5$
$\overline{4} \cdot 778\ 3$

6. Evaluate:

(a) $5(0 \cdot 174\ 8)$ (b) $3(1 \cdot 467\ 2)$
(c) $2(\overline{1} \cdot 480\ 5)$ (d) $4(\overline{1} \cdot 450\ 6)$

7. Evaluate:

(a) $\dfrac{3 \cdot 451\ 6}{4}$ (b) $\dfrac{\overline{5} \cdot 970\ 8}{5}$ (c) $\dfrac{\overline{1} \cdot 170\ 8}{4}$

(d) $\dfrac{\overline{1} \cdot 981\ 3}{7}$ (e) $\dfrac{2(\overline{1} \cdot 497\ 2)}{3}$ (f) $\dfrac{3(\overline{2} \cdot 864\ 5)}{5}$

Answers to Problems 1.2

1. (a) $a + b$ (b) $a + c$
(c) $b + d$ (d) $a + b + c + d$
(e) $a + b + d$ (f) $a - b$
(g) $c - d$ (h) $(a + b) - (c + d)$
(j) $a + b + c - d$ (k) $2a$
(l) $2a + b$ (m) $2(a + b)$

(n) $2a + b + 2c + d$ (o) $\dfrac{a}{2}$

(p) $\dfrac{a}{4}$ (q) $\dfrac{a + b}{2}$

(r) $\dfrac{2a + b}{3}$ (s) $a + \left(\dfrac{b + 2c}{3}\right)$

(t) $a + b + 2c - \dfrac{d}{2}$ (u) $\dfrac{a}{2} + b + c - \dfrac{d}{3}$

(v) $4a + b - \dfrac{2d}{5}$ (w) $1 + a$

(x) $2 + d$ (y) $a + b - 2$

(z) $2 + a + b - \dfrac{3c}{2}$ (aa) $2c - \left(\dfrac{2 + a}{2}\right)$

(ab) $3a - \left(\dfrac{3 + c + 2d}{3}\right)$

2. (a) 1·913 8   (b) 1·977 7   (c) 0·845 1
   (d) 2·638 5   (e) 2·240 5   (f) 3·058 1
   (g) 3·073 0   (h) 0·690 2   (j) $\bar{3}$·690 2
   (k) $\bar{4}$·954 2   (l) $\bar{2}$·725 9   (m) $\bar{2}$·328 8
   (n) 2·328 8   (o) 0·070 0   (p) 4·000 0
   (q) $\bar{2}$·000 0   (r) 4·730 2   (s) $\bar{5}$·912 1
   (t) 2·847 7   (u) 4·907 8   (v) 0·011 8
   (w) 1·229 6   (x) 0·027 8   (y) 1·199 6

3. (a) 2·439   (b) 24 390   (c) 2 439
   (d) 0·243 9   (e) 1·000   (f) 0·025 12
   (g) 22·65   (h) 2·000   (j) 0·486 5
   (k) 339·7   (l) 1·371   (m) 0·000 389 2

4. (a) 4·623 9   (b) $\bar{3}$·142 5   (c) 2·334 0   (d) $\bar{2}$·707 7
5. (a) 0·628 1   (b) $\bar{1}$·332 8   (c) 2·370 7   (d) 1·603 2
6. (a) 0·874 0   (b) 4·401 6   (c) $\bar{2}$·961 0   (d) $\bar{3}$·802 4
7. (a) 0·862 9   (b) $\bar{1}$·194 2   (c) $\bar{1}$·792 7
   (d) $\bar{1}$·997 3   (e) $\bar{1}$·664 8   (f) $\bar{1}$·318 7

1.3 The Setting Out of Calculations

There are many similarities between the manufacture of an article in industry and the solution of a problem in mathematics or science. In industry, the raw material is processed using the tools available, according to a planning schedule, often with intermediary checks, the article eventually being submitted for final inspection. The raw material of a problem in mathematics and science is the data provided in the question; the processing tools are the various rules of arithmetic, formulae, mathematical tables, slide rules, and so on.

Raw materials can be processed in many ways; for instance, metal can be removed by milling, shaping or turning. A workman will only use those tools that he feels competent to handle skilfully. There are many short cuts and trick methods that a competent artisan can use, but he rarely employs them unless he knows exactly what he is doing.

Furthermore, if the engineering trainee uses his eyes in the workshop, it will soon become evident that the accurate, respected craftsman is the one who invariably lays out, uses and stores his tools in an efficient manner.

The same basic principles apply to the solution of problems in mathematics. An orderly manner of setting out calculations is desirable, since:

- (*a*) it shows the reader the various steps by which the solution was obtained;
- (*b*) it allows an easier detection of errors when such errors unfortunately occur;
- (*c*) it encourages pride in achievement. Industry has no vacancies for untidy, slovenly and inaccurate engineers.

The expression 'rough check' is in quite common use, but in some instances the adjective 'rough' is somewhat unfortunate. So-called rough checks can be surprisingly accurate. The purpose of a rough check is to give an indication of the accuracy of an answer by using approximations. If the approximations are made with care, and chosen so that the errors of the approximations tend to neutralize each other, then rough checks will most certainly indicate violent errors, such as the misplacing of a decimal point.

The use of logarithms and rough checks is demonstrated in the worked examples which follow.

Example

The volume of a cylinder is given by the formula:

$$V = 0.785\ 4\ d^2h$$

and 1 m³ contains 1 000 litres. What is the capacity, in litres, of a cylindrical tank of diameter 1·05 m and length 2·16 m?

$$V \text{ (in m}^3) = 0.785\ 4\ d^2h$$
$$\text{Capacity in litres} = 1\ 000 \times 0.785\ 4\ d^2h$$
$$= 785.4\ d^2h$$
$$\therefore \text{Capacity} = 785.4 \times 1.05^2 \times 2.16 = 1\ 871$$

No.	Log
785·4	2·895 1
1·05	0·021 2
1·05	0·021 2
2·16	0·334 5
1 871	3·272 0

Rough check:
750 × 1 × 1 × 2 = 1 500

Answer: Capacity = 1 870 litres

Example

The time t seconds for one complete oscillation of a simple pendulum is given by the formula:

$$t = 2\pi \sqrt{\frac{L}{g}}$$

Find the value of t if $\pi = 3\cdot142$, $L = 0\cdot5$ and $g = 9\cdot81$.

$$t = 2\pi \sqrt{\frac{L}{g}} = (2 \times 3\cdot142) \times \sqrt{\frac{0\cdot5}{9\cdot81}} = 1\cdot419$$

No.	Log
0·5 9·81	$\bar{1}$·699 0 0·991 7
Subt	$\bar{2}$·707 3
Root | 2	$\bar{1}$·353 6
2 3·142	0·301 0 0·497 2
1·419	0·151 8

Rough check:

$$6 \times \sqrt{\frac{1}{20}}$$
$$= 6 \times \text{(between } \tfrac{1}{4} \text{ and } \tfrac{1}{5})$$
$$= \text{between } 1\cdot5 \text{ and } 1\cdot2$$

Answer: Time $= 1\cdot42$ s

Example

The area A of a triangle with sides of length a, b and c is given by the formula:

$$A = \sqrt{\{s(s-a)(s-b)(s-c)\}}$$

where s is the semi-perimeter, i.e.

$$s = \frac{a+b+c}{2}$$

Find the area of a triangle having sides of length 78·6, 117·4 and 154·8 mm. Give the answer in square millimetres.

We must note carefully that the formulae include additions and subtractions and these must be eliminated before logarithms are used.

$$s = \frac{a+b+c}{2} = \frac{78\cdot6 + 117\cdot4 + 154\cdot8}{2} = \frac{350\cdot8}{2} = 175\cdot4$$

$$s - a = 175\cdot4 - 78\cdot6 \ = 96\cdot8$$
$$s - b = 175\cdot4 - 117\cdot4 = 58\cdot0$$
$$s - c = 175\cdot4 - 154\cdot8 = 20\cdot6$$
$$A = \sqrt{(175\cdot4 \times 96\cdot8 \times 58\cdot0 \times 20\cdot6)} = 4\,504$$

B

No.		Log
175·4		2·244 0
96·8		1·985 9
58·0		1·763 4
20·6		1·313 9
Root	2	7·307 2
4 504		3·653 6

Rough check:

$\sqrt{(175 \times 100 \times 60 \times 20)}$
$= \sqrt{14\,000\,000}$
$=$ about 4 000

Answer: Area $= 4\,500$ mm²

Example

The centre distance C millimetres for helical gears with shafts at right angles is given by the formula:

$$C = \frac{Nm(1 + \sqrt[3]{R^2})^{1\cdot5}}{2}$$

where
$N =$ number of teeth on the pinion
$m =$ metric module, in millimetres
$R =$ gear ratio

Find the centre distance for a gear ratio of 3, the metric module being 2 mm and the pinion having 24 teeth.

$$C = \frac{24 \times 2\,(1 + \sqrt[3]{9})^{1\cdot5}}{2}$$

$\sqrt[3]{9}$ from tables (page 26) $= 2\cdot080$
$C = 24\,(1 + 2\cdot080)^{1\cdot5}$ $= 24\,(3\cdot080)^{1\cdot5}$

Log $3\cdot080^{1\cdot5} = 1\cdot5 \log 3\cdot080$ $= 1\cdot5 \times 0\cdot488\,6 = 0\cdot732\,9$
Log answer $= \log 24 + 0\cdot732\,9 = 1\cdot380\,2 + 0\cdot732\,9 = 2\cdot113\,1$
Answer $=$ antilog $2\cdot113\,1$ $= 129\cdot7$

Rough check: $24(3)^{1\cdot5} = 24 \times \sqrt[2]{3^3}$ $= 24 \times \sqrt[2]{27}$
$= 24 \times$ about $5 =$ about 120

Answer: Centre distance $= 130$ mm

Problems 1.3

The student should note that all formulae which follow are commonly used in engineering and will gradually become of use to him as his studies develop. The problems below are to give him practice in the use of logarithms, but the formulae which have been selected are not just haphazard collections of symbols. They all have a practical application.

You are reminded that when four-figure tables are used, answers should be rounded off to three significant figures.

1. If $I = \dfrac{BD^3}{12}$, find I when $B = 5\cdot75$ and $D = 12$.

2. If $F = \dfrac{4\pi^2 EI}{L^2}$, find F when $\pi = 3\cdot142$, $E = 30 \times 10^6$, $I = 5\cdot7$ and $L = 64$. (Give the answer in standard form.)

3. If $V = \dfrac{4\pi R^3}{3}$, find V when $\pi = 3\cdot142$ and $R = 0\cdot815$.

4. If $y = \dfrac{Fa^2b^2}{3\,EIL}$ find y when $F = 4\,480$, $a = 36$, $b = 84$, $E = 30 \times 10^6$, $I = 192$ and $L = 120$.

5. If $s = \dfrac{v^2 - u^2}{2a}$, find s when $v = 88$, $u = 22$, and $a = 1\cdot135$.

6. If $R_1 = \dfrac{RR_2}{R_2 - R}$, find R_1 when $R = 10\cdot54$ and $R_2 = 16\cdot23$.

7. If $D = \sqrt[3]{\dfrac{6V}{\pi}}$, and $\pi = 3\cdot142$, find D when
   (*a*) $V = 10\cdot4$;   (*b*) $V = 0\cdot472$.

8. If $V = c\sqrt{mi}$, find V when $c = 120$, $m = 1\cdot508$ and $i = 3\cdot2 \times 10^{-3}$.

9. If $Q = 3\cdot09\ BH^{1\cdot5}$ and $B = 3\cdot5$, find the value of Q when
   (*a*) $H = 1\cdot414$;   (*b*) $H = 0\cdot507$.

10. If $K = 0\cdot275\ \sqrt{\left(\dfrac{D^5 - d^5}{D^2 - d^2}\right)}$, find K when
    (*a*) $D = 2\cdot2$ and $d = 1\cdot6$;   (*b*) $D = 0\cdot45$ and $d = 0\cdot37$.

11. If $L = \dfrac{1}{C(2\pi f)^2}$, find the value of L when $C = 0\cdot4 \times 10^{-6}$, $\pi = 3\cdot142$ and $f = 24 \times 10^3$.

29

12. Evaluate $H = \dfrac{M}{(d^2 + l^2)^{3/2}}$ when $M = 333, d = 15\cdot5$ and $l = 5\cdot2$.

13. If $P = kB^n f$, calculate by logarithms the value of P when $k = 0\cdot04$, $B = 1\cdot5$, $n = 1\cdot6$ and $f = 50$.

14. The A0 size of drawing paper is a rectangle having an area of 1 square metre with lengths of sides in the proportion of $\sqrt{2}$ to 1. Determine the lengths of the sides, in millimetres, each to three significant figures.

15. A pipe, of outside diameter D millimetres and inside diameter d millimetres, is used as a beam as part of the structure of a shipyard crane. The maximum stress σ N/mm^2 (which is incidentally equal to σ MN/m^2) for a particular loading can be determined from the formula:

$$\sigma = \frac{17\cdot6\ D}{\pi(D^4 - d^4)} \times 10^8 \text{ N/mm}^2$$

Find the value of σ when $D = 200$ mm and $d = 180$ mm. (Take π as $\frac{22}{7}$.)

16. If a barrel has a largest diameter of D, a diameter of the ends d and a length of L, a close approximation to its volume V is given by the formula:

$$V = \frac{\pi L}{12}(2D^2 + d^2)$$

If 1 cubic metre contains 1 000 litres, find the capacity, in litres, of a barrel where $D = 1\cdot2$ m, $d = 0\cdot8$ m and $L = 1\cdot5$ m. (Take π as $\frac{22}{7}$.)

17. A zone of a sphere reveals two circles of radii R and r, their distance apart being h. The diameter D of the sphere from which the zone was cut can be obtained from the formula:

$$\frac{D}{2} = \sqrt{\left\{R^2 + \left(\frac{R^2 - r^2 - h^2}{2h}\right)^2\right\}}$$

Find the value of D when $R = 75$ mm, $r = 51$ mm and $h = 28$ mm.

18. A circular blank is drawn into a circular shell in such a manner that the thickness of the base of the shell differs from the wall thickness.

    If a = outside diameter
              b = inside diameter
              h = depth of shell
              t = thickness of base
              B = approximate diameter of circular blank

    then $B = \sqrt{\left\{a^2 + (a^2 - b^2)\dfrac{h}{t}\right\}}$

    Determine B when $a = 80$ mm, $b = 78 \cdot 4$ mm, $h = 54$ mm and $t = 1 \cdot 2$ mm.

19. A close approximation to the length L of the perimeter of an ellipse whose axes have lengths a and b is given by the formula:

    $$L = \pi\sqrt{\left\{\frac{a^2 + b^2}{2} - \frac{(a - b)^2}{8 \cdot 8}\right\}}$$

    Find L when $a = 40$ mm, $b = 24$ mm and $\pi = 3 \cdot 142$.

20. In a particular turning operation, if S is the surface cutting speed in m/min and T the tool life in hours, then S and T are connected by the formula:

    $$S \times \sqrt[6]{T} = \text{a constant}$$

    It is known when $S = 80$ m/min, T is 45 minutes. What must be the values of S to give a tool life of:

    (*a*) 1 hour;   (*b*) 30 minutes?

21. The Brinell hardness number of a material is given by the formula:

    $$\frac{2F}{\pi D \left\{D - \sqrt{(D^2 - d^2)}\right\}}$$

    Calculate the Brinell hardness number (to the nearest whole number) when $F = 3\,000$, $D = 10$, $d = 3 \cdot 51$ and $\pi = 3 \cdot 142$.

22. (*a*) From the results of a science experiment, the following equation was obtained:

    $$\log W = \log m + 2 \log v - 0 \cdot 301\,0$$

    Deduce a formula connecting W, m and v which does not include logarithms.

(b) The efficiency η of a particular turbine is given by the formula:

$$\eta = \frac{2u\,(v - u)\,(1 + \cos \theta)}{v^2}$$

(i) Find the efficiency under theoretical conditions when $u = \dfrac{v}{2}$ and $\theta = 0°$.

(ii) Find the efficiency (as a percentage, to the nearest whole number) under practical conditions when $u = 37$ m/s, $v = 80$ m/s and $\theta = 20°$.

Answers to Problems 1.3

1. 828
2. $1·65 \times 10^6$
3. 2·27
4. 0·019 8
5. 3 200
6. 30·1
7. (a) 2·71   (b) 0·966
8. 8·34
9. (a) 18·2   (b) 3·90
10. (a) 1·17   (b) 0·115
11. $1·10 \times 10^{-4}$
12. 0·076 2
13. 3·83
14. 1 190 mm $\times$ 841 mm
15. 204 N/mm^2
16. 1 380 litres
17. 170 mm
18. 133 mm
19. 102 mm
20. (a) 76·3 m/min   (b) 85·6 m/min
21. 300
22. (a) $W = \dfrac{mv^2}{2}$ (b) (i) 100%; (ii) 96·4%

1.4   The Slide Rule

1.4.1   THE SCALES OF A SLIDE RULE

The slide rule is a useful aid when performing certain mathematical processes. Like any other tool used in engineering, the accuracy of the results obtained depends upon the accuracy of the tool itself and upon the skill of the user. An accuracy of three significant figures is easily obtained with a slide rule if the first figure is 1 or 2, not so easily if the first figure is 8 or 9. In industry, the rapid introduction of calculating machines has generally led to the slide rule losing favour for exact calculations. In technical studies, the slide rule can be very valuable in the speeding up of calculations, but its use is no invitation to inaccurate working. As a general guide, until skill has been obtained, the slide rule should be used for checking purposes only. The student is recommended initially to purchase a cheap rule to develop skill, and then to purchase a more expensive and accurate rule having a wider selection of scales when his studies and skill call for an article of better quality.

We shall confine our attention to the use of the slide rule for multiplication, division and computing of square roots and squares. Since the principle of its use is based on logarithms, addition and subtraction processes cannot be performed on a slide rule. The slide rule consists of three basic parts, these being the *stock*, the *slide*, and a moving frame, known as a *cursor*, which carries an engraved reference line. The cursor slides in guides on the stock. There are four basic scales, known as the *A*, *B*, *C* and *D* scales. The *B* scale is uppermost on the slide, the *C* scale being the lower scale on the slide. The *A* scale is on the stock and is opposite to and identical with the *B* scale on the slide. The *D* scale is on the stock and is opposite to and identical with the *C* scale on the slide.

If the scales are observed carefully, it will be noted that divisions are not of equal width. Furthermore, one division may represent 0·01 at one part of the scale, 0·1 at another, and other values elsewhere. This is because the scales are logarithmic and not linear. The log of 1 is zero, the log of 10 is 1, and the log of 100 is 2. Hence on the *A* and *B* scales the value of 10 lies halfway along the rule. The slide rule is usually used to produce the significant figures of an answer only; the position of the decimal point is invariably found by means of a rough check.

1.4.2. MULTIPLICATION

The principle for multiplication on the slide rule is that $\log (ab) = \log a + \log b$. Fig. 1.1 shows how this operation is performed.

Example

Multiply 58·7 by 0·178.

Move 1 on the slide opposite 5·87 on the *A* scale.
Bring cursor over 1·78 on the *B* scale.

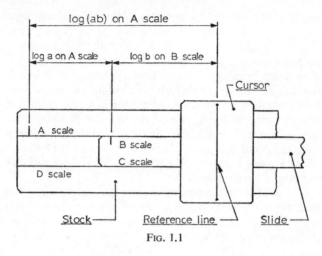

FIG. 1.1

Read off the answer on the *A* scale (significant figures are 1045). Position the decimal point by a rough check.

$$60 \times \frac{1}{6} = 10$$

Answer: 10·45

1.4.3 DIVISION

Division is accomplished by reversing the sequence of the previous example, noting that if the 1 of the scale *B* comes out of the stock, the value on scale *A* can be found opposite 10 or 100 on scale *B*.

Example

Divide 4·33 by 82·64.

Move line on cursor over 4·33 on scale *A*.

Move slide until 82·64 on scale *B* comes under cursor line.

Answer is read on scale *A*, opposite 1, 10, or 100 of scale *B*. (In this case, opposite 100, significant figures are 524.) Find decimal point by trial.

$$4 \div 80 = \frac{1}{20} = 0·05$$

Answer: 0·052 4

1.4.4 COMBINED MULTIPLICATION AND DIVISION

To avoid unnecessary movements of the slide and the cursor, it is advisable to perform multiplications and divisions alternately.

Example

Evaluate $\dfrac{58 \cdot 7 \times 1 \cdot 92 \times 0 \cdot 071}{63 \cdot 4 \times 0 \cdot 027}$.

This is obtained with the sequence:

$$58 \cdot 7 \times 1 \cdot 92 \div 63 \cdot 4 \times 0 \cdot 071 \div 0 \cdot 027$$

Move slide to bring 1 on scale *B* opposite 5·87 on scale *A*.

Move cursor line over 1·92 on scale *B*. (The cursor line indicates 5·87 × 1·92 on scale *A*.)

Move slide to bring 6·34 on scale *B* under cursor line. (The 1 on scale *B* is opposite the answer to $\dfrac{5 \cdot 87 \times 1 \cdot 92}{6 \cdot 34}$ on scale *A*.)

Move cursor line over 7·1 on scale *B*. (The answer to $\dfrac{5 \cdot 87 \times 1 \cdot 92 \times 7 \cdot 1}{6 \cdot 34}$ is now under the cursor line on scale *A*.)

Move slide so that 2·7 on scale *B* is under the cursor line. (The answer to $\dfrac{5 \cdot 87 \times 1 \cdot 92 \times 7 \cdot 1}{6 \cdot 34 \times 2 \cdot 7}$ is found on scale *A* opposite the 1 on scale *B* on the slide (significant figures are 467).)

Check on the decimal point.

$$\frac{60 \times 2 \times 0 \cdot 07}{60 \times 0 \cdot 028} = 5$$

Answer: 4·67

1.4.5 SQUARE ROOTS AND SQUARES

If the slide is removed completely from the rule, the square roots of numbers on the *A* scale are found on scale *D* directly below. Similarly, the squares of the numbers on the *D* scale are found directly above on the *A* scale. No difficulties are caused with the determination of squares, but care should be taken in the determination of square roots that the correct range (1 to 10 or 10 to 100) is chosen on the *A* scale.

Example

Find $\sqrt{161}$.

$$161 = 1 \cdot 61 \times 100$$
$$\sqrt{161} = \sqrt{(1 \cdot 61 \times 100)} = \sqrt{1 \cdot 61} \times 10$$

Move slide away from 1·61 on the *A* scale.
Move cursor over 1·61 on the *A* scale.
Read $\sqrt{1 \cdot 61}$ under the cursor line on the *D* scale (= 1·27).

$$\sqrt{1 \cdot 61} = 1 \cdot 27 \times 10 = 12 \cdot 7$$

Answer: 12·7

Example

Find $\sqrt{0 \cdot 697}$.

$$0 \cdot 697 = \frac{69 \cdot 7}{100}$$

$$\sqrt{\frac{69 \cdot 7}{100}} = \frac{\sqrt{69 \cdot 7}}{10}$$

Move the slide away from 69·7 on the *A* scale.
Move the cursor line over 69·7 on the *A* scale.
Read $\sqrt{69 \cdot 7}$ under the cursor line on the *D* scale (= 8·35).

$$\sqrt{0 \cdot 697} = \frac{8 \cdot 35}{10} = 0 \cdot 835$$

Answer: 0·835

Scales *C* and *D* can be used for multiplication and division in a similar manner to scales *A* and *B*, and since scales *C* and *D* are larger, theoretically greater accuracy can be obtained. On the other hand, since they only run from 1 to 10 instead of 1 to 100, there are many more occasions when a sub-answer has to be nominally multiplied or divided by 10 to keep it on the rule. The student is advised initially to sacrifice the greater accuracy obtainable with the *C* and *D* scales until he is competent in multiplying and dividing on the *A* and *B* scales.

The correct evaluation of problems involving combined multiplication and division including squares and/or square roots needs considerable care. It is advisable to perform operations one at a time rather than to run the risk of an incorrect answer due to incorrect manipulation. A slide rule is like any other engineer's tool. The skilled artisan can use a tool with dexterity only when he has practised its use over a suitable period. The reader is urged to have patience while learning the use of a slide rule. It is advisable to concentrate initially on multiplication and division, first with the *A* and *B* scales, then with the *C* and *D* scales, and to master these processes fully before proceeding further. This can then be followed by square roots, squares and combined multiplication and division. Other processes involving the use of other scales, such as reciprocals, log-log and so on, are better left to a later stage of studies.

If the reader cares to practise in the use of the slide rule, he may solve problems 1.3 with its aid, omitting questions involving powers higher than the square, and roots of a degree other than the square root.

1.5 Mathematical Tables Other Than Logarithms

1.5.1 USE OF TABULATED DATA

Many students refer to books which contain tabulated data as 'log tables'. It must be admitted that considerable use is made of logarithms and antilogarithms, but the use of the expression 'log tables' often leads a student to the view that the tables of logs and antilogs are the only important tables in such a publication. The reader has been impressed with the importance of not using logarithms unless it is essential. Let us consider certain other tables in Castle's *Four-figure Mathematical Tables*.

At times during a complete Technicians' course the reader will refer to every set of tables in Castle's *Four-figure Mathematical Tables*, but our employment of certain of the tables must be left until we have studied the topics which involve their use. The various tables will be introduced at appropriate times during the course. We shall now consider tables of square roots and of reciprocals.

1.5.2 TABLES OF SQUARE ROOTS (AND OF SQUARES)

Castle's *Four-figure Mathematical Tables* include tables which are entitled 'square roots', but before these are considered in detail let us look at the interesting tables on pages 38 and 39. These will be found to be most useful if a number has only one or two significant figures. If we take as an example the number 54, the tables indicate:

$$54^2 = 2\,916 \qquad\qquad 54^3 = 157\,464$$
$$\text{(exactly, not to four significant figures)}$$
$$\sqrt{54} = 7{\cdot}348 \qquad\qquad \sqrt[3]{54} = 3{\cdot}780$$
$$\sqrt{540} = 23{\cdot}238 \qquad\qquad \sqrt[3]{540} = 8{\cdot}143$$
$$\sqrt[3]{5\,400} = 17{\cdot}544 \qquad \text{and} \qquad \tfrac{1}{54} = 0{\cdot}018\,52$$

37

If we wish to find the square root of a number with three or four significant figures, the tables shown on pages 40–43 inclusive are used. The square roots fall into 2 groups, those of numbers 1 to 10 and those of numbers 10 to 100. The square roots of numbers from 1 to 100 are extracted in a manner similar to logarithms. The reader should check the values:

$$\sqrt{8 \cdot 78} = 2 \cdot 963$$
$$\sqrt{5 \cdot 507} = 2 \cdot 346$$
$$\sqrt{42 \cdot 4} = 6 \cdot 512$$
$$\sqrt{15 \cdot 84} = 3 \cdot 980$$

The tables can be used for positive numbers outside the range of 1 to 100 by adjusting the decimal point of the result.

We write the number in the form $a \times 10^n$, where n is an *even* number (positive or negative) and a lies between 1 and 100.

Now $$\sqrt{(a \times 10^n)} = \sqrt{a} \times 10^{n/2}$$

Hence for $\sqrt{847}$, we note that $847 = 8 \cdot 47 \times 10^2$, look up the root of $8 \cdot 47$ and multiply it by 10^1. Similarly, for $\sqrt{0 \cdot 164\,2}$, we note that $0 \cdot 164\,2 = 16 \cdot 42 \times 10^{-2}$, look up $\sqrt{16 \cdot 42}$ and multiply by 10^{-1}, i.e. divide by 10. As examples:

$$\sqrt{59\,600} = \sqrt{(5 \cdot 96 \times 10^4)} = \sqrt{5 \cdot 96} \times 10^2$$
$$= 2 \cdot 441 \times 100 = 244 \cdot 1$$
$$\text{and } \sqrt{0 \cdot 189\,4} = \sqrt{(18 \cdot 94 \times 10^{-2})} = \sqrt{18 \cdot 94} \times 10^{-1}$$
$$= \frac{4 \cdot 352}{10} = 0 \cdot 435\,2$$

Although the tables are headed 'square roots', we can use them to find squares by reversing the former procedure. If we wish to know the square of $5 \cdot 642$, we have to determine the number of which $5 \cdot 642$ is the square root. Using the tables, we find the nearest value below $5 \cdot 642$. This is $5 \cdot 639$, the square root of $31 \cdot 8$. The difference to be added is 3, which could be a last significant figure of 3 or 4. If it could be either, we may as well be consistent and compute to an even value, so we take $31 \cdot 84$ as the number. If the number whose square is required lies outside the range 1 to 10, we can express the number in standard form, and note:

$$(a \times 10^n)^2 = a^2 \times 10^{2n}$$

For example
$$0 \cdot 021\,74^2 = (2 \cdot 174 \times 10^{-2})^2$$
$$= 2 \cdot 174^2 \times 10^{-4}$$
$$= 4 \cdot 724 \times 10^{-4}$$
$$= 0 \cdot 000\,472\,4$$

(The reader should note that in this example, the last significant figure could apparently be 3, 4, 5 or 6. The mean is 4·5, which we round off evenly to 4.)

1.5.3 RECIPROCALS OF NUMBERS

The *reciprocal* of a number is its direct inversion. The number 8·47 can be written as $\frac{8·47}{1}$, hence its reciprocal is $\frac{1}{8·47}$. The reciprocal of a single number is therefore unity divided by that number. The reciprocal of a fraction such as $\frac{23}{37}$ is $\frac{37}{23}$.

Tables of reciprocals of numbers appear in Castle's *Four-figure Mathematical Tables*. On pages 38 and 39, the end column headed $\frac{1}{n}$ gives directly the reciprocals of whole numbers from unity to 100 inclusive. If the number has three significant figures or more, the reciprocal can be found with the aid of the tables on pages 44 and 45.

As a number tends to increase, its reciprocal tends to decrease. The reader should now open Castle's *Four-figure Mathematical Tables* to pages 44 and 45, and note that the groups of four-figure numbers tend to diminish. Consequently the mean differences in the end column have to be subtracted, and our reader is therefore advised to write plainly in large capitals in red, at the top of each table, SUBTRACT MEAN DIFFERENCES.

Example

If resistors of magnitude R_1, R_2 and R_3 are connected in parallel, the equivalent single resistance R can be obtained from the formula:

$$\frac{1}{R} = \frac{1}{R_1} + \frac{1}{R_2} + \frac{1}{R_3}$$

Find the value of R when $R_1 = 5·37$ ohms, $R_2 = 1·714$ ohms and $R_3 = 12·3$ ohms.

$$\frac{1}{R_1} = \frac{1}{5·37} = 0·186\ 2$$

$$\frac{1}{R_2} = \frac{1}{1·714} = 0·583\ 5$$

$$\frac{1}{R_3} = \frac{1}{12·3} = 0·081\ 3$$

By addition:

$$\frac{1}{R_1} + \frac{1}{R_2} + \frac{1}{R_3} = 0.186\ 2 + 0.583\ 5 + 0.081\ 3 = 0.851\ 0$$

$$\frac{1}{R} = 0.851\ 0$$

$$\therefore R = \frac{1}{0.851\ 0} = 1.175$$

Answer: $R = 1.18$ ohms

Example

If a segment of a circle has a height of h and a chord length of w, an approximate formula for the area of the segment is:

$$A = \frac{4h^2}{3} \sqrt{\left(\frac{w^2}{4h^2} + 0.4\right)}$$

Use this formula to find the area of a segment when $h = 0.8$ mm and $w = 4.8$ mm.

$$\frac{w^2}{4h^2} = \frac{4.8 \times 4.8}{4 \times 0.8 \times 0.8} = 9 \text{ (by cancellation)}$$

$$9 + 0.4 = 9.4$$

$$\sqrt{9.4} = 3.066 \text{ (from tables of square roots)}$$

$$A = \frac{4h^2}{3} \times 3.066 = \frac{4 \times 0.8 \times 0.8 \times 3.066}{3}$$

$$= 2.56 \times 1.022 \text{ (by simplification and cancellation)}$$

$$= 2.616\ 32 \text{ (by formal multiplication)}$$

Since we have used four-figure tables during the sequence of operations, as a final step we should now round off to three significant figures.

Answer: Area $= 2.62$ mm^2

Problems 1.5

None of the questions which follow should be solved with the aid of logarithms.

1. Find, to three significant figures, values for the following, taking π as 3.142:

(a) $\dfrac{1}{\pi}$ (b) $\dfrac{1}{2\pi}$ (c) π^2 (d) $\dfrac{1}{\pi^2}$

2. Find, to three significant figures, values for the following, taking g as 9·81:

(a) $\dfrac{1}{g}$ (b) $\sqrt{(2g)}$ (c) $\dfrac{1}{\sqrt{(2g)}}$

3. A geometrical property M, of a circle, is found from the formula:

$$M = \frac{r^4}{2}$$

Find the positive value of r, to three significant figures, when $M = 37\cdot5$.

4. A square has a side of length 5 mm. The length of the side is reduced so that a new square is formed which is 0·81 of the area of the old square. Find the new length of the side.

5. Find the value, to three significant figures, of $\sqrt{(b^2 - 4ac)}$ when $b = 5\cdot72$, $a = 2$ and $c = 1\cdot6$.

6. If the longest side of a right-angled triangle is represented by c, and the sides containing the right angle by a and b, then:

$$a = \sqrt{(c^2 - b^2)}$$

Find the value of a when
(a) $c = 4\cdot1$ and $b = 0\cdot9$;   (b) $c = 5\cdot372$ and $b = 3\cdot828$.

7. A formula which occurs in optics is:

$$\frac{1}{v} - \frac{1}{u} = \frac{1}{f}$$

Find the value of f, to three significant figures, when $v = 2\cdot7$ and $u = 8\cdot35$.

8. When resistances R_1, R_2 and R_3 are connected in parallel, the equivalent single resistance R is found from the formula:

$$\frac{1}{R} = \frac{1}{R_1} + \frac{1}{R_2} + \frac{1}{R_3}$$

Find the value of R, to three significant figures, when $R_1 = 5\cdot72$ ohms, $R_2 = 8\cdot36$ ohms and $R_3 = 3\cdot17$ ohms.

Answers to Problems 1.5

1. (*a*) 0·318　　(*b*) 0·159　　(*c*) 9·87　　(*d*) 0·101
2. (*a*) 0·102　　(*b*) 4·43　　(*c*) 0·226
3. 2·94
4. 4·5 mm
5. 4·46
6. (*a*) 4　　(*b*) 3·77
7. 3·99
8. 1·64 ohms

1.6　Averages and Percentages

1.6.1　THE ARITHMETICAL MEAN

Most people are aware of the idea of an average, particularly in the sporting sphere. In cricket there are three well known averages, those concerned with batting, bowling, and points per game. The purpose of an average is to give an idea of the general size of a collection of various values. The three averages referred to in connection with cricket are all obtained in the same manner, that is, by totalling the items in a set and dividing by the number of individual items. Thus the average of the five individual numbers 16, 12, 28, 17 and 22 is evaluated as:

$$\frac{16 + 12 + 28 + 17 + 22}{5} = \frac{95}{5} = 19$$

This simple average is not the only type of average. Engineers invent all kinds of averages to suit particular purposes. For instance, an engineer might require an *average length* x between 4 mm and 16 mm, so that x is as many times 4 as 16 is times x. The value for this particular average is 8 mm but this is not our usual idea of a simple average, which for 4 mm and 16 mm would be 10 mm.

The word *average* is a general term for a whole variety of different indications, and we must be very careful to describe exactly which particular type of average is under consideration. For the purpose of this book only one type of average need be considered. It is the simple average originally referred to, and to distinguish it from other averages we specifically refer to it as the *arithmetical mean*.

Suppose we have 50 bars of varying length, according to the following table:

Length (mm)	5	6	7	8	9
Number of this length	4	11	22	8	5

If we require the arithmetical mean we place them end to end, find the overall length, and divide by 50. Hence the arithmetical mean is:

$$\frac{\{(4 \times 5) + (11 \times 6) + (22 \times 7) + (8 \times 8) + (5 \times 9)\}}{4 + 11 + 22 + 8 + 5} \text{ mm}$$

$$= \frac{\{20 + 66 + 154 + 64 + 45\}}{50} \text{ mm}$$

$$= \frac{349}{50} \text{ mm} = 6 \cdot 98 \text{ mm}$$

For convenience in condensing the data, items having the same length were put in the same *cell*. The formal name given to the cell is the *variate*, to which we give the symbol x.

The number of items we put into a particular cell is called the *frequency* of the variate, given by the symbol f. The arithmetical mean is denoted by $\bar{x}$, called 'bar x'. Hence:

$$\bar{x} = \frac{\text{the sum of all the different } (fx) \text{ values}}{\text{the sum of all the different } (f) \text{ values}}$$

The sum of all the different f values is the total number of items N. The reader is well aware of what is meant by the Greek letter π. We will now introduce him to the Greek letter *capital sigma*, Σ. This is the mathematician's shorthand way of writing 'the sum of all such things as . . .' We are now in a position to be far more exact about the particular average we are discussing, by using a definition.

The arithmetical mean $\bar{x}$, of a total of N items, consisting of variates x with various frequencies f, is given by the formula:

$$\bar{x} = \frac{\Sigma(fx)}{N} \qquad \text{where } N = \Sigma f$$

The reader should note that if the word 'mean' is used by itself, without qualification, the arithmetical mean is implied.

Example

Spot checks were made of the number of machines idle in a particular workshop, 80 different observations producing the following data:

Machines idle	0	1	2	3	4	5
Observations	11	22	19	16	8	4

What is the mean number of machines idle?

x	f	fx
0	11	0
1	22	22
2	19	38
3	16	48
4	8	32
5	4	20

$$\bar{x} = \frac{\Sigma(fx)}{N}$$
$$= \frac{160}{80}$$
$$= 2$$

$\Sigma f = 80 = N \quad \Sigma(fx) = 160$

Answer: Mean number of machines idle = 2

Example

50 samples were extracted from consignments of goods. Each sample was inspected, and the number of defectives per sample tabulated as follows:

$$3 \quad 4 \quad 2 \quad 3 \quad 4 \quad 1 \quad 1 \quad 6 \quad 1 \quad 0$$
$$0 \quad 0 \quad 2 \quad 3 \quad 6 \quad 1 \quad 6 \quad 7 \quad 0 \quad 3$$
$$1 \quad 0 \quad 3 \quad 2 \quad 7 \quad 4 \quad 7 \quad 2 \quad 4 \quad 0$$
$$3 \quad 1 \quad 1 \quad 1 \quad 0 \quad 3 \quad 4 \quad 3 \quad 1 \quad 6$$
$$4 \quad 2 \quad 7 \quad 4 \quad 2 \quad 1 \quad 2 \quad 1 \quad 7 \quad 4$$

Compile a table of frequencies and determine the arithmetical mean of the number of defectives per sample.

x	Occurrences	f	(fx) value
0	++++ ll	7	0
1	++++ ++++ l	11	11
2	++++ ll	7	14
3	++++ lll	8	24
4	++++ lll	8	32
5		0	0
6	llll	4	24
7	++++	5	35

$\Sigma f = 50 = N \quad \Sigma(fx) = 140$

$$\bar{x} = \frac{\Sigma(fx)}{N} = \frac{140}{50} = 2 \cdot 8$$

Answer: Mean defectives per sample = 2·8

(The student should note the method of obtaining frequencies from a list of numbers. As a value is read off, a dash is put against the appropriate variate. A fifth dash crosses the previous four, and totals are then easily computed using groups of five plus the remaining dashes.)

1.6.2 PERCENTAGES

With a cursory inspection, it is impossible to detect which of the vulgar fractions $\frac{138}{169}$, $\frac{196}{239}$ or $\frac{210}{257}$ is the largest. An assistance in effecting a decision would be to express the fractions with a common denominator which is the least common multiple of 169, 239 and 257. Such calculations would prove extremely laborious.

Another way would be to divide each individual denominator into the appropriate numerator, to as many decimal places as becomes necessary to establish differences between the values. For the given fractions, to four decimal places:

$$\frac{138}{169} = 0.816\ 6 \qquad \frac{196}{239} = 0.820\ 1 \qquad \frac{210}{257} = 0.817\ 1$$

showing that $\frac{196}{239}$ is the largest.

Assuming that four decimal places provides sufficient accuracy, we could write the three decimal fractions as:

$$\frac{81.66}{100} \qquad \frac{82.01}{100} \qquad \text{and} \qquad \frac{81.71}{100}$$

The first vulgar fraction implies 81·66 parts in one hundred. A conventional way of expressing such a relationship is to call it a *percentage* and to use the % sign. Thus:

$$\frac{138}{169} = \frac{81.66}{100} = 81.66\%$$

If we require to know what percentage a is of b, then:

$$\frac{a}{b} = \frac{x}{100}$$

and by cross-multiplication $x = \dfrac{100a}{b}$

Percentages are very useful for indicating changes. An amount of change would be a new value minus an original value. Hence:

$$\text{Percentage change} = \frac{\text{new value} - \text{original value}}{\text{original value}} \times 100\%$$

Example

The stress in a particular tie-bar is given by the formula:

$$\text{Stress} = \frac{\text{load}}{\text{cross-sectional area}}$$

When installed, a tie-bar has a rectangular section 50 mm × 25 mm. Due to corrosion its width and breath are each reduced by 1 mm. If the load (F) remains unchanged, what is the percentage increase in stress?

$$\text{Original stress} = \frac{\text{load}}{50 \times 25} = \frac{F}{1\ 250}$$

$$\text{Final stress} = \frac{\text{load}}{49 \times 24} = \frac{F}{1\ 176}$$

$$\text{Increase in stress} = \frac{F}{1\ 176} - \frac{F}{1\ 250}$$

$$= \frac{1\ 250F - 1\ 176F}{1\ 176 \times 1\ 250}$$

$$= \frac{74F}{1\ 176 \times 1\ 250}$$

$$\text{Percentage increase in stress} = \frac{\text{increase in stress}}{\text{original stress}} \times 100\%$$

$$= \frac{74F}{1\ 176 \times 1\ 250} \times \frac{1\ 250}{F} \times 100\%$$

$$= \frac{7\ 400\%}{1\ 176} = 6 \cdot 290\%$$

No.	Log
7 400	3·869 2
1 176	3·070 4
6·290	0·798 6

Rough check:
$$\frac{7\ 200}{1\ 200} = 6$$

Answer: Increase in stress = 6·29%

If a value depends on several variables, there are occasions when only one variable changes.

Let $y_1 = Kx_1$, where K is a constant or product of constants, and let this change to $y_2 = Kx_2$.

$$\text{Percentage change} = \frac{Kx_2 - Kx_1}{Kx_1} (100\%)$$

$$= \frac{x_2 - x_1}{x_1} (100\%)$$

We conclude that in establishing percentage changes it is only necessary to consider the changes in those values which vary.

Example

If $C = \dfrac{10rH \tan \theta}{2\pi n}$, calculate:

(a) the values of C when $r = 20$, $n = 50$, $H = 0.18$, $\pi = 3.142$ and $\theta = 40°$;

(b) the percentage increase in C if θ changes from $40°$ to $50°$, the other values remaining unchanged.

(a) $\quad C = \dfrac{10rH \tan \theta}{2\pi n} = \dfrac{10 \times 20 \times 0.18 \times \tan 40°}{2 \times 3.142 \times 50}$

$\quad\quad = \dfrac{36}{314.2} (\tan 40°) = 0.096\ 12$

No.	Log
36	1·556 3
tan 40°	$\bar{1}$·923 8
Num.	1·480 1
314·2	2·497 2
0·096 14	$\bar{2}$·982 9

Rough check:
$$\frac{36 \times 0.84}{300} = 0.100\ 8$$

(b) $\quad\quad C = K \tan \theta$ where $K = \dfrac{36}{314.2}$

Percentage change $= \left(\dfrac{\tan \theta_2 - \tan \theta_1}{\tan \theta_1} \right) \times 100\%$

$\quad\quad\quad\quad = \left(\dfrac{\tan 50° - \tan 40°}{\tan 40°} \right) \times 100\%$

$\quad\quad\quad\quad = \left(\dfrac{1.191\ 8 - 0.839\ 1}{0.839\ 1} \right) \times 100\%$

$\quad\quad\quad\quad = \left(\dfrac{0.352\ 7}{0.839\ 1} \right) \times 100\% = \dfrac{35.27}{0.839\ 1} \%$

$\quad\quad\quad\quad = 42.03\%$

No.	Log
35·27	1·547 4
0·839 1	$\bar{1}$·923 9
42·03	1·623 5

Rough check:

$$\frac{35}{0·8} = 43·75$$

Answers: (*a*) $C = 0·096\ 1$ (*b*) Increase = $42·0\%$

Problems 1.6

1. If 1 370 castings have a total mass of one metric tonne, what is the arithmetical mean of the weight of a single casting, in grammes, to three significant figures? (One metric tonne = 1 000 kg.)

2. Ten forgings were extracted at random from a large batch. Their masses were stated to be:

4·8 kg	4·9 kg	5·0 kg	5·1 kg
1	4	3	2

If these ten can be considered representative, how many complete forgings can be expected from a batch of mass one metric tonne?

3. Samples of small screws are delivered to a factory in packets of 100. An analysis of the defective screws in 30 packets yielded the following data:

Defective screws	0	1	2	3	4
No. of packets	14	9	4	2	1

How many packets should be ordered to allow for 100 000 acceptable screws?

4. The production of articles from nine successive shifts was:

$$116 \quad 121 \quad 115 \quad 122 \quad 121 \quad 120 \quad 117 \quad 119 \quad 120$$

(*a*) What is the mean rate of production?
(*b*) How many are required from a tenth shift to bring the mean rate of production over all 10 shifts to 120 articles per shift?

5. The root-mean-square of a set of numbers is found by squaring them, determining the mean of the squares and finding the square root of this mean.

(*a*) Find the root-mean-square of 15, 12, 20, 16 and 17.

(*b*) Find the mean of the five numbers.

6. Fifty articles were measured on a dimension nominally 25 mm and put into categories as follows:

L (mm)	24·6	24·8	25·0	25·2	25·4
Number in this category	7	12	16	9	6

Determine the arithmetical mean of L for this particular sample of 50.

7. Four castings were chosen at random from a batch of 64 similar fettled castings and their masses were 15·7, 16·5, 15·3 and 16·7 kg. The cupola melt for the batch was 1·25 metric tonnes. Determine:

(*a*) The mean mass of the four castings.

(*b*) The percentage of the cupola melt that appeared in the fettled castings, assuming that the four chosen at random were representative of the whole batch.

8. The average number of articles produced in 19 successive shifts was 283. How many must be produced on the twentieth shift to raise the overall average to 285?

9. Six rivet-making machines are producing identical components. 80 different observations of the number of machines idle were as follows:

Machines idle	0	1	2	3	4	5	6
Frequency	15	15	21	18	7	3	1

Obtain a value for the average number of machines idle, and hence determine an estimation of the total production of rivets from the group of six machines for an 8-hour shift if each machine is capable of producing 150 articles per hour when operating continually.

10. The following are the production figures for 50 different shifts:

390	407	372	407	411	385	377	406	399	387
401	397	407	383	395	415	395	381	416	417
388	402	410	424	407	404	416	409	406	387
407	381	396	397	375	395	398	394	379	425
387	399	416	397	413	416	405	395	427	397

The true arithmetical mean of the values obtained by totalling all 50 quantities and dividing by 50 is 400. Make a frequency table by putting all the values 370–379 inclusive in one cell, 380–389 in another and so on. Use the value 374·5 as the variate for the first cell, 384·5 for the next and so on. Evaluate the arithmetical mean, and determine the percentage error of the arithmetical mean obtained by this approximate method.

11. In an experiment five lines were measured, and their lengths in millimetres and inches were stated to be:

Length in millimetres	151	178	203	229	254
Length in inches	6	7	8	9	10

Determine:
(*a*) the average length in millimetres;
(*b*) the average length in inches;
(*c*) an 'experimental' value for the number of millimetres in an inch, to three significant figures.

12. Express the following fractions as percentages:
(*a*) $\frac{1}{2}$ (*b*) $\frac{1}{5}$ (*c*) $\frac{3}{4}$ (*d*) $\frac{5}{8}$

13. Express the following percentages as vulgar fractions:
(*a*) $33\frac{1}{3}\%$ (*b*) $31\frac{1}{4}\%$ (*c*) $14\frac{2}{7}\%$ (*d*) $44\frac{4}{9}\%$

14. An article purchased for £4 is resold for £5·40. What percentage of the purchase price is the profit?

15. Trains hauled by steam locomotives complete a journey between two towns 75 kilometres apart in an hour and a half. The introduction of diesel haulage raises the mean speed by 20%. What time is saved by the use of diesel locomotives?

16. Producing at 'standard rate', a firm can complete an order in 20 working days. After producing for 8 days at standard rate, the production rate is accelerated by $33\frac{1}{3}\%$. How many working days are saved by accelerating production?

17. The conversion factor between metric and British units of length is that 1 in = 25·4 mm. What is the percentage error, to two significant figures, if 1 mm is taken as 0·040 in?

18. A lighting fitment is considered to be 80% efficient when first installed. At the end of every month its efficiency has fallen by 10% of the value of efficiency at the commencement of that month. What is the efficiency of the fitment at the end of four successive months after installation?

19. A firm receives its supplies of resistors from three sources, A, B and C. Source A supplies as many as B and C together, while B supplies 3 times as many as C. Of those supplied, the acceptable articles from A, B and C are 80%, 80% and 100% respectively. If a random collection of 825 acceptable resistors is issued by the firm's stores, how many can be expected to have originated from each supplier?

20. When two resistors R_1 and R_2 are connected in parallel, the equivalent resistor R can be obtained from the formula:

$$\frac{1}{R} = \frac{1}{R_1} + \frac{1}{R_2}$$

In a circuit, the values of R_1 and R_2 are originally 3 ohms and 6 ohms respectively. If R is to remain unchanged, what percentage change must be made to R_2 when the value of R_1 is increased by $33\frac{1}{3}\%$.

21. If C is the distance across corners of a hexagon, the approximate area of the hexagon is $0·65\ C^2$. Find the percentage reduction in volume when a circular bar of diameter 20 mm is milled into hexagonal form 20 mm across corners. (π can be taken as $\frac{22}{7}$, and give the answer to the nearest whole number.)

22. In a particular measurement of angles using a unit called a radian, four-figure mathematical tables quote one minute as being equal to 0·000 3 radian. The accurate value is obtained by multiplying

the angle in degrees by $\frac{\pi}{180}$. Taking π as 3·142, calculate, to two significant figures, the percentage inaccuracy of four-figure tables for the value of one minute in radian measure.

23. 10 kg of scrap brass having a composition of 60% copper to 40% zinc are melted down with 20 kg of a different brass having a composition of 70% of copper to 30% of zinc. Determine the percentage composition of the new alloy.

24. A contract of 4 800 articles is scheduled to be completed in twelve weeks at the rate of 400 articles per week and commences at this rate. After six weeks of production at this rate the contract is re-scheduled so that completion is to be effected one week early. By what percentage must the weekly production rise if a constant rate of production is to be maintained over the last five weeks?

25. What is the percentage increase in the area of a circle when its diameter of 50 mm is increased by 8%?

26. Ohm's Law can be stated symbolically as:

$$V = IR$$

If the resistance R is increased by 5% and the current I decreased by 7%, find the percentage change in the potential difference V.

27. If a lamp of power P is placed d m from a screen, the intensity of illumination I at the screen is given by:

$$I = \frac{kP}{d^2}$$

k being a constant. A lamp is initially 5 m from a screen. By what percentage is I increased if the lamp is moved 1 m nearer the screen?

28. What is the percentage change in the volume of a cylinder if its radius increases by 10% and its length decreases by 4%?

29. The bore of a water pipe has a diameter of 20 mm. Calculate, to two significant figures, the percentage reduction in cross-sectional area when the bore becomes coated with scale to a depth of 0·3 mm.

Answers to Problems 1.6

1. 730 g
2. 201
3. 1 010
4. (*a*) 119/shift   (*b*) 129
5. (*a*) 16·2   (*b*) 16·0
6. 24·98 mm
7. (*a*) 16·05 kg   (*b*) 82·2%
8. 323
9. 2 machines idle, 4 800
10. Mean = 399·1, error = 0·225%
11. (*a*) 203 mm   (*b*) 8 in   (*c*) 25·4
12. (*a*) 50%   (*b*) 20%   (*c*) 75%   (*d*) 62·5%
13. (*a*) $\frac{1}{3}$ (*b*) $\frac{5}{16}$ (*c*) $\frac{1}{7}$ (*d*) $\frac{4}{9}$
14. 35%
15. 15 min
16. 3
17. 1·6%
18. 52·5%
19. $A = 400$, $B = 300$, $C = 125$
20. R_2 decreased by $33\frac{1}{3}$% to 4 ohms
21. 17%
22. 3·1%
23. $66\frac{2}{3}$% of copper with $33\frac{1}{3}$% of zinc
24. 20%
25. 16·6%
26. Reduced by 2·35%
27. 56·25%
28. Increased by 16·2%
29. 5·9%

Chapter Two

Algebra

2.1 Basic Algebraic Processes

2.1.1 ALGEBRAIC TERMS

Engineers often use symbols to obtain a general solution to a number of problems of a similar nature. With the aid of this general solution or *formula*, they are able to solve subsequent problems of the same type. As an example, the area of any rectangle of length L and width W is $L \times W$. If we require the area of a particular rectangle, we substitute appropriate values for L and for W.

The product of two symbols, such as x multiplied by y, is written as xy. If no arithmetical sign is indicated, a positive value is assumed. It is conventional practice with the product of symbols to write them in alphabetical order, thus:

$$c \times b \text{ is usually indicated as } bc$$

The method can be continued to more than two symbols, for example:

$$a \times d \times b \times e \times c \text{ is usually indicated as } abcde$$

The product of a number and symbols is indicated by writing the number first, thus:

$$3 \times a \times b = 3ab$$
$$4a \times 5b = (4 \times 5)(a \times b) = 20ab$$
$$5x \times 3y \times 4z = (5 \times 3 \times 4)(x \times y \times z) = 60xyz$$

The mathematical name for a multiplier is a *coefficient*. A product of numbers and symbols together with either a positive or negative sign, or implied positive sign, is called an *algebraic term*.

Hence, in the algebraic term $60xyz$, the coefficient of xyz is 60, the coefficient of yz is $60x$, and the coefficient of y is $60xz$. If no numerical coefficient is indicated, the coefficient is understood to be unity; for example, $ab = 1ab$.

2.1.2 ARITHMETICAL SIGNS

The rule for the determination of signs in multiplication and division, is that *a manipulation between two like signs produces a positive result, while a manipulation between two unlike signs produces a negative result.* The reader will find it safer, for the time being, to regard all symbols as positive and to carry out a separate manipulation to find the correct arithmetical sign. As examples:

$$5a \times -4b = (+ \times -)(5 \times 4)(a \times b)$$
$$= -20ab$$

and $-2a \times -b \times 7c = (- \times - \times +)(2 \times 1 \times 7)(a \times b \times c)$
$$= (+ \times +)(14)(abc)$$
$$= +14abc$$
$$= 14abc$$

Division of a pair of algebraic symbols or terms is indicated similarly to a vulgar fraction. Thus:

$$a \div b \text{ is written } \frac{a}{b}$$

and $\qquad\qquad 2x \div 3y \text{ is written } \dfrac{2x}{3y}$

(In this case, the coefficient of $\dfrac{x}{y}$ is $\dfrac{2}{3}$, the coefficient of $\dfrac{1}{y}$ is $\dfrac{2x}{3}$, and so on.)

2.1.3 THE LAWS OF INDICES

The product of like algebraic symbols is indicated by using that symbol with an *index* to show how many of that particular symbol are multiplied together.

$$a \times a \times a \times a = 4 \text{ '}a\text{s' multiplied together}$$
$$= a^4$$
$$x \times x = 2 \text{ '}x\text{s' multiplied together}$$
$$= x^2$$

Let us now deduce some rules for the manipulation of indices.

$$x^2 \times x^3 = (x \times x) \times (x \times x \times x) = x^5$$
$$a^4 \times a = (a \times a \times a \times a) \times (a) = a^5$$

Hence, in general $\qquad x^m \times x^n = x^{m+n}$

For division $\dfrac{x^5}{x^3} = \dfrac{x \times x \times x \times x \times x}{x \times x \times x} = x^2$

and $\qquad \dfrac{a^6}{a^5} = \dfrac{a \times a \times a \times a \times a \times a}{a \times a \times a \times a \times a} = a^1 = a$

We observe that certain of the 'as' in the denominator cancel with some of those in the numerator, and in general:

$$\frac{x^m}{x^n} = x^{m-n}$$

For powers $(a^2)^3 = a^2 \times a^2 \times a^2$
$$= (a \times a) \times (a \times a) \times (a \times a)$$
$$= 6 \text{ 'as' multiplied together}$$
$$= a^6$$

and in general $(x^m)^n = x^{mn}$

The reader will observe that we have quietly introduced a new topic, a pair of brackets. This has been done to indicate quite clearly that x^m is to be raised to the nth power. A pair of brackets indicates that any operation has to be conducted on everything inside the brackets, *and that what is inside the brackets has to be treated as a complete entity.*

For roots, we can work back from the rule for products.

$\sqrt[5]{x} = x$ raised to some power so that when five of them are multiplied together they produce x^1

$$= x^{1/5}$$

Similarly $\sqrt[3]{x} = x^{1/3}$

because $x^{1/3} \times x^{1/3} \times x^{1/3} = x^{(1/3+1/3+1/3)} = x^1 = x$

Finally $\sqrt[4]{x^3} = x^{3/4}$

because $x^{3/4} \times x^{3/4} \times x^{3/4} \times x^{3/4} = x^{(3/4+3/4+3/4+3/4)} = x^3$

Hence, in general $\sqrt[n]{x} = x^{1/n}$

and $\sqrt[n]{x^m} = x^{m/n}$

Before we leave the laws of indices, let us see if we can reason what is meant by x^0 and by x^{-m}

$$x^0 = x^{3-3} \text{ or } x^{5-5} \text{ or } x^{m-m}$$
$$= (x^3 \div x^3) \text{ or } (x^5 \div x^5) \text{ or } (x^m \div x^m)$$
$$= \text{unity in every case}$$

The answer of unity does not involve x, hence *anything raised to the power of zero is unity.*

Now $$\frac{1}{x^2} = x^0 \div x^2 = x^{0-2} = x^{-2}$$

and $$\frac{1}{a^3} = a^0 \div a^3 = a^{0-3} = a^{-3}$$

Hence, in general $x^{-m} = \dfrac{1}{x^m}$

Summarizing the rules for indices:

$$x^m \times x^n = x^{m+n}$$
$$\frac{x^m}{x^n} = x^{m-n}$$
$$(x^m)^n = x^{mn}$$
$$\sqrt[n]{x^m} = x^{m/n}$$

and we note that
$$x^{-m} = \frac{1}{x^m}$$

and that anything to the power of zero is unity.

We will now illustrate all our information on fundamental symbolic notation with some examples. They are intentionally worked out in detail. As the reader acquires skill in algebraic manipulation, he will find that it is unnecessary to write down many of the intermediary steps which are indicated. Nevertheless, it is advisable to proceed cautiously and accurately. The spending of a little extra time in clearly indicating steps towards a solution is not really as wasteful as it may seem.

Example

Express in the simplest terms:

(a) $5a^2b \times 5a^3b^2$ (b) $42x^2y^2 \div 7xy$ (c) $27a^3b \div 2ab^3$

All symbols to have positive indices.

(a)
$$5a^2b \times 5a^3b^2 = (5 \times 5)(a^2 \times a^3)(b \times b^2)$$
$$= 25(a^{2+3})(b^{1+2})$$
$$= 25a^5b^3$$

(b)
$$42x^2y^2 \div 7xy = \left(\frac{42}{7}\right)\left(\frac{x^2}{x}\right)\left(\frac{y^2}{y}\right)$$
$$= 6(x^{2-1})(y^{2-1})$$
$$= 6x^1y^1$$
$$= 6xy$$

(c)
$$27a^3b \div 2ab^3 = \left(\frac{27}{2}\right)\left(\frac{a^3}{a}\right)\left(\frac{b}{b^3}\right)$$
$$= \frac{27}{2}(a^{3-1})(b^{1-3})$$
$$= \frac{27}{2}a^2b^{-2} \qquad \text{(cont. overleaf)}$$

$$= \frac{27}{2}a^2\left(\frac{1}{b^2}\right)$$

$$= \frac{27a^2}{2b^2}$$

Answers: (a) $25a^5b^3$

(b) $6xy$

(c) $\dfrac{27a^2}{2b^2}$

If square roots are taken, the sign $\pm$, read as 'plus or minus', is applied to the numerical coefficient, together with the positive value of the symbolic term. Furthermore, it is considered quite satisfactory to leave answers in an indicial form. If no numerical value is quoted for a root, a square root is implied.

Example

Express in simplest terms:

(a) $\sqrt{(36x^4y^2)}$ (b) $\sqrt{(x^2y)}$ (c) $\sqrt[3]{(-27x^6y^3)}$

(a)
$$\begin{aligned}
\sqrt{\{36x^4y^2\}} &= \sqrt{\{(36)(x^4)(y^2)\}} \\
&= (\pm 6)(x^{4/2})(y^{2/2}) \\
&= (\pm 6)(x^2)(y^1) \\
&= \pm 6x^2y
\end{aligned}$$

(b)
$$\begin{aligned}
\sqrt{\{x^2y\}} &= \sqrt{\{(1)(x^2)(y^1)\}} \\
&= (\pm 1)(x^{2/2})(y^{1/2}) \\
&= (\pm 1)(x^1)(y^{1/2}) \\
&= \pm\, xy^{1/2}
\end{aligned}$$

(c)
$$\begin{aligned}
\sqrt[3]{\{-27x^6y^3\}} &= \sqrt[3]{\{(-27)(x^6)(y^3)\}} \\
&= (-3)(x^{6/3})(y^{3/3}) \\
&= (-3)(x^2)(y^1) \\
&= -3x^2y
\end{aligned}$$

Answers: (a) $\pm 6x^2y$

(b) $\pm xy^{1/2}$

(c) $-3x^2y$

Example

Simplify:

(a) $\dfrac{6a^2bc}{15a^3b^2c^2} \times \dfrac{24bc^3}{3ac}$ (b) $\dfrac{-5a^2b}{4ab^3} \div \dfrac{25ab^2}{-16a^4}$

58

(a) $\dfrac{6a^2bc}{15a^3b^2c^2} \times \dfrac{24bc^3}{3ac} = \left(\dfrac{6 \times 24}{15 \times 3}\right)\left(\dfrac{a^2}{a^3 \times a}\right)\left(\dfrac{b \times b}{b^2}\right)\left(\dfrac{c \times c^3}{c^2 \times c}\right)$

$$= \left(\dfrac{16}{5}\right)\left(\dfrac{a^2}{a^{3+1}}\right)\left(\dfrac{b^{1+1}}{b^2}\right)\left(\dfrac{c^{1+3}}{c^{2+1}}\right)$$

$$= \left(\dfrac{16}{5}\right)\left(\dfrac{a^2}{a^4}\right)\left(\dfrac{b^2}{b^2}\right)\left(\dfrac{c^4}{c^3}\right)$$

$$= \left(\dfrac{16}{5}\right)\left(a^{2-4}\right)\left(b^{2-2}\right)\left(c^{4-3}\right)$$

$$= \left(\dfrac{16}{5}\right)\left(a^{-2}\right)\left(b^0\right)\left(c^1\right)$$

$$= \left(\dfrac{16}{5}\right)\left(\dfrac{1}{a^2}\right)\left(\dfrac{1}{1}\right)\left(c\right)$$

$$= \dfrac{16c}{5a^2}$$

(b) $\dfrac{-5a^2b}{4ab^3} \div \dfrac{25ab^2}{-16a^4} = \dfrac{-5a^2b}{4ab^3} \times \dfrac{-16a^4}{25ab^2}$

$$= \left(\dfrac{- \times -}{+ \times +}\right)\left(\dfrac{5 \times 16}{4 \times 25}\right)\left(\dfrac{a^2 \times a^4}{a \times a}\right)\left(\dfrac{b}{b^3 \times b^2}\right)$$

$$= \left(\dfrac{+}{+}\right)\left(\dfrac{4}{5}\right)\left(\dfrac{a^{2+4}}{a^{1+1}}\right)\left(\dfrac{b}{b^{3+2}}\right)$$

$$= \left(+\right)\left(\dfrac{4}{5}\right)\left(\dfrac{a^6}{a^2}\right)\left(\dfrac{b^1}{b^5}\right)$$

$$= \left(\dfrac{4}{5}\right)\left(a^{6-2}\right)\left(b^{1-5}\right)$$

$$= \left(\dfrac{4}{5}\right)\left(a^4\right)\left(b^{-4}\right)$$

$$= \left(\dfrac{4}{5}\right)\left(a^4\right)\left(\dfrac{1}{b^4}\right)$$

$$= \dfrac{4a^4}{5b^4}$$

Answers: (a) $\dfrac{16c}{5a^2}$ (b) $\dfrac{4a^4}{5b^4}$

c

Problems 2.1

Express questions 1–7 in the simplest manner, all symbols to have positive indices:

1. (a) $3a \times 7b$ (b) $2a \times 4b \times 3c$
   (c) $2a \times -5b \times 2c$ (d) $-5c \times -3b \times -4a$
   (e) $a \times -b \times 2c \times -3d$ (f) $7x \times -2y \times -5z$

2. (a) $36xy \div 3x$ (b) $28xyz \div 4xy$
   (c) $8abc \div 4abc$ (d) $81xyz \div -3x$
   (e) $-15xy \div -3xz$ (f) $-2xy \div 8z$

3. (a) $4a \times 6b \div 8c$ (b) $6ab \times -3c \div 4d$
   (c) $8ab \div 2a \times -4c$ (d) $-4abc \div 2a \times 3d$

4. (a) $x^2 \times x^4$ (b) $x^2 \times x^3 \times x^4$
   (c) $-x \times x^5$ (d) $x^2 \times x^3 \times y^3$
   (e) $x \times x^4 \times y^2 \times y^3 \times z$ (f) $2x \times 3x^2 \times -4y$

5. (a) $a^5 \div a^2$ (b) $a^2 \div a^5$
   (c) $-a^2 \div a$ (d) $15a^4 \div 5a^2$
   (e) $-27x^5 \div 3x$ (f) $-125x \div -25x^2$

6. (a) $(x^2)^3$ (b) $\sqrt[3]{x^9}$
   (c) $(\sqrt{x})^4$ (d) $\sqrt[2]{x^5}$
   (e) $\sqrt{(9x^4)}$ (f) $\sqrt[3]{(-125x^6y^3)}$

7. (a) $\dfrac{27a^2b^3}{3ab^2}$ (b) $\dfrac{-64a^4b^3}{4ab}$

   (c) $\dfrac{16a^2 \times 5b^2}{4ab}$ (d) $\dfrac{-27a \times 4b^2}{2b \times 3a}$

   (e) $\sqrt{\left(\dfrac{5a^6 \times 25a^4}{8a}\right)}$ (f) $\left(\dfrac{2a^2 \times 3a}{4b}\right)^2$

8. Simplify:
   (a) $\dfrac{4a^2c^2}{3bd^2} \times \dfrac{9bd}{16a^3c}$ (b) $\dfrac{9a^2b^2}{16c^4} \div \dfrac{3}{4c^2}$

9. Simplify:
   (a) $\dfrac{2a^3}{3bc} \times \dfrac{5b^2}{4ca^2} \times \dfrac{3c^2}{2ab^4}$ (b) $\sqrt[4]{(81a^4b^8)}$

10. Simplify:

(a) $\dfrac{6a^2b \times 2ab^2c}{(ab)^2 \times 24abc^2}$　　(b) $x^{1/2} \times y^{1/3} \times x^{3/2} \times y^{5/3}$

11. Simplify:

(a) $10^5 \times 10^{-2} \div 10^{-3}$　　(b) $(9x^2y^6)^{3/2}$

12. Simplify, giving answers with positive indices:

(a) $\dfrac{10x^{-3/8}}{5x^{-3/4}}$　　(b) $\dfrac{14a^{-3}b^{-2}}{7a^2b^3}$　　(c) $\sqrt{(36p^{3/4}q^{1/2})} \times p^{-1/4}q^{1/2}$

13. Simplify, giving answers with positive indices only:

(a) $\dfrac{4e^{-2}f^{-3/4} \times 3g^{4/3}}{18e^3f^{1/4}g^{1/3}}$　　(b) $\dfrac{\sqrt[3]{(27p^4q^5)}}{p^{-2/3}q^{-1/3}}$

14. Simplify:

(a) $\dfrac{x^{2/3} \times y^{1/2} \times z^{3/2}}{x^{-1/3} \times y^2 \times z^{2/3}}$

15. Simplify:

$(a^{2/3}b^{2/5})^4 \div (a^{1/6}b^{1/5})^{-2}$

16. Simplify:

(a) $(x^{3/5}y^{1/4})^2 \times (x^{2/5}y^{1/2})^{-3}$　　(b) $32^{3/5}$

17. Simplify, writing answers with positive indices only:

(a) $10^3 \times 10^{-4} \div 10^{-2}$　　(b) $(a^{-2}b^{1/2})^{-3}$　　(c) $\dfrac{3x^{-2}y}{y^{-2}}$

18. Simplify:

(a) $7^{3/2} \times 28^{1/2}$　　(b) $a^{-3/2} \times (4a)^{1/2}$
(c) $9^n \times 3^{-2n}$　　(d) $16^{3/2} \times 9^{1/2} \div 6$

19. Simplify the following:

(a) $\dfrac{2a^2b}{3ab^2} \times \dfrac{7a}{5b^2}$　　(b) $\sqrt{\left(\dfrac{9a^2b^2}{16c^4}\right)} \div \dfrac{3}{4c^2}$
(c) $\dfrac{4a^2c^2}{bd^2} \times \dfrac{9bd}{16a^3c}$

61

Mathematics for Mechanical Technicians 1

Answers to Problems 2.1

1. (a) $21ab$ (b) $24abc$ (c) $-20abc$
   (d) $-60abc$ (e) $6abcd$ (f) $70xyz$

2. (a) $12y$ (b) $7z$ (c) 2

   (d) $-27yz$ (e) $\dfrac{5y}{z}$ (f) $-\dfrac{xy}{4z}$

3. (a) $\dfrac{3ab}{c}$ (b) $\dfrac{9abc}{2d}$
   (c) $-16bc$ (d) $-6bcd$

4. (a) x^6 (b) x^9 (c) $-x^6$
   (d) x^5y^3 (e) x^5y^5z (f) $-24x^3y$

5 (a) a^3 (b) $\dfrac{1}{a^3}$ (c) $-a$

   (d) $3a^2$ (e) $-9x^4$ (f) $\dfrac{5}{x}$

6. (a) x^6 (b) x^3 (c) x^2
   (d) $\pm x^{5/2}$ (e) $\pm 3x^2$ (f) $-5x^2y$

7. (a) $9ab$ (b) $-16a^3b^2$ (c) $20ab$
   (d) $-18b$ (e) $\dfrac{5a^3}{2}$ (f) $\dfrac{9a^6}{4b^2}$

8. (a) $\dfrac{3c}{4ad}$ (b) $\dfrac{3a^2b^2}{4c^2}$

9. (a) $\dfrac{5}{4b^3}$ (b) $\pm 3ab^2$

10. (a) $\dfrac{1}{2c}$ (b) x^2y^2

11. (a) 10^6 (b) $27x^3y^9$

12. (a) $2x^{3/8}$ (b) $\dfrac{2}{a^5b^5}$ (c) $\pm 6p^{1/8}q^{1/2}$

13. (a) $\dfrac{2g}{3e^5f}$ (b) $3p^2q^2$

14. $\dfrac{xz^{5/6}}{y^{3/2}}$

15. a^3b^2

16. (a) $\dfrac{1}{y}$ (b) 8

17. (*a*) 10　　　(*b*) $\dfrac{a^6}{b^{3/2}}$　　　(*c*) $\dfrac{3y^3}{x^2}$

18. (*a*) 98　　　(*b*) $\pm\,\dfrac{2}{a}$

19. (*a*) $\dfrac{14a^2}{15b^3}$　　　(*b*) $\pm\,ab$　　　(*c*) $\dfrac{3c}{4ad}$

2.2　Manipulation of Algebraic Expressions

2.2.1　ADDITION OF ALGEBRAIC EXPRESSIONS

The work on algebra that has been undertaken thus far has been confined to the multiplication and division of single algebraic terms, such as $3x, -5a^4, \dfrac{2\sqrt{x}}{ab^3}$, etc.

An *algebraic expression* is a collection of single terms, such as:

$$2x^4 + 3x^3 + 3x^2 - 5x$$

Algebraic expressions can be added, subtracted, multiplied and divided by methods closely similar to those used in ordinary arithmetic. Just as in arithmetical work we distinguish between units, tens, hundreds, etc. so in algebraic work we must distinguish between the different symbolic portions of algebraic expressions. In arithmetic we keep units under units, tens under tens and so on, in columns. In algebraic operations we keep x^2 terms in one column, x terms in another column and so on.

If we consider the expression:

$$3x^4 - x^3 + \frac{x^2}{4} - 5x - 15 + \frac{4}{x} - \frac{7}{x^2}$$

we observe that the power of x is decreased by one as we proceed from term to term. The expression is said to be arranged in *descending powers of x*. Until the reader becomes familiar with the layout of problems involving the manipulation of algebraic expressions, he is advised to keep as near as possible to descending powers of symbols, leaving a space for a particular term in an expression if one of the logical descending powers is omitted.

As an example, $2x^3 - x + 5$ should be spaced as:

$$2x^3 \boxed{} - x + 5$$

and $x^4 - 2x^2 + 8$ as:

$$x^4 \boxed{} - 2x^2 \boxed{} + 8$$

If we add 7 583 and 204, what we really do in denary arithmetic is add coefficients in the following manner, giving an answer of 7 787.

$$
\begin{array}{llll}
7(10^3) & + 5(10^2) & + 8(10^1) & + 3(10^0) \\
        & + 2(10^2) &   & + 4(10^0) \\
\hline
7(10^3) & + 7(10^2) & + 8(10^1) & + 7(10^0)
\end{array}
$$

We do exactly the same thing when adding algebraic expressions, by adding the coefficients in the columns just as we do in arithmetic.

Example

Find the sum of $2x^2 - 3x + 5$, $x^2 + x - 11$ and $3x + 4x^2 + 2$.

$$
\begin{array}{l}
2x^2 - 3x + 5 \\
x^2 + x - 11 \\
3x^2 + 4x + 2 \\
\hline
6x^2 + 2x - 4
\end{array}
$$

Answer: $6x^2 + 2x - 4$

Example

Find the sum of $x^3 + 5x$, $2x^2 - 7x + 4$, $-x^3 + 3x^2 - 5x + 2$ and $3x^3 + 2x^2 - 7$.

In this case we have descending powers of x from x^3 to the constants, which are multiples of x^0. Some of the expressions do not include all the descending powers, but columns for x^3, x^2, x and constant terms have to be included.

$$
\begin{array}{llll}
x^3 &   & + 5x &   \\
     & 2x^2 & - 7x & + 4 \\
-x^3 & + 3x^2 & - 5x & + 2 \\
3x^3 & + 2x^2 &   & - 7 \\
\hline
3x^3 & + 7x^2 & - 7x & - 1
\end{array}
$$

Answer: $3x^3 + 7x^2 - 7x - 1$

2.2.2 SUBTRACTION OF ALGEBRAIC EXPRESSIONS

The terms are again arranged in vertical columns and we operate on the coefficients. Since 'minus minus' is plus, we can adopt the simple rule of 'change the sign of the bottom line and add'.

Example

Subtract $3a^2 - 5a + 8$ from $5a^2 + a - 4$.

$$5a^2 + a - 4$$
$$3a^2 - 5a + 8$$
$$\overline{}$$
$$2a^2 + 6a - 12$$

Answer: $2a^2 + 6a - 12$

Example

Subtract $5x^2 - 4x + 14$ from $2x^3 - 8x + 9$.

$$2x^3 - 8x + 9$$
$$5x^2 - 4x + 14$$
$$\overline{}$$
$$2x^3 - 5x^2 - 4x - 5$$

Answer: $2x^3 - 5x^2 - 4x - 5$

2.2.3 MULTIPLICATION OF ALGEBRAIC EXPRESSIONS

Let us consider the multiplication of 3 457 by 745 in denary arithmetic. We can lay this out as follows:

$$3\overset{\cdot}{}457$$
$$745$$
$$\overline{}$$
$$17\,285$$
$$138\,28$$
$$2\,419\,9$$
$$\overline{}$$
$$2\,575\,465$$

We follow this method in algebra, keeping the terms with like symbols in the same column. With multiplication (and division) a partial check on the accuracy is to let each symbol be unity. For multiplication, the sum of the coefficients and the constant in the answer should be the product of the sums of the coefficients and constant of the expressions that are multiplied together.

Example

Multiply $3x^2 - 8x + 4$ by $2x^2 - 5x + 2$.

$$3x^2 - \ 8x + 4$$
$$2x^2 - \ 5x + 2$$

Multiply top line by 2: $\qquad\qquad 6x^2 - 16x + 8$
Multiply top line by $-5x$: $\qquad -15x^3 + 40x^2 - 20x$
Multiply top line by $2x^2$: $\ 6x^4 - 16x^3 + \ 8x^2$

Add: $\qquad\qquad\qquad 6x^4 - 31x^3 + 54x^2 - 36x + 8$

Partial check by letting $x = 1$: $\quad 3 - 8 + 4 = -1$
$$2 - 5 + 2 = -1$$
$$-1 \times -1 = 1$$
and $\qquad\qquad 6 - 31 + 54 - 36 + 8 = 1$

Answer: $6x^4 - 31x^3 + 54x^2 - 36x + 8$

Example

Multiply $2x^3 - x + 3$ by $x^2 - 5$.

$$2x^3 \qquad - x \ + \ 3$$
$$x^2 \qquad - \ 5$$

Multiply top line by -5: $\qquad -10x^3 \qquad + 5x - 15$
Multiply top line by x^2: $\ 2x^5 - \ x^3 + 3x^2$

Add: $\qquad\qquad 2x^5 - 11x^3 + 3x^2 + 5x - 15$

Partial check by letting $x = 1$: $\quad 2 - 1 + 3 = 4$
$$1 - 5 = -4$$
$$4 \times -4 = -16$$
and $\qquad\qquad 2 - 11 + 3 + 5 - 15 = -16$

Answer: $2x^5 - 11x^3 + 3x^2 + 5x - 15$

2.2.4 DIVISION OF ALGEBRAIC EXPRESSIONS

With division, we divide the first term of the dividend by the first term of the divisor, to obtain the first term of the quotient. A remainder is established, and the next term brought down in a somewhat similar manner to ordinary arithmetic. We continue in the same manner to obtain the remaining terms of the quotient. A partial check should again be applied by summating coefficients and constants.

Example

Divide $6a^4 - 17a^3 + 21a^2 - 27a + 10$ by $2a^2 - 5a + 2$.

$$2a^2 - 5a + 2 \overline{\big)\,\underline{\begin{array}{l} 6a^4 - 17a^3 + 21a^2 - 27a + 10 \\ 6a^4 - 15a^3 + 6a^2 \end{array}}} \quad 3a^2 - a + 5$$

$$\underline{\begin{array}{l} -2a^3 + 15a^2 - 27a \\ -2a^3 + 5a^2 - 2a \end{array}}$$

$$\overline{\begin{array}{l} 10a^2 - 25a + 10 \\ 10a^2 - 25a + 10 \end{array}}$$

Partial check: $6 - 17 + 21 - 27 + 10 = -7$
$2 - 5 + 2 = -1$
$-7 \div -1 = 7$
and $3 - 1 + 5 = 7$

Answer: $3a^2 - a + 5$

Example

Divide $x^3 - 8$ by $x - 2$.

In order to allow for x^2 and x terms if they should appear, the dividend of $x^3 - 8$ will be written as:

$$x^3 \;\boxed{}\quad \boxed{}\; - 8$$

$$x - 2 \overline{\big)\; x^3 \;\boxed{}\quad \boxed{}\; - 8\,} \quad x^2 + 2x + 4$$

$$\underline{x^3 - 2x^2}$$

$$\begin{array}{l} 2x^2 \\ \underline{2x^2 - 4x} \end{array}$$

$$\overline{\begin{array}{ll} 4x & - 8 \\ 4x & - 8 \end{array}}$$

Partial check: $1 - 8 = -7$
$1 - 2 = -1$
$-7 \div -1 = 7$
and $1 + 2 + 4 = 7$

Answer: $x^2 + 2x + 4$

2.2.5 BRACKETS

It was convenient to introduce brackets at an earlier stage of this volume. The reader will recall that if there are numbers and/or algebraic terms inside a pair of brackets they must be treated as a single entity. Any coefficient outside a bracket operates on every term inside the bracket. A bracketed expression should be simplified as far as possible before the coefficient operates. In simplification, we follow the rule used in arithmetic which states that multiplication and division signs have preference over addition and subtraction signs.

Examples

$$3(a^2 + b^2 + c) = 3a^2 + 3b^2 + 3c$$
$$4a(2x^2 + y^2 - 3z) = 8ax^2 + 4ay^2 - 12az$$
$$4(x^4 - x^2 \times x) = 4(x^4 - x^3) = 4x^4 - 4x^3$$
$$-5(a^2 + b^2) = -5a^2 - 5b^2$$
$$-8x(3x^3 - 4x + 2) = -24x^4 + 32x^2 - 16x$$

It will be observed from the above examples that if the coefficient is positive, after it has operated on the bracket the signs are unchanged. If the coefficient is negative, after it has been operated on all the signs are changed.

Remembering that an expression within brackets must be treated as a single entity, if a coefficient is itself bracketed, each term of the coefficient operates on each of the terms of the other bracketed expression.

Examples

$$
\begin{aligned}
(x + y)(x + 2y) &= x(x + 2y) + y(x + 2y) \\
&= x^2 + 2xy + xy + 2y^2 \\
&= x^2 + 3xy + 2y^2
\end{aligned}
$$

$$
\begin{aligned}
(3a - 4b)(3a + 4b) &= 3a(3a + 4b) - 4b(3a + 4b) \\
&= 9a^2 + 12ab - 12ab - 16b^2 \\
&= 9a^2 - 16b^2
\end{aligned}
$$

$$
\begin{aligned}
(4x + 5)(2x - 7) &= 4x(2x - 7) + 5(2x - 7) \\
&= 8x^2 - 28x + 10x - 35 \\
&= 8x^2 - 18x - 35
\end{aligned}
$$

$$
\begin{aligned}
-(3a + 2b)(a - b) &= (-3a - 2b)(a - b) \\
&= -3a(a - b) - 2b(a - b) \\
&= -3a^2 + 3ab - 2ab + 2b^2 \\
&= -3a^2 + ab + 2b^2
\end{aligned}
$$

In order to indicate precisely how entities have to be considered, there are occasions when we find it convenient to have a bracketed expression appearing within another bracket. We adopt a convention that the innermost brackets have to be removed first. In order to distinguish between sets of brackets, the innermost are shown ( ), the next { } and the next [ ]. For the scope of studies for which this volume was intended, it is not necessary to indicate more than three types of bracket sign. When brackets are removed, it is advisable to simplify before proceeding to the removal of the next pair of brackets.

Example

Simplify $2[8x^2 - 2x\{3x - 5(2x)\}]$.

$$2[8x^2 - 2x\{3x - 5(2x)\}]$$
$$= 2[8x^2 - 2x\{3x - 10x\}]$$
$$= 2[8x^2 - 2x\{-7x\}]$$
$$= 2[8x^2 + 14x^2]$$
$$= 2[22x^2]$$
$$= 44x^2$$

Answer: $44x^2$

Example

Simplify $2a[3a^2 - 4\{(a + 3b)(a - 3b) - 2b^2\} + 6]$.

$$2a[3a^2 - 4\{(a + 3b)(a - 3b) - 2b^2\} + 6]$$
$$= 2a[3a^2 - 4\{a^2 - 3ab + 3ab - 9b^2 - 2b^2\} + 6]$$
$$= 2a[3a^2 - 4\{a^2 - 11b^2\} + 6]$$
$$= 2a[3a^2 - 4a^2 + 44b^2 + 6]$$
$$= 2a[-a^2 + 44b^2 + 6]$$
$$= -2a^3 + 88ab^2 + 12a$$

Answer: $-2a^3 + 88ab^2 + 12a$

If we have fractions such as $\dfrac{2x - 3y}{2}$ and $\dfrac{8x^2 - 3y^2}{4x}$, we could express these as $x - \dfrac{3y}{2}$ and $2x - \dfrac{3y^2}{4x}$ respectively. It will be observed that the denominator has been divided into each term of the numerator. Consequently, although the dividing line of a fraction has not the appearance of a pair of brackets, it can be regarded as a pair of brackets for the purposes of algebraic manipulation. Thus:

$$\frac{2x - 3y}{2} \text{ can be indicated as } \frac{1}{2}(2x - 3y)$$

and $\qquad \dfrac{8x^2 - 3y^2}{4x}$,, ,, ,, ,,$\dfrac{1}{4x}$ $(8x^2 - 3y^2)$

Problems 2.2

1. Add:

    (a) $a + 2b + 3c$, $2a + 3b + 4c$ and $3a + 4b + 5c$
    (b) $2x + 3y - z$, $5x - 3y + 2z$ and $-3x - 5y + 6z$
    (c) $x^3 + 3x^2 - 5x + 2$, $2x^3 + 7x + 5$ and $3x^2 - 2x - 7$
    (d) $a^2 + 5ab + b^2$, $-7ab + 3b^2 + 4$ and $3a^2 - b^2 - 7$

2. Subtract:

    (a) $2x^2 + 5x + 8$ from $3x^2 + 8x + 15$
    (b) $2a^2 + 3a - 5$ from $5a^2 - 6a + 2$
    (c) $2x^2 - 5x + 7$ from $-3x^3 + 2x - 15$
    (d) $2a^2 - 7ab + 5b^2$ from $3a^3 - 5a^2 + 2b^2 - 7$

3. Multiply:

    (a) $2x^2 - 5x + 6$ by $x - 3$
    (b) $a^2 + 3a - 4$ by $2a^2 + 6a - 3$

4. Multiply:

    (a) $5x^2 - 4xy + y^2$ by $3x - 7y$
    (b) $2a^2 + 3a - 4$ by $a^2 - 5a + 2$
    (c) $4x^2 - 10xy + 25y^2$ by $2x + 5y$

5. Multiply (and in each case check your result by division):

    (a) $x + 3$ by $x + 5$
    (b) $2x - 3$ by $x - 4$
    (c) $4x + 3y$ by $4x - 3y$
    (d) $x^2 + 3x - 5$ by $2x - 3$
    (e) $x^2 + xy + y^2$ by $x - y$
    (f) $3a^2 + 5a - 7$ by $2a^2 + 3a - 2$

6. Divide:

    (a) $2x^3 + 9x^2 + 5x - 12$ by $x + 3$
    (b) $2a^4 + a^3 - 20a^2 + 29a - 12$ by $2a^2 - 5a + 3$

7. Divide:

   (*a*) $6x^2 + 13xy - 28y^2$ by $2x + 7y$

   (*b*) $2x^3 - 13x^2 + 19x - 6$ by $2x - 3$

   (*c*) $a^3 - 64$ by $a^2 + 4a + 16$

8. Divide (and in each case check your result by multiplication):

   (*a*) $x^2 + 10x + 21$ by $x + 7$

   (*b*) $2x^2 + 5x - 3$ by $x + 3$

   (*c*) $x^2 - xy - 6y^2$ by $x - 3y$

   (*d*) $8a^3 - b^3$ by $2a - b$

   (*e*) $12x^4 + 28x^3 - 53x^2 - 72x + 45$ by $6x^2 - x - 15$

9. Add $2x^2 + 5x - 7$ to $3x^2 - 28x + 19$ and divide the result by $x - 4$.

10. Subtract $x^3 - 2x^2y + 3xy^2 + 4y^3$ from $2x^3 - 2x^2y + 3xy^2 + 12y^3$, and divide the result by $x + 2y$.

11. Simplify:

   (*a*) $3(a^2 + 4a + 7) - 2a(a - 15) - 5(-3a + 4)$

   (*b*) $2\{4a^2 - 5(3a - 2)\} - 3\{2a(a - 8) - 5\}$

   (*c*) $3[8x^3 - 3x\{x^2 - 2(4x - 3) + 7\}]$

   (*d*) $2a[3a^2 - 5a\{-2a + 7(a + 6) - 5(3a + 2)\}]$

12. Simplify:

   (*a*) $3(2x + 5) + 4(3x + 2)$

   (*b*) $7(3x - 2) - 5(x - 5)$

   (*c*) $8(2a^2 - 5a + 3) + 3(2a + 1) - 5(2a^2 - 4)$

   (*d*) $2\{23x - 5(4x + 2) + 7\}$

   (*e*) $3[8a^2 - 2\{15 - 3a(2a + 6) + 4(a + 2)\}]$

Answers to Problems 2.2

1. (*a*) $6a + 9b + 12c$ (*b*) $4x - 5y + 7z$
   (*c*) $3x^3 + 6x^2$ (*d*) $4a^2 - 2ab + 3b^2 - 3$

2. (*a*) $x^2 + 3x + 7$ (*b*) $3a^2 - 9a + 7$
   (*c*) $-3x^3 - 2x^2 + 7x - 22$ (*d*) $3a^3 - 7a^2 + 7ab - 3b^2 - 7$

3. (*a*) $2x^3 - 11x^2 + 21x - 18$
   (*b*) $2a^4 + 12a^3 + 7a^2 - 33a + 12$

4. (*a*) $15x^3 - 47x^2y + 31xy^2 - 7y^3$
   (*b*) $2a^4 - 7a^3 - 15a^2 + 26a - 8$
   (*c*) $8x^3 + 125y^3$

5. (*a*) $x^2 + 8x + 15$ (*b*) $2x^2 - 11x + 12$
   (*c*) $16x^2 - 9y^2$ (*d*) $2x^3 + 3x^2 - 19x + 15$
   (*e*) $x^3 - y^3$ (*f*) $6a^4 + 19a^3 - 5a^2 - 31a + 14$
6. (*a*) $2x^2 + 3x - 4$ (*b*) $a^2 + 3a - 4$
7. (*a*) $3x - 4y$ (*b*) $x^2 - 5x + 2$ (*c*) $a - 4$
8. (*a*) $x + 3$ (*b*) $2x - 1$ (*c*) $x + 2y$
   (*d*) $4a^2 + 2ab + b^2$ (*e*) $2x^2 + 5x - 3$
9. $5x - 3$
10. $x^2 - 2xy + 4y^2$
11. (*a*) $a^2 + 57a + 1$ (*b*) $2a^2 + 18a + 35$
    (*c*) $15x^3 + 72x^2 - 117x$ (*d*) $106a^3 - 320a^2$
12. (*a*) $18x + 23$ (*b*) $16x + 11$ (*c*) $6a^2 - 34a + 47$
    (*d*) $6x - 6$ (*e*) $60a^2 + 84a - 138$

2.3   Factors of Algebraic Expressions

2.3.1   COMMON FACTORS

A factor of a number or an algebraic term is a quantity which will divide into that number or algebraic term without leaving a remainder. The numbers 2, 3, 5 and 7 all divide into 210 without leaving a remainder, and hence 2, 3, 5 and 7 are all factors of 210. Similarly since $(x - 1)$, $(x + 1)$ and $(x + 2)$ all divide into $x^3 + 2x^2 - x - 2$ without leaving a remainder, $(x - 1)$, $(x + 1)$ and $(x + 2)$ are all factors of $x^3 + 2x^2 - x - 2$. Although unity divides into all quantities without leaving a remainder, unity itself is not considered to be a factor.

An algebraic expression consists of two, three or more than three terms. An expression containing two terms is known as a *binomial*, one containing three terms is a *trinomial*, while one containing more than three terms is called a *polynomial*. The first step in determining the factors of any algebraic expression is to see whether or not there are common factors. If so, these should be combined into a single highest common factor.

Example

Find the factors of $9a^2 - 12a$.

Inspection shows that each term is divisible by 3 and by a, hence 3 and a are factors, whilst $3a$ is the highest common factor. (It is true that $-3a$ is also a common factor, but it is conventional practice to consider only positive common factors.)

$$\frac{9a^2 - 12a}{3a} = 3a - 4$$

$$\therefore 9a^2 - 12a = 3a(3a - 4)$$

$3a - 4$ cannot be factorized. Hence the factors of $9a^2 - 12a$ are 3 and $(3a - 4)$.

Answer: $9a^2 - 12a = 3a(3a - 4)$

2.3.2 FACTORS OF BINOMIALS

Apart from a common factor, the most commonly occurring type of binomial with which we are interested in our study of factors is the difference of two perfect squares. (We will leave the sum or difference of two perfect cubes till a little later.) By multiplication:

$$(x + y)(x - y) = x^2 - xy + xy - y^2 = x^2 - y^2$$

Reversing this procedure, the factors of the difference of two perfect squares are the sum and difference of the positive values of the square roots of the terms of the binomial.

Example

Factorize $9a^2 - 16b^2$.

Inspection reveals no common factor.
Considering positive values only, $9a^2 = (3a)^2$ and $16b^2 = (4b)^2$. Hence the factors of $9a^2 - 16b^2$ are $(3a + 4b)$ and $(3a - 4b)$.

Answer: $9a^2 - 16b^2 = (3a + 4b)(3a - 4b)$

Example

Factorize $9y - 36y^3$.

Inspection reveals that $9y$ is the highest common factor.

$$\frac{9y - 36y^3}{9y} = 1 - 4y^2$$

A further inspection reveals that 1 and $4y^2$ are perfect squares.

$$1 = (1)^2 \quad \text{and} \quad 4y^2 = (2y)^2$$
Hence $\quad 1 - 4y^2 = (1 + 2y)(1 - 2y)$
The factors of $9y - 36y^2$ are $9y$, $(1 + 2y)$ and $(1 - 2y)$

Answer: $9y - 36y^2 = 9y(1 + 2y)(1 - 2y)$

Example

Factorize $(5x - 2y)^2 - (4x - 2y)^2$.

The expression is the difference of two squares.

$$(5x - 2y) + (4x - 2y) = 5x - 2y + 4x - 2y = 9x - 4y$$
$$(5x - 2y) - (4x - 2y) = 5x - 2y - 4x + 2y = x$$

Answer: $(5x - 2y)^2 - (4x - 2y)^2 = x(9x - 4y)$

2.3.3 FACTORS OF TRINOMIALS

After it has been checked for common factors, a trinomial should be inspected to see whether or not it is the square of a binomial.

Now
$$(a + b)^2 = a^2 + 2ab + b^2$$
and
$$(a - b)^2 = a^2 - 2ab + b^2$$

The form of a trinomial which is the square of a binomial can be deduced from the above. The square of a binomial is (square of the first term) plus (twice the product of the terms) plus (square of the second term). If the second term of a trinomial is negative, the first and last terms being positive, and the trinomial is a perfect square, it is the square of the difference of two algebraic terms.

Example

Factorize $x^2 + 6x + 9$.

There is no common factor.

$$x^2 = (x)^2 \qquad 9 = (3)^2 \qquad 6x = 2(x)(3)$$

Hence $x^2 + 6x + 9$ is the square of $x + 3$.

Answer: $x^2 + 6x + 9 = (x + 3)^2$

Example

Factorize $9a^2 - 12ab + 4b^2$.

There is no common factor.

$$9a^2 = (3a)^2 \qquad 4b^2 = (2b)^2 \qquad 12ab = 2(3a)(2b)$$

We note that the second term of the trinomial is negative. Hence $9a^2 - 12ab + 4b^2$ is the square of $3a - 2b$.

Answer: $9a^2 - 12ab + 4b^2 = (3a - 2b)^2$

Example

Factorize $75a^2b - 60ab^2 + 12b^3$.

On inspection, 3 and b are common factors; $3b$ is the highest common factor.

$$\frac{75a^2b - 60ab^2 + 12b^3}{3b} = 25a^2 - 20ab + 4b^2$$

$$25a^2 = (5a)^2 \qquad 4b^2 = (2b)^2 \qquad 20ab = 2(5a)(2b)$$

The second term of $25a^2 - 20ab + 4b^2$ is negative. Hence $25a^2 - 20ab + 4b^2$ is the square of $5a - 2b$.

Answer: $75a^2b - 60ab^2 + 12b^3 = 3b(5a - 2b)^2$

Apart from common factors and perfect squares, the only other trinomials which we may be called upon to factorize at our present stage of studies are those trinomials which are the product of two binomials. In general terms:

$$(ax + b)(cx + d) = acx^2 + axd + bcx + bd$$
$$= ac(x^2) + (ad + bc)x + bd$$

What we shall be seeking will be values for a, b, c and d, with correct mathematical signs, so that:

   (i) ac is the coefficient of the first term of the trinomial;
   (ii) bd is the last term of the trinomial; and
   (iii) $ad + bc$ is the coefficient of the second term of the trinomial.

It is now very important to proceed methodically to avoid wasted effort. As always, we first look for a common factor. Following this, on the rare occasions that the first term is negative, we can take out -1 as a temporary common factor to make the first term positive. We now look at the signs in the trinomial. If the signs of the trinomial are all positive, the factors (which are binomials) have positive signs. If the sign of the second term of the trinomial is negative while the sign of the third term is positive, the signs in the brackets are negative. If the sign of the last term of the trinomial is negative, one binomial is an addition, the other is a subtraction. In general:

$$\boxed{} + \boxed{} + \boxed{}$$

$$= \left(\boxed{} + \boxed{} \right) \left(\boxed{} + \boxed{} \right)$$

$$\boxed{} - \boxed{} + \boxed{}$$

$$= \left(\boxed{} - \boxed{} \right) \left(\boxed{} - \boxed{} \right)$$

and $\boxed{} \begin{array}{c} + \\ \text{or} \\ - \end{array} \boxed{} - \boxed{}$

$$= \left(\boxed{} + \boxed{} \right) \left(\boxed{} - \boxed{} \right)$$

Having decided on the pattern of signs, we proceed to find the possible combinations to produce the first term, arranging that the larger factor is quoted first, and not proceeding further if the first factor becomes less than the second. For instance, for $16x^2$, we have:

$$16x \text{ and } x, \qquad 8x \text{ and } 2x, \qquad 4x \text{ and } 4x$$

and it is not necessary to consider reversals such as $2x$ and $8x$, or x and $16x$.

We now list the factors of the third term, including reversals, bearing in mind some of them can be discounted because of the sequence of the signs. We shall now find a pattern where we can patiently try every combination, without duplication, to find the correct combination to produce the second term. Let us illustrate the method with a series of examples.

Example

Factorize $x^2 + 8x + 7$.

There is no common factor, and it is not a perfect square.

Factors of x^2		*Factors of* 7	
x	x	7	1
		1	7

(No need to consider -7 and -1, or -1 and -7, due to the pattern of signs.)

Our combination here is obvious; the factors are $(x + 7)$ and $(x + 1)$.

Answer: $x^2 + 8x + 7 = (x + 7)(x + 1)$

Example

Factorize $2x^2 - 5x + 3$.

There is no common factor, and it is not a perfect square.

Factors of $2x^2$		*Factors of* $+3$	
$2x$	x	-3	-1
		-1	-3

(The pattern of signs eliminates positive factors.)

The combinations possible are:

$$(2x - 3)(x - 1)$$
and
$$(2x - 1)(x - 3)$$

Of these, only the former produces the second term of $-5x$.

Answer: $2x^2 - 5x + 3 = (2x - 3)(x - 1)$

Example

Factorize $4x^2 + 5x - 6$.

There is no common factor, and it is not a perfect square.

Factors of $4x^2$		*Factors of* -6	
$4x$	x	6	-1
$2x$	$2x$	-6	1
		3	-2
		-3	2

We now have to try patiently all possible combinations, and the above layout assists us to list them without duplication. They are:

$(4x + 6)(x - 1)$*	$(2x + 6)(2x - 1)$*
$(4x - 6)(x + 1)$*	$(2x - 6)(x + 1)$*
$(4x + 3)(x - 2)$	$(2x + 3)(x - 2)$
$(4x - 3)(x + 2)$	$(2x - 3)(x + 2)$

We can immediately dismiss those marked with an asterisk, since the first bracket in each case would imply a common factor. Of the others, only $(4x - 3)(x + 2)$ produces the second term of $+5x$.

Answer: $4x^2 + 5x - 6 = (4x - 3)(x + 2)$

2.3.4 POLYNOMIALS OF FOUR TERMS

Having checked for common factors, and dividing by the highest common factor, should common factors occur, the polynomial should be rearranged if necessary into pairs of terms, each pair having a different common factor.

Example

Factorize $3ac + 8bd + 6bc + 4ad$.

. There is no complete common factor, but

$(3ac + 4ad)$ has a common factor of a
$(6bc + 8bd)$ has a common factor of $2b$
$$3ac + 8bd + 6bc + 4ad = (3ac + 4ad) + (6bc + 8bd)$$
$$= a(3c + 4d) + 2b(3c + 4d)$$
$$= (a + 2b)(3c + 4d)$$

Answer: $3ac + 8bd + 6bc + 4ad = (a + 2b)(3c + 4d)$

Example

Factorize $6ac - 2bd + 3bc - 4ad$.

There is no common factor.

$$(6ac + 3bc) = 3c(2a + b)$$
$$(-2bd - 4ad) = 2d(-b - 2a)$$
$$(6ac + 3bc) + (-2bd - 4ad) = 3c(2a + b) + 2d(-b - 2a)$$

We observe that the last bracketed expression can be made identical to the last but one by changing the sign of the coefficient and reversing the order of the terms.

$$(6ac + 3bc) + (-2bd - 4ad) = 3c(2a + b) - 2d(2a + b)$$
$$= (3c - 2d)(2a + b)$$

Answer: $6ac - 2bd + 3bc - 4ad = (2a + b)(3c - 2d)$

2.3.5 GENERAL PROCEDURE FOR OBTAINING FACTORS

The recommended approach to obtaining the factors of an algebraic expression is to look first for common factors. If there is a common factor, or common factors which combine to form a highest common factor, these should be divided into the original expression.

The next step is to recognize the form of the original expression, or the expression which remains after division. It will be a binomial, a trinomial or a polynomial. If it is a binomial, at our present stage of studies it will either not factorize or be the difference of two perfect squares. If it is a trinomial, the first thing to investigate is the possibility of a perfect square. If it is not, it will usually be the product of two different binomials. A polynomial of four terms will also usually be the product of two binomials.

Occasionally it may be necessary for a simplification to be performed before the form can be recognized.

Example

Factorize $4x(x - 3y) + y(12x - 9y)$.

$$4x(x - 3y) + y(12x - 9y) = 4x^2 - 12xy + 12xy - 9y^2$$
$$= 4x^2 - 9y^2$$

This is a binomial without a common factor, and is the difference of two perfect squares.

$$4x^2 = (2x)^2 \quad \text{and} \quad 9y^2 = (3y)^2$$

Hence $\quad 4x^2 - 9y^2 = (2x + 3y)(2x - 3y)$

Answer: $4x(x - 3y) + y(12x - 9y) = (2x + 3y)(2x - 3y)$

2.3.6 FUNCTIONAL NOTATION AND THE FACTOR THEOREM

If two variables are connected by a formula, say y and x, so that the value of y depends upon the value we give to x, we say that y is *a function of x*. There are various mathematical conventions for indicating the statement 'a function of x'. The most common one, which we shall use, is $f(x)$. Others are $\phi(x)$ and $F(x)$. Instead of $y = x^2 + 3x - 4$ we could state $f(x) = x^2 + 3x - 4$.

If we want to indicate the value of $f(x)$ when a specific value is given to x, such as the value of a particular function when $x = 4$, we indicate this as $f(4)$. Thus:

if $\qquad\qquad f(x) = x^2 + 3x - 4$
$\qquad\qquad\qquad f(1) = 1 + 3 - 4 = 0$
$\qquad\qquad\qquad f(0) = 0 + 0 - 4 = -4$
and $\qquad\qquad f(a) = a^2 + 3a - 4$

The following statement, known as the factor theorem, can often assist in determining factors, and is presented without proof:

$$(x - a) \text{ is a factor of } f(x) \text{ if } f(a) = 0$$

As examples:

If $f(x) = x^2 - 1, f(1) = 0$, hence $(x - 1)$ is a factor of $x^2 - 1$
If $f(x) = x^3 - 1, f(1) = 0$, hence $(x - 1)$ is a factor of $x^3 - 1$
If $f(x) = 4x^2 - 13x - 12, f(4) = 64 - 52 - 12 = 0$
hence $x - 4$ is a factor of $4x^2 - 13x - 12$.

The other factor could be found by division.

$$x - 4 \overline{)\begin{array}{l} 4x^2 - 13x - 12 \end{array}} \, 4x + 3$$
$$\underline{4x^2 - 16x}$$
$$3x - 12$$
$$\underline{3x - 12}$$

Thus $4x^2 - 13x - 12 = (x - 4)(4x + 3)$.

The use of the factor theorem can be of assistance in determining which binomials are NOT factors, by using the theorem in reverse:
If $(x - a)$ is to be a factor of $f(x)$ then $f(a) = 0$.
Thus $(x - 1)$ cannot be a factor of $x^3 + 1$, because $f(1) = 2$.
On the other hand, $(x + 1)$ is a factor, since $f(-1) = 0$.

Let us put the factor theorem to use for the factors of the sum and of the difference of two perfect cubes.

If $\qquad\qquad f(a) = a^3 + b^3$
then $\qquad\qquad f(-b) = -b^3 + b^3 = 0$
hence $\qquad \{a-(-b)\} = (a + b)$ is a factor of $a^3 + b^3$

By dividing out, we find the second factor to be:

$$a^2 - ab + b^2 = \{(a + b)^2 - 3ab\} = \{(a - b)^2 + ab\}$$
Hence $\qquad a^3 + b^3 = (a + b)(a^2 - ab + b^2)$
$$= (a + b)\{(a + b)^2 - 3ab\}$$
$$= (a + b)\{(a - b)^2 + ab\}$$

Let us proceed to the difference of two cubes, by factorizing $a^3 - b^3$.

If $\qquad\qquad f(a) = a^3 - b^3$
we note $\qquad\qquad f(b) = b^3 - b^3 = 0$
hence $\qquad\qquad a - b$ is a factor of $a^3 - b^3$

By dividing out, we find that the second factor is $a^2 + ab + b^2$.
$$a^2 + ab + b^2 = \{(a + b)^2 - ab\} = \{(a - b)^2 + 3ab\}$$
Hence $\qquad a^3 - b^3 = (a - b)(a^2 + ab + b^2)$
$$= (a - b)\{(a + b)^2 - ab\}$$
$$= (a - b)\{(a - b)^2 + 3ab\}$$

Unless the reader has an above average memory it is advisable not to remember the factors of the sum and of the difference of two cubes but to work from first principles, remembering that one factor of $(a^3 + b^3)$ is $(a + b)$ and that one factor of $(a^3 - b^3)$ is $(a - b)$.

Example

Factorize $8x^3 - 27y^3$

$$\sqrt[3]{(8x^3)} = 2x \qquad \sqrt[3]{(27y^3)} = 3y$$

Hence $2x - 3y$ is a factor.

$$2x - 3y \begin{array}{|l}
8x^3 \qquad\qquad\qquad\quad - 27y^3 \\
8x^3 - 12x^2y \\
\hline
\quad 12x^2y \\
\quad 12x^2y - 18xy^2 \\
\hline
\qquad\qquad 18xy^2 - 27y^3 \\
\qquad\qquad 18xy^2 - 27y^3 \\
\hline
\end{array} \Big| 4x^2 + 6xy + 9y^2$$

Answer: $8x^3 - 27y^3 = (2x - 3y)(4x^2 + 6xy + 9y^2)$

2.3.7. FRACTIONS OF ALGEBRAIC EXPRESSIONS

In article 2.2.1, the reader was shown how the processes of addition, subtraction, multiplication and division with algebraic expressions follow very closely the rules of fundamental arithmetic. We shall now proceed to a similar application of arithmetical rules to problems dealing with fractions of algebraic expressions. In the addition and subtraction of vulgar fractions we had to express fractions with a common denominator. We follow the same method with algebraic fractions by obtaining a common denominator which is the least common multiple of the various denominators.

Example

Simplify $\dfrac{3}{2a^2} + \dfrac{4b}{3a} - \dfrac{5}{4a^2}$.

We require the L.C.M. of $2a^2$, $3a$ and $4a^2$.

$$2a^2 = 2 \times a \times a$$
$$3a = 3 \times a$$
$$4a^2 = 2 \times 2 \times a \times a$$
$$\text{L.C.M.} = (2 \times 2 \times 3) \times a^2 = 12a^2$$
$$\frac{3}{2a^2} + \frac{4b}{3a} - \frac{5}{4a^2} = \frac{6(3)}{6(2a^2)} + \frac{4a(4b)}{4a(3a)} - \frac{3(5)}{3(4a^2)}$$
$$= \frac{18 + 16ab - 15}{12a^2} = \frac{16ab + 3}{12a^2}$$

Answer: $\dfrac{16ab + 3}{12a^2}$

Example

Simplify $\dfrac{5x + 3}{x + 1} + \dfrac{2x + 5}{x - 1} - \dfrac{5}{2(x^2 - 1)}$.

We require the L.C.M. of $x + 1$, $x - 1$, and $2(x^2 - 1)$.

Now $\qquad\qquad\qquad 2(x^2 - 1) = 2(x + 1)(x - 1)$

so $\qquad\qquad\qquad 2(x^2 - 1)$ is the L.C.M.

since $x + 1$ and $x - 1$, the other two denominators, are factors of $2(x^2 - 1)$.

$$\dfrac{5x + 3}{x + 1} + \dfrac{2x + 5}{x - 1} - \dfrac{5}{2(x^2 - 1)}$$

$$= \dfrac{2(x - 1)(5x + 3)}{2(x - 1)(x + 1)} + \dfrac{2(x + 1)(2x + 5)}{2(x + 1)(x - 1)} - \dfrac{5}{2(x^2 - 1)}$$

$$= \dfrac{2(5x^2 - 2x - 3) + 2(2x^2 + 7x + 5) - 1(5)}{2(x^2 - 1)}$$

$$= \dfrac{(10x^2 - 4x - 6) + (4x^2 + 14x + 10) - (5)}{2(x^2 - 1)}$$

$$= \dfrac{14x^2 + 10x - 1}{2(x^2 - 1)}$$

This last expression cannot be simplified further.

Answer: $\dfrac{14x^2 + 10x - 1}{2(x^2 - 1)}$

With multiplication and division, we have to investigate whether cancelling can take place. This usually involves factorizing algebraic expressions in order to cancel factors. With division, where necessary, we follow the arithmetical rule of 'invert the divisor and multiply'.

Example

Simplify $\dfrac{2x^2 + x - 15}{x^2 - 9}$.

$$2x^2 + x - 15 = (2x - 5)(x + 3)$$
$$x^2 - 9 = (x + 3)(x - 3)$$
$$\dfrac{2x^2 + x - 15}{x^2 - 9} = \dfrac{(2x - 5)(x + 3)}{(x + 3)(x - 3)} = \dfrac{2x - 5}{x - 3}$$

(The expression $x + 3$ cancels.)

Answer: $\dfrac{2x - 5}{x - 3}$

Example

Simplify $\dfrac{x^2 - 4x + 4}{2x^2 - 11x + 14} \div \dfrac{x^2 - 4}{3x^2 + 4x - 4}$.

$$x^2 - 4x + 4 = (x - 2)(x - 2)$$
$$2x^2 - 11x + 14 = (x - 2)(2x - 7)$$
$$x^2 - 4 = (x + 2)(x - 2)$$
$$3x^2 + 4x - 4 = (3x - 2)(x + 2)$$

$$\frac{x^2 - 4x + 4}{2x^2 - 11x + 14} \div \frac{x^2 - 4}{3x^2 + 4x - 4}$$

$$= \frac{x^2 - 4x + 4}{2x^2 - 11x + 14} \times \frac{3x^2 + 4x - 4}{x^2 - 4}$$

$$= \frac{(x - 2)(x - 2)(3x - 2)(x + 2)}{(x - 2)(2x - 7)(x + 2)(x - 2)}$$

$$= \frac{3x - 2}{2x - 7}$$

Answer: $\dfrac{3x - 2}{2x - 7}$

The reader is advised to use a partial check on the validity of answers by letting $x = 1$, or some other simple value if one of the expressions results in zero. In this case $x = 1$ and $x = 2$ makes certain expressions zero, so let $x = 3$. A further check could be let $x = $ zero, in which case we only check the constants.

With $x = 3$, we have $\dfrac{1}{-1} \div \dfrac{5}{35} = \dfrac{1 \times 35}{-1 \times 5} = -7$

and $\dfrac{3x - 2}{2x - 7} = \dfrac{7}{-1} = -7$

With $x = 0$, we have $\dfrac{4}{14} \div \dfrac{-4}{-4} = \dfrac{4 \times -4}{14 \times -4} = \dfrac{2}{7}$

and $\dfrac{3x - 2}{2x - 7} = \dfrac{-2}{-7} = \dfrac{2}{7}$

The reader may now care to return to the penultimate example, $\dfrac{2x^2 + x - 15}{x^2 - 9}$, and check the validity of the answer $\dfrac{2x - 5}{x - 3}$.

Problems 2.3

1. Factorize:
    (a) $x^2 - 9$
    (b) $a^2 - b^2$
    (c) $4a^2 - 9b^2$
    (d) $ay^2 - a$
    (e) $(4x - y)^2 - (2x + y)^2$
    (f) $4 - \dfrac{a^2}{16}$

2. Factorize:
    (a) $a^2 + 6a + 9$
    (b) $x^2 - 4x + 4$
    (c) $a^2 + 6ab + 9b^2$
    (d) $2x^3 + 12x^2y + 18xy^2$
    (e) $9a^2 - 3a + \frac{1}{4}$

3. Factorize:
    (a) $x^2 + 6x + 5$
    (b) $x^2 + 6x + 8$
    (c) $x^2 + 2x - 15$
    (d) $x^2 - 9x + 20$
    (e) $2x^2 + 3x + 1$
    (f) $3x^2 - 10x + 3$
    (g) $10a^2b - 7ab - 12b$
    (h) $48x^2z - 26xyz - 4y^2z$

4. Factorize:
    (a) $ac + ad + bc + bd$
    (b) $6ac + 4bd + 3bc + 8ad$
    (c) $8ax - 5by + 4ay - 10bx$
    (d) $abd + 2cd - bd - 2acd$

5. Factorize:
    (a) $5x^2 - 6x - 8$
    (b) $4a^2c - 12abc + 9b^2c$
    (c) $3ac - 8bd + 6bc - 4ad$
    (d) $x^3 - xy^2 + 2x^2y - 2y^3$

6. One of the factors of $2x^3 + 9x^2 - 11x - 30$ is $x + 5$. Find the other two.

7. Factorize:
    (a) $18 + 3a - 6a^2$
    (b) $5y + 2xy - 6x - 15$
    (c) $16x^3y^2 - 9x$

8. Factorize:
    (a) $6a^2 + 7ab - 3b^2$
    (b) $27a^2b - 3b$
    (c) $4a^2 - 4ab + b^2$
    (d) $pq - qr + 2ps - 2rs$

9. Find the four factors of:

$$2x^4 - x^3 - 20x^2 + 13x + 30$$

knowing that this expression can be divided by $x^2 + x - 6$ without leaving a remainder.

10. Express $\dfrac{5}{x-3} - \dfrac{3}{x-1}$ as a single algebraic fraction in its simplest form.

11. Simplify $\dfrac{1}{x+4} - \dfrac{8}{x^2-16} + \dfrac{1}{x-4}$.

12. Express as a single fraction in its simplest form:

$\dfrac{3}{x+1} + \dfrac{2}{x-2} - \dfrac{2x-7}{x^2-x-2}$.

13. Simplify:

   (a) $\dfrac{x^2-1}{x^2+4x-5}$ (b) $\dfrac{a^2+6a+9}{a^2-9}$ (c) $\dfrac{x^3-1}{x^2-1}$

14. Simplify:

   (a) $\dfrac{x^2+3x-10}{x^2+5x-14}$ (b) $\dfrac{bx+ay+by+ax}{cx+dy+cy+dx}$

15. Simplify $\left(\dfrac{x^2-x-12}{2x^2-9x+4}\right)\left(\dfrac{4x^2+4x-15}{2x^2+11x+15}\right)$.

16. Simplify $\dfrac{a^2+8a+16}{2a^2+17a+21} \times \dfrac{2a^2+11a-21}{2a^2+5a-12} \div \dfrac{a+4}{2a-3}$.

17. If $f(a) = 2a^2 - 11a - 21$, find the values of:
   (a) $f(1)$ (b) $f(0)$ (c) $f(-7)$ (d) $f(1{\cdot}5)$

18. If $f(x) = 5x^2 - 7x - 24$, show that $f(3) = 0$. Hence obtain the factors of $5x^2 - 7x + 24$.

19. If $f(x) = x^3 - 8x^2 + x + 42$, show that $f(7) = 0$. Hence obtain the factors of $x^3 - 8x^2 + x + 42$.

20. If $f(a) = 125a^3 - 27b^3$, show that $f\left(\dfrac{3b}{5}\right) = 0$. Hence, or otherwise, find the factors of $125a^3 - 27b^3$.

21. Simplify:

   (a) $\dfrac{x+5}{4} + \dfrac{3x+2}{6} + \dfrac{x+5}{3}$ (b) $\dfrac{2}{ab} - \dfrac{3}{bc} + \dfrac{1}{ac}$

Mathematics for Mechanical Technicians 1

21. (c) $\dfrac{5x + 2}{x^2 - 1} + \dfrac{7}{x + 1}$ (d) $\left(\dfrac{x + 3}{x^2 + 4x + 4}\right)\left(\dfrac{x + 2}{x^2 + x - 6}\right)$

(e) $\left(\dfrac{x^2 - 7x + 12}{2x - 5}\right) \div \left(\dfrac{x^2 - 9}{2x^2 + x - 15}\right)$

Answers to Problems 2.3

1. (a) $(x + 3)(x - 3)$ (b) $(a + b)(a - b)$
   (c) $(2a + 3b)(2a - 3b)$ (d) $a(y + 1)(y - 1)$
   (e) $12x(x - y)$ (f) $\left(2 + \dfrac{a}{4}\right)\left(2 - \dfrac{a}{4}\right)$

2. (a) $(a + 3)(a + 3)$ (b) $(x - 2)(x - 2)$
   (c) $(a + 3b)(a + 3b)$ (d) $2x(x + 3y)(x + 3y)$
   (e) $(3a - \frac{1}{2})(3a - \frac{1}{2})$

3. (a) $(x + 5)(x + 1)$ (b) $(x + 4)(x + 2)$
   (c) $(x + 5)(x - 3)$ (d) $(x - 4)(x - 5)$
   (e) $(2x + 1)(x + 1)$ (f) $(3x - 1)(x - 3)$
   (g) $b(2a + 3)(5a - 4)$ (h) $2z(8x + y)(3x - 2y)$

4. (a) $(a + b)(c + d)$ (b) $(2a + b)(3c + 4d)$
   (c) $(2x + y)(4a - 5b)$ (d) $d(a - 1)(b - 2c)$

5. (a) $(5x + 4)(x - 2)$ (b) $c(2a - 3b)(2a - 3b)$
   (c) $(a + 2b)(3c - 4d)$ (d) $(x + y)(x - y)(x + 2y)$

6. $(2x + 3)$ and $(x - 2)$

7. (a) $3(2 - a)(3 + 2a)$ (b) $(2x + 5)(y - 3)$
   (c) $x(4xy + 3)(4xy - 3)$

8. (a) $(2a + 3b)(3a - b)$ (b) $3b(3a + 1)(3a - 1)$
   (c) $(2a - b)(2a - b)$ (d) $(p - r)(q + 2s)$

9. $x + 3, x - 2, 2x - 5,$ and $x + 1$

10. $\dfrac{2(x + 2)}{(x - 3)(x - 1)}$ or $\dfrac{2x + 4}{x^2 - 4x + 3}$

11. $\dfrac{2}{x + 4}$

12. $\dfrac{3}{x - 2}$

13. (a) $\dfrac{x + 1}{x + 5}$ (b) $\dfrac{a + 3}{a - 3}$ (c) $\dfrac{x^2 + x + 1}{x + 1}$

14. (a) $\dfrac{x + 5}{x + 7}$ (b) $\dfrac{a + b}{c + d}$

86

15. $\dfrac{2x - 3}{2x - 1}$

16. $\dfrac{2a - 3}{2a + 3}$

17. (*a*) -30 (*b*) -21 (*c*) 154 (*d*) -33

18. $(x - 3)(5x + 8)$

19. $(x - 7)(x - 3)(x + 2)$

20. $(5a - 3b)(25a^2 + 15ab + 9b^2)$

21. (*a*) $\dfrac{13x + 39}{12}$ (*b*) $\dfrac{-3a + b - 2c}{abc}$

   (*c*) $\dfrac{12x - 5}{x^2 - 1}$ (*d*) $\dfrac{1}{x^2 - 4}$

   (*e*) $x - 4$

2.4 Simple Equations

2.4.1 SOLUTION OF SIMPLE EQUATIONS

An *equation* is a statement indicating an equality, and in its mathematical form is characterized by the appearance of an equals sign. With most equations an algebraic symbol occurs which represents an unknown quantity. Such an equation is said to be *solved* when a value (numerical or algebraic) is found for the unknown quantity so that when this value is substituted for the unknown quantity the state of equality is maintained. An equation can be regarded as a balance between the quantities on either side of the equals sign. Equations are solved by conducting operations which do not disturb that balance. Whatever operation is performed on one side of an equation must be performed on the other side.

A *simple equation* is one which contains the first power of the unknown quantity. If a simple equation is solved there is one value, and one value only, for the unknown quantity. A little later we shall meet equations which contain the second power of the unknown. If such an equation is solved, there will be two values for the unknown quantity. In general, an equation which contains the nth power of the unknown will have n values for the unknown.

The major proportion of the work involved in solving a simple equation is usually carried out by performing a sequence of operations so that eventually all the terms containing the unknown are brought to one side of the equation, the remaining terms appearing on the other side. The operations will vary according to the construction of the original equation. We shall illustrate the different types of operations with worked examples. When a solution has been obtained, the value should be put in the original equation to check its validity.

Example

Solve the equation $\quad x - 2 = 2(x - 4)$.

Remove the brackets: $\quad x - 2 = 2x - 8$

Bring the numerical terms to one side by adding 2 to each side.

$$x - 2 + 2 = 2x - 8 + 2$$
$$x = 2x - 6$$

Bring the algebraic terms to the other side by subtracting $2x$ from each side.

$$x - 2x = 2x - 6 - 2x$$
$$-x = -6$$

The equation cannot be simplified further, and now we leave just x on the left-hand side by dividing by its coefficient, in this case -1.

$$\frac{-x}{-1} = \frac{-6}{-1}$$
$$x = 6$$

We now check the validity of the answer by substituting its value in the original equation.

$$Check\colon x - 2 = 2(x - 4)$$
$$6 - 2 = 2(6 - 4)$$
$$4 = 2(2)$$
$$4 = 4$$

The balance is maintained and hence the answer is correct. As is usual, we complete the solution by writing out the answer.

Answer: $x = 6$

Let us investigate the effect of adding (or subtracting) to eliminate certain quantities.

Consider $\quad\quad\quad\quad x = 2x - 6$

and the elimination of $2x$ from the right-hand side by subtracting $2x$ from each side.

$$x - 2x = 2x - 6 - 2x$$
$$x - 2x = -6$$

If we compare this last equation with the original equation, we note that the $2x$ term has moved to the other side of the equals sign but its sign has changed from positive to negative. This indicates a useful rule which can save time in effecting solutions. Any complete term can be transferred from one side of the equals sign to the other providing its sign is changed.

Example

Solve the equation $\dfrac{5x + 7}{4} - \dfrac{3x - 8}{7} = \dfrac{x + 9}{2}$.

When fractions appear, it is generally favourable to commence by eliminating the fractions. We should remember from previous work in this book that the lines denoting the fractions group terms into single entities. Let us never be afraid of introducing brackets to ensure that we treat them as such. We will rewrite the equation as:

$$\frac{(5x + 7)}{4} - \frac{(3x - 8)}{7} = \frac{(x + 9)}{2}$$

We can eliminate the fractions by multiplying everything by the least common multiple of 4, 7 and 2, which is 28.

$$\frac{28}{4}(5x + 7) - \frac{28}{7}(3x - 8) = \frac{28}{2}(x + 9)$$

$$7(5x + 7) - 4(3x - 8) = 14(x + 9)$$

Remove brackets:

$$35x + 49 - 12x + 32 = 14x + 126$$

Collect like terms:

$$35x - 12x - 14x = 126 - 49 - 32$$
$$9x = 45$$
$$x = 5$$

$$Check: \frac{5x + 7}{4} - \frac{3x - 8}{7} = \frac{x + 9}{2}$$

$$\frac{25 + 7}{4} - \frac{15 - 8}{7} = \frac{5 + 9}{2}$$

$$\frac{32}{4} - \frac{7}{7} = \frac{14}{2}$$

$$8 - 1 = 7$$

$$7 = 7$$

Answer: $x = 5$

Let us now consider an equation in which two fractions are equated, such as:

$$\frac{x + 2}{2} = \frac{5x - 11}{3}$$

The denominator on the left-hand side can be eliminated by multiplying both sides of the equation by 2, obtaining:

$$x + 2 = \frac{2(5x - 11)}{3}$$

The denominator 3 on the right-hand side of this latter equation can be eliminated by multiplying both sides of the equation by 3, to obtain:

$$3(x + 2) = 2(5x - 11)$$

If we compare this last equation with the original equation, we observe it to be

(denominator, right-hand side)(numerator, left-hand side)

= (denominator, left-hand side)(numerator, right-hand side)

that is, if $\frac{a}{b} = \frac{c}{d}$, then $(a \times d) = (b \times c)$.

We note that the multiplication takes place across the equals sign, hence the process is called *cross-multiplication*. We have deduced another rule which could prove to be convenient in certain cases. If an equation is formed by equating two fractions, another equation can be formed by cross-multiplication. It should be noted that any algebraic term which is not a fraction can be put in the form of a fraction by using a denominator of unity.

Example

Solve the equation $\frac{7(x - 4)}{8} = 2x - 12 \cdot 5$.

Rearrange as an equation of two fractions, and use a bracket to treat $2x - 12 \cdot 5$ as a complete entity.

$$\frac{7(x - 4)}{8} = \frac{(2x - 12 \cdot 5)}{1}$$

By cross-multiplication:

$$7(x - 4) = 8(2x - 12 \cdot 5)$$

Remove brackets:

$$7x - 28 = 16x - 100$$

Collect like terms:

$$7x - 16x = -100 + 28$$
$$-9x = -72$$
$$x = \frac{-72}{-9}$$
$$x = 8$$

$$Check: \frac{7(x - 4)}{8} = 2x - 12 \cdot 5$$
$$\frac{7(8 - 4)}{8} = 16 - 12 \cdot 5$$
$$\frac{28}{8} = 3 \cdot 5$$
$$3 \cdot 5 = 3 \cdot 5$$

Answer: $x = 8$

The notes which have been put down alongside the solutions in this article were used to indicate the operations being performed, and as skill is acquired the use of such notes by students can be discarded. Now let us demonstrate how algebra can be used to help us solve engineering problems.

2.4.2 PRACTICAL APPLICATIONS OF THE SOLUTION OF SIMPLE EQUATIONS

Example

If a channel section has a width of W, a depth of D and a constant thickness of t, the cross-sectional area A can be found from the formula:

$$A = t(2D + W - 2t)$$

D

Find the value of D when $A = 600$ mm^2, $W = 70$ mm, and $t = 5$ mm.

$$A = t(2D + W - 2t)$$
$$600 = 5(2D + 70 - 10)$$
$$600 = 5(2D + 60)$$
$$600 = 10D + 300$$
$$600-300 = 10D$$
$$300 = 10D$$
$$D = 30$$

Answer: $D = 30$ mm

Example

The length s, measured from its lowest point, of a heavy cable suspended between two points, and the vertical height y, are connected by the equation:

$$(y + c)^2 = s^2 + c^2$$

where c is constant. If $y = 4$ when $s = 8$, show that $c = 6$. Find s when $y = 10$.

$$(y + c)^2 = s^2 + c^2$$
$$(4 + c)^2 = 8^2 + c^2$$
$$16 + 8c + c^2 = 64 + c^2$$
$$8c = 64 - 16 = 48$$
$$c = \frac{48}{8} = 6$$
$$\therefore (y + 6)^2 = s^2 + 6^2$$
$$(10 + 6)^2 = s^2 + 36$$
$$16^2 = s^2 + 36$$
$$256 = s^2 + 36$$
$$s^2 = 256 - 36 = 220$$
$$s = \sqrt{220} = \pm 14.83$$

The negative value cannot apply $\therefore s = 14.83$

Answer: $c = 6$
$$s = 14.8 \text{ when } y = 10$$

Example

The mass of an amount of liquid, in grammes, can be found by multiplying its relative density by its volume in millilitres. The relative density of 800 millilitres of a dilute sulphuric acid is 1·12. What

volume of dilute sulphuric acid of relative density 1·27 must be added
to produce an acid of relative density 1·22?

Let $\qquad$ volume added be x millilitres
then $\qquad$ mass added = volume × relative density
$$= 1\cdot27x \text{ grammes}$$
$$\text{Mass of original acid} = 800 \times 1\cdot12 = 896 \text{ grammes}$$
$$\text{Mass after addition} = 896 + 1\cdot27x \text{ grammes}$$
$$\text{Volume after addition} = 800 + x$$
$$\text{Relative density after addition} = \frac{\text{mass}}{\text{volume}}$$
$$1\cdot22 = \frac{896 + 1\cdot27x}{800 + x}$$

By cross-multiplication:

$$(800 + x)\,1\cdot22 = 896 + 1\cdot27x$$
$$976 + 1\cdot22x = 896 + 1\cdot27x$$
$$976 - 896 = 1\cdot27x - 1\cdot22x$$
$$80 = 0\cdot05x$$
$$x = \frac{80}{0\cdot05} = 1\,600$$

Answer: Volume added = 1 600 millilitres

Example

An employee produces a total of 910 articles. He commences at the
rate of 20 articles per hour and, having completed a part of the total,
increases his rate to 25 articles per hour. The time taken overall was
40 hours. How many articles had been made when production was
changed?

Let $\qquad N$ = number of articles made when rate changed
then $910 - N$ = number of articles made at a faster rate

$$\text{Time taken at initial rate} = \frac{N}{20}$$
$$\text{Time taken at faster rate} = \frac{910 - N}{25}$$
$$\text{Total time} = 40 \text{ hours}$$
$$\therefore \frac{N}{20} + \frac{910 - N}{25} = 40$$

L.C.M. of 20 and 25 is 100.

$$100\left(\frac{N}{20}\right) + \frac{100(910 - N)}{25} = 100(40)$$
$$5N + 4(910 - N) = 4\,000$$
$$5N + 3\,640 - 4N = 4\,000$$
$$5N - 4N = 4\,000 - 3\,640$$
$$N = 360$$

Answer: Rate changed after 360 articles had been made.

Example

Referring to the holes shown in Fig. 2.1, obtain two different expressions for the height h in terms of x. Equate these expressions and hence determine the value of x.

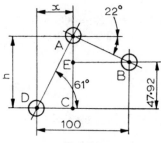

Fig. 2.1

In triangle ADC, $h = AC = DC \tan 61°$
$$= x \times 1 \cdot 804\,0$$
$$= 1 \cdot 804\,0\,x$$

In triangle ABE, $BE = 100 - x$
$$AE = BE \tan 22°$$
$$= (100 - x)\,0 \cdot 404\,0$$
$$= 40 \cdot 4 - 0 \cdot 404\,0\,x$$

$h = AE + 47 \cdot 92 = 40 \cdot 4 - 0 \cdot 404\,0\,x + 47 \cdot 92 = 88 \cdot 32 - 0 \cdot 404\,0\,x$

By equating values of h:

$$1 \cdot 804\,0\,x = 88 \cdot 32 - 0 \cdot 404\,0\,x$$
$$1 \cdot 804\,0\,x + 0 \cdot 404\,0\,x = 88 \cdot 32$$
$$2 \cdot 208\,0\,x = 88 \cdot 32$$
$$x = \frac{88 \cdot 32}{2 \cdot 208} = 40$$

Answer: $x = 40$ mm

Problems 2.4

1. Solve the following equations:

   (a) $2(2x - 5) + 3(x + 2) = 6x + 4$

   (b) $3(x + 4) - 2(x - 3) = 3x + 6$

   (c) $\dfrac{3x + 5}{4} + \dfrac{5x - 7}{6} = \dfrac{5x - 1}{3}$

   (d) $\frac{1}{2}(3x + 4) + \frac{2}{3}(x + 2) = 3x$

   (e) $3(x - 2) = \dfrac{3x + 1}{4} + 7x - 1{\cdot}5$

   (f) $\dfrac{x + 8}{x - 2} = \dfrac{x + 26}{x + 1}$

   (g) $\{2x - 3(x - 7)\} = \dfrac{3x + 2}{2}$

   (h) $5x - 3\{x - 2(2x - 4)\} = 7x - 3$

2. The following equation resulted from a problem dealing with mixing steam and water:

$$5\,400 + 10(100 - T) = 610(T - 20)$$

   Determine the value of T.

3. An approximate relationship between the number of teeth on a milling cutter T, the diameter of cutter D and the depth cut d is:

$$T = \frac{12{\cdot}5D}{D + 4d}$$

   Find the value of D when $T = 10$ and $d = 5$ mm.

4. If a shaft has a diameter D, the depth of cut d to produce a flat of width W can be obtained from the formula:

$$D - 2d = \sqrt{(D^2 - W^2)}$$

   Find the value of d when $D = 34$ mm and $W = 16$ mm.

5. A keyway of width W is cut in a shaft of diameter D so that the nominal depth at the side of the keyway is h. The depth at the centre of the keyway H can be found from the formula:

$$\sqrt{\left(\frac{D^2 - W^2}{4} \right)} = \frac{D}{2} - H + h$$

Find the value of H when $D = 26$ mm, $W = 10$ mm and $h = 4$ mm.

6. A rectangle has a length which is 4 mm greater than its breadth. By letting the length be x, obtain an expression for the perimeter of the rectangle. Hence obtain the dimensions of such a rectangle whose perimeter is 28 mm.

7. Without using tooling, articles cost £0·90 each to produce. By investing £120 in tooling, the cost is reduced to £0·30 per article. At what number of articles is the 'break even' point reached, i.e. the number of articles when the total cost by either method is identical?

8. A rectangular plate of uniform thickness originally has a length of 250 mm and a width of 120 mm. Four rectangular lightening holes are to be cut in the plate, each of length 60 mm and width x mm so that the weight of the plate is reduced by 20%. Determine the value of x.

9. A traveller starts a journey at an average speed of 30 kilometres per hour and continues at this rate for 2 hours. He rests for half an hour and then continues his journey at the rate of 40 kilometres per hour. Obtain an expression for the total distance travelled x hours after the start, when x is greater than $2\frac{1}{2}$, and hence find the total time to travel 120 kilometres.

10. The current I which flows in a simple series circuit is found by dividing the electromotive force E by the resistance R of that circuit. The original resistance of the circuit R was not known, but when R was increased by 3 ohms, the e.m.f. had to be increased by 60% to cause the same current to flow. Find the value of R.

11. When a body passes a datum with an initial velocity u and a constant acceleration of a, the distance s from datum after a time t is given by:

$$s = ut + \frac{at^2}{2}$$

A body passes datum with a velocity of 40 m/s and after 4 seconds has travelled 200 m. Find the value of a, stating both its magnitude and its unit.

12. A brass ingot has a mass of 30 kg and contains 60% of copper. An amount of x kg of copper is melted into this ingot to produce a new ingot of mass $(30 + x)$ kg. In this new ingot there is 70% of copper. Find the amount x which was added.

13. A bin of electrical components totalling 2 000 components consists of deliveries from two suppliers A and B, of which supplier A has contributed 70%. How many components must be added, entirely from supplier B, so that his contribution is increased to 44%?

14. During an experiment using heat transfer in order to determine the specific heat c of a light mineral oil, the following equation was developed:

$$m_1c_1(t_2 - t_1) = (m_2c_2 + mc)(t_1 - t_0)$$

Find the value of c given that:

$$m = 156 \qquad m_1 = 50 \qquad m_2 = 100 \qquad c_1 = c_2 = 504$$
$$t_2 = 100 \qquad t_1 = 25 \qquad t_0 = 20$$

15. Fig. 2.2 shows an angle bracket made out of a piece of material of length 180 mm. Determine the distance x so that the two ends, after bending, are 120 mm apart.

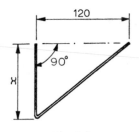

FIG. 2.2

16. Two parallel conveyor belts move in the same direction at speeds of 5 m/min. and 8 m/min. The entry points to both conveyors are at the same level. A sub-assembly enters the slower conveyor and 3 minutes later a matching sub-assembly enters the faster conveyor. How far are the sub-assemblies from the entry point when they are level?

97

17. If R_0 is the resistance of a particular conductor at 0°C, the resistance R_t of that conductor at a temperature of t°C is given by the equation:

$$R_t = R_0(1 + \alpha t)$$

If a conductor has a resistance of 81·6 ohms at 5°C and 88·0 ohms at 25°C, form two separate equations each containing R_0. Divide these two equations and hence find the value of α.

18. An indicator needle is oscillating about its final steady reading x. A first reading is 39, the second reading is 24, so that the first deviation is $39 - x$ and the second deviation is $x - 24$. The third reading is 34. The ratio of the first deviation to the second deviation is the same as the ratio of the second to the third. Calculate the final steady reading x.

Answers to Problems 2.4

1. (*a*) $x = 8$ (*b*) $x = 6$ (*c*) $x = 5$ (*d*) $x = 4$
   (*e*) $x = -1$ (*f*) $x = 4$ (*g*) $x = 8$ (*h*) $x = 3$
2. $T = 30$
3. $D = 80$ mm
4. $d = 2$ mm
5. $H = 5$ mm
6. $4x + 8$, 5 mm × 9 mm
7. 200
8. $x = 25$ mm
9. $40x - 40$, $x = 4$ hours
10. $R = 5$ ohms
11. 5 m/s²
12. 10 kg
13. 500
14. $c = 2\,100$
15. 50 mm
16. 40 m
17. 0·004
18. 30

2.5 Simultaneous Equations

The equation $x = y + 3$ provides an infinite number of values of x, each value of x depending upon the value that is given to y. There is one, and only one, value of x, and hence only one associated value of y, which satisfies the equation $x = y + 3$, and at the same time (or *simultaneously*) satisfies an equation containing x and/or y which is not a multiple of the first equation. Let us suppose this second equation is $x + 3y = 19$.

$x = y + 3$ and $x + 3y = 19$ are a pair of *simultaneous equations*. If there are two unknowns, two separate and distinct equations will be necessary to effect a solution. Three unknowns will require three separate and distinct equations. Expressed in general terms, n unknowns require n separate and distinct equations to effect a solution. At present we are only concerned with simultaneous equations of two unknowns.

Just as with other equations, simultaneous equations can be solved by algebraic processes or by graphs. We will first consider the algebraic processes, leaving the graphical method until a later chapter. There are several methods of solution, and it takes a little experience to decide which method is quickest for a particular problem.

Example

Solve the simultaneous equations:

$$5x = 8y + 3$$
$$x + 3y = 19$$

First method: Equating coefficients

With this method one or both equations are multiplied to produce a pair of equations where the coefficients of one of the unknowns are numerically equal. If the coefficients have the same sign, subtracting the equations eliminates one unknown and leaves a simple equation. If the coefficients have opposite signs, adding the equations will eliminate an unknown.

We first rearrange the equations, if necessary, to bring the unknowns on one side of the equals sign.

$$5x = 8y + 3$$

$\therefore 5x - 8y = 3$	... equation (1)
$x + 3y = 19$	... equation (2)

Equation (2) × 5: $5x + 15y = 95$

Equation (1): $5x - 8y = 3$

The coefficients of x are now alike, and since they both have the same sign, we shall subtract one equation from the other.

$$23y = 92$$
$$y = 4$$

Substituting this value in one of the original equations:

$$5x = 8y + 3 = 32 + 3 = 35$$
$$x = 7$$

Check: $5x = 8y + 3$, $35 = 32 + 3$, $35 = 35$
$x + 3y = 19$, $7 + 12 = 19$, $19 = 19$

Answer: $x = 7 \quad y = 4$

Second method: *Substitution of one equation in the other*

The first step is to obtain from one equation an expression either for x or for y. In this particular problem, a value for x from the second equation is easiest.

$$x + 3y = 19$$
$$\therefore x = 19 - 3y$$

We now substitute this value in the first equation:

$$5x = 8y + 3$$
$$5(19 - 3y) = 8y + 3$$
$$95 - 15y = 8y + 3$$
$$-15y - 8y = -95 + 3$$
$$-23y = -92$$
$$y = \frac{-92}{-23} = 4, \text{ as before}$$
$$x = 19 - 3y = 19 - 12 = 7 \text{ as before}$$

Hence
$$x = 7 \text{ and } y = 4$$

The validity of these values has already been checked.

For most of the problems which occur in our present stage of studies, the method of equating coefficients will generally prove to be the most rapid. On some occasions the reader may prefer to arrange a substitution before the method of equating coefficients is used.

Example

Solve the simultaneous equations:

$$\frac{5}{x} + \frac{8}{y} = 9$$
$$\frac{7}{x} - \frac{6}{y} = 4$$

Let
$$\frac{1}{x} = a \text{ and } \frac{1}{y} = b$$

then	$5a + 8b = 9$	. . . equation (1)
and	$7a - 6b = 4$	. . . equation (2)

Equation (1) $\times$ 7: $\quad 35a + 56b = 63$

Equation (2) $\times$ 5: $\quad 35a - 30b = 20$

Subtract: $\qquad\qquad\qquad 86b = 43 \qquad b = \frac{43}{86} = \frac{1}{2}$

Substitute this value in equation (1).

$$5a + 8b = 9, \; 5a + 4 = 9, \; 5a = 9 - 4 = 5$$
$$a = 1$$
$$\frac{1}{x} = a \quad \therefore x = \frac{1}{a} = \frac{1}{1} = 1$$
$$\frac{1}{y} = b \quad \therefore y = \frac{1}{b} = \frac{1}{\frac{1}{2}} = 2$$

Check: $\dfrac{5}{x} + \dfrac{8}{y} = 9, \; \dfrac{5}{1} + \dfrac{8}{2} = 9, \; 5 + 4 = 9, \; 9 = 9$

$\qquad\quad \dfrac{7}{x} - \dfrac{6}{y} = 4, \; \dfrac{7}{1} - \dfrac{6}{2} = 4, \; 7 - 3 = 4, \; 4 = 4$

Answers: $x = 1, \; y = 2$

Problems 2.5

1. Solve the following simultaneous equations:

(a) $x + 2y = 11$
     $2x + y = 7$

(b) $7x - 5y = 13$
     $2x + 3y = 17$

(c) $3x - 2y = 4$
     $5x = 2y$

(d) $4x + 5y = 2$
     $x - y = \dfrac{1}{20}$

(e) $\dfrac{1}{v} - \dfrac{1}{u} = \dfrac{1}{20}$
     $\dfrac{2}{v} + \dfrac{7.5}{u} = 2$

2. Solve the simultaneous equations:
$$3a - 4b = 0$$
$$2a + 6b = 13$$

3. Solve the simultaneous equations:
$$2x + 9y = 19$$
$$7x - 6y = 4$$

4. Determine the values of V_1 and V_2, given that:
$$5V_1 + 12V_2 = 36.1$$
$$11V_1 + 8V_2 = 37.1$$

5. If $W = KL + c$, find K and c given that when $L = 3$, $W = 15$ and when $L = 4$, $W = 18$.

6. Solve the simultaneous equations:
$$3x - 6y = 0$$
$$2x + 5y = 45$$

7. Solve the simultaneous equations:
$$4(x - 2) = 5(1 - y)$$
$$26x + 3y + 4 = 0$$

8. Solve the following simultaneous equations for I_1 and I_2:
$$0{\cdot}05I_1 + (I_1 + I_2) = 2{\cdot}05$$
$$0{\cdot}08I_2 + 2(I_1 + I_2) = 4{\cdot}30$$

9. Solve the simultaneous equations:
$$2R = A - \frac{1}{0{\cdot}25}$$
$$A = 3R + 1$$

10. Solve the simultaneous equations:
$$4x = 3y + 16$$
$$4y = x + 9$$

11. Solve for x and y the simultaneous equations:
$$\frac{1}{x} + \frac{1}{y} = \frac{1}{4}$$
$$\frac{5}{x} + \frac{2}{y} = 2$$

12. By writing $\dfrac{1}{x + 3y} = a$ and $\dfrac{1}{3x - y} = b$, find the values of x and y that satisfy the equations:
$$\frac{2}{x + 3y} - \frac{1}{3x - y} = 4$$
$$\frac{1}{x + 3y} + \frac{2}{3x - y} = 7$$

13. If twice the sum of two numbers exceeds four times their difference by 10 and the two numbers are in the ratio of 4:1, calculate each number.

14. The relation between the load W and the required effort E of a particular lifting machine is given by the formula:

$$E = aW + b$$

A lifting machine can lift 100 N with an effort of 15 N, and 400 N with an effort of 30 N. Determine the value of the constants a and b, and hence the value of the load when the effort is 40 N.

15. The length of a compression spring can be found from its free length L and a shortening due to the load W and stiffness S, so that the length is given by $L - (W \div S)$. Such a spring has a length of 38 mm under a load of 400 N and a length of 35·5 mm under a load of 900 N. Find the values of L and S, and hence determine the load on the spring when it has a length of 37·5 mm.

16. If a body has an initial velocity of u and has a uniform acceleration of a, its velocity v after time t is obtained from the formula:

$$v = u + at$$

Such a body has a velocity v of 40 m/s when $t = 3$ seconds and a velocity v of 100 m/s when $t = 15$ seconds. Determine the values of u and a, indicating both the magnitude and the unit in each case.

17. The selling price P of a hand tool consists of a fixed amount A plus a variable amount which is proportional to the square of the nominal size S, so that:

$$P = A + BS^2$$

where A and B are constants. If a 20 mm tool costs £0·70 and a 50 mm tool cost £3·32½, determine the values of A and B, and hence the cost of a 60 mm tool.

Answers to Problems 2.5

1. (a) $x = 1, y = 5$ (b) $x = 4, y = 3$
   (c) $x = -2, y = -5$ (d) $x = \frac{1}{4}, y = \frac{1}{5}$
   (e) $v = 4, u = 5$
2. $a = 2, b = 1\frac{1}{2}$
3. $x = 2, y = 1\frac{2}{3}$
4. $V_1 = 1·7, V_2 = 2·3$

5. $K = 3$, $c = 6$
6. $x = 10$, $y = 5$
7. $x = -\frac{1}{2}$, $y = 3$
8. $I_1 = -10$, $I_2 = 12\cdot55$
9. $A = 10$, $R = 3$
10. $x = 7$, $y = 4$
11. $x = 2$, $y = -4$
12. $x = \dfrac{11}{60}$, $y = \dfrac{1}{20}$
13. -20 and -5
14. $a = \dfrac{1}{20}$, $b = 10$ N; $W = 600$ N
15. $L = 40$ mm, $S = 200$ N/mm; 500 N
16. $u = 25$ m/s, $a = 5$ m/s^2
17. $A = £0\cdot20$, $B = £0\cdot12\frac{1}{2}$; £4·70

2.6 Quadratic Equations

2.6.1 SOLUTION BY FACTORS

In article 2.4, we met equations which we called simple equations. When the equations were solved, for each separate equation there was only one value for the unknown. In the language of mathematics, we say that a simple equation has only one root. Now let us consider the equation:

$$x^2 - 5x = -6$$

which can be written as $x^2 - 5x + 6 = 0$

If we factorize the left-hand side, we obtain:

$$(x - 3)(x - 2) = 0$$

If we require that when two items are multiplied together they produce zero, we can provide this result by making one of those items equal to zero. So:

if $\qquad (x - 3)(x - 2) = 0,$
then either $\qquad x - 3 = 0$, when $x = 3$
or $\qquad x - 2 = 0$, when $x = 2$

Having obtained an answer to an equation, we should always check that the answer is correct. Try $x = 3$:

$$x^2 - 5x = -6, 9 - 15 = -6, -6 = -6$$

Now try $x = 2$:

$$x^2 - 5x = -6, 4 - 10 = -6, -6 = -6$$

Hence $x = 2$ and $x = 3$ are both roots of the equation $x^2 - 5x = -6$. An equation which contains the square of an unknown, but no higher power, is called a *quadratic equation*. A quadratic equation has two roots. This is because the equation includes a second power, and there are always two separate values which, when squared, produce a number. A very simple quadratic equation is:

$$x^2 = 9$$

for which x is plus three or minus three

which we write as $\qquad x = \pm\, 3$

and which we read as 'x = plus or minus three'.

We could easily use the previous *method of factors* to solve $x^2 = 9$. Writing as:

$$x^2 - 9 = 0$$

and noting that $x^2 - 9$ is the difference of two squares,

then $\qquad\qquad (x + 3)(x - 3) = 0$
So that either $\qquad x + 3 = 0, \qquad x = -3$
or $\qquad\qquad x - 3 = 0, \qquad x = 3$
Hence, as before $\qquad x = \pm\, 3$

Now let us consider the quadratic equation:

$$x^2 - 6x = -9,$$

which we can write as $x^2 - 6x + 9 = 0$.
Factorizing: $\qquad\quad (x - 3)(x - 3) = 0$
So, as before $\qquad\quad x - 3 = 0, \qquad x = 3$
or $\qquad\qquad\quad x - 3 = 0, \qquad x = 3$.

In this unusual case, we still have two roots, but they are equal. Let us still check their validity.

$$x^2 - 6x = -9, \qquad 9 - 18 = -9, \qquad -9 = -9$$

Now let us consider the equation:

$$x^2 - 3x = 0$$

Factorizing the left-hand side, we obtain:

$$x(x - 3) = 0$$

105

Equating each factor in turn to zero, we obtain:

either $x = 0$

or $x - 3 = 0, \quad x = 3$

Hence $x = 0 \text{ or } 3.$

Checking these values:

$$x = 0, \quad x^2 - 3x = 0, \quad 0 - 0 = 0, \quad 0 = 0$$
$$x = 3, \quad x^2 - 3x = 0, \quad 9 - 9 = 0, \quad 0 = 0$$

Let us now summarize what has been introduced in this article:

1. A quadratic equation is an equation which contains the square (but no higher power) of an unknown quantity.

2. Some quadratic equations can be solved by a method of factors. The steps of this method are:

   (*a*) Rearrange the equation, if necessary, to make one side of the equation zero, by bringing all the terms to one side.

   (*b*) Factorize the side of the equation which contains these terms.

   (*c*) Equate each of the factors in turn to zero to obtain the roots of the equation.

   (*d*) Check that each root satisfies the equation.

3. For every quadratic equation there are two roots. The roots can be different, and one of them could be zero. In certain rare cases the roots are equal.

Example

Find the smallest number so that the sum of the number and its reciprocal is 2·9.

$$\text{Let the number} = x$$
$$\text{Reciprocal of the number} = \frac{1}{x}$$
$$x + \frac{1}{x} = 2 \cdot 9$$
$$x^2 + 1 = 2 \cdot 9x$$
$$x^2 - 2 \cdot 9x + 1 = 0$$
$$10x^2 - 29x + 10 = 0$$
$$(2x - 5)(5x - 2) = 0$$

Either $2x - 5 = 0, \quad 2x = 5, \quad x = 2 \cdot 5$

or $5x - 2 = 0, \quad 5x = 2, \quad x = 0 \cdot 4$

$$x = 2 \cdot 5 \text{ or } 0 \cdot 4$$

Proof: $2·5 + \dfrac{1}{2·5} = 2·5 + 0·4 = 2·9$

$$0·4 + \dfrac{1}{0·4} = 0·4 + 2·5 = 2·9$$

Both $x = 2·5$ and $x = 0·4$ satisfy the equation, but the problem asked for the smallest value, hence $x = 2·5$ is discarded.

Answer: $x = 0·4$

Example

The length and breadth of a rectangular workshop 30 m × 20 m are increased by the same amount x m. If this alteration increases the floor space by 56 per cent of the original area, calculate x.

Working in units of metres:

$$\text{Original area} = 30 \times 20 = 600$$
$$\text{New length} = 30 + x, \text{ new breadth} = 20 + x$$
$$\text{New area} = (30 + x)(20 + x) = 600 + 50x + x^2$$

and

$$\text{increase in area} = (600 + 50x + x^2) - (600)$$
$$= 50x + x^2$$

$$\text{Percentage increase} = \frac{\text{increase in area}}{\text{original area}} \times 100$$

$$\therefore 56 = \frac{(50x + x^2) \times 100}{600}$$

$$56 = \frac{50x + x^2}{6}$$

$$336 = 50x + x^2$$
$$x^2 + 50x - 336 = 0$$
$$(x - 6)(x + 56) = 0$$
$$\therefore \text{either } x - 6 = 0, x = 6$$
$$\text{or } x + 56 = 0, x = -56 \text{ (this root not logical)}$$

Check: New area = 36 × 26 = 936
Increase = 936 − 600 = 336

$$\text{Percentage increase} = \frac{336}{600} \times 100 = 56$$

Answer: $x = 6$ m

We have already stated that a quadratic equation has two roots. When a practical problem results in a quadratic equation, the solution usually provides two answers. In certain circumstances, both roots apply. The more usual case is that only one satisfies the practical circumstances of the problem, and one root has to be discarded as inappropriate, as illustrated in the previous example.

Example

Form a quadratic equation whose roots are $x = 4$ and $x = -5$.

$$\text{If } x = 4, \qquad \text{then } x - 4 = 0$$
$$\text{If } x = -5, \qquad \text{then } x + 5 = 0$$
$$\therefore (x - 4)(x + 5) = 0$$
$$x^2 + x - 20 = 0$$

Check: Put $x = 4$ $16 + 4 - 20 = 0$ $0 = 0$
              Put $x = -5$ $25 - 5 - 20 = 0$ $0 = 0$

Answer: $x^2 + x - 20 = 0$

2.6.2 SOLUTION BY COMPLETING THE SQUARE

In many quadratic equations, when one side is made zero, the other side may not factorize, or occasionally the factors may be difficult to determine. We must therefore proceed to methods of solving any quadratic equation. One method includes the moving of all the terms involving the unknown to one side of the equation and then converting this side of the equation into a perfect square.

Consider $(x + a)^2 = x^2 + 2ax + (a^2)$
and $(x - a)^2 = x^2 - 2ax + (a^2)$

If we have an expression such as $(x^2 + 2ax)$ or $(x^2 - 2ax)$ we can convert it into a perfect square by adding to it the square of half of the coefficient of x. For instance with $x^2 + 6x$:

the coefficient of x is $+ 6$,
half the coefficient of x is $+ 3$,
the square of half the coefficient is $+9$
and $x^2 + 6x(+9)$ is a perfect square,
being $(x +$ half the coefficient of $x)^2$
in this case $(x + 3)^2$

Similarly, with $x^2 - 10x$:

the coefficient of x is -10,
half the coefficient of x is -5
the square of this is $+25$
and $x^2 - 10x + 25$ is $(x - 5)^2$

Let us show the use of the method of completing the square by a worked example, indicating special points as they occur. The reader should note that the examiner in setting this particular question specifically requested the method of completing the square. A method of solution by formula is another method of solution. This will be introduced in the next article, but it is debatable if in answering this question any credit at all would be given for a solution by formula.

Example

Solve, by completing the square, the quadratic equation:

$$2x^2 - 5x - 4 = 0$$

giving roots to two decimal places.

$$2x^2 - 5x - 4 = 0$$

Make the coefficient of x^2 unity:

$$x^2 - \frac{5x}{2} - 2 = 0$$

Transpose to keep only the terms involving x on one side of the equation:

$$x^2 - \frac{5x}{2} = 2$$

The coefficient of x is $-\frac{5}{2}$.

$$(\text{Half the coefficient})^2 = \left(-\frac{5}{4}\right)^2 = \frac{25}{16}$$

Add this to both sides, the left-hand side is then $\left(x - \frac{5}{4}\right)^2$

$$x^2 - \frac{5x}{2} + \frac{25}{16} = 2 + \frac{25}{16}$$
$$\left(x - \frac{5}{4}\right)^2 = 2 + \frac{25}{16} = \frac{57}{16}$$

Let us now take the square root of both sides, and note carefully that we have to associate a $\pm$ sign to the square root of the right-hand side.

$$x - \frac{5}{4} = \pm \sqrt{\frac{57}{16}}$$

$$x - 1.25 = \frac{\pm \sqrt{57}}{4}$$

$$x - 1.25 = \pm \frac{7.550}{4}$$

$$x - 1.25 = \pm 1.89, \text{ to two decimal places}$$

Either $\quad x - 1.25 = 1.89, x = 1.89 + 1.25 = 3.14$

or $\qquad x - 1.25 = -1.89, x = -1.89 + 1.25 = -0.64$

We will check these values by substitution in the original equation.

$$2x^2 - 5x - 4 = 0$$

$x = 3.14$:
$$2(3.14)^2 - 5(3.14) - 4 = 0$$
$$2(9.859\ 6) - 15.70 - 4 = 0$$
$$19.719\ 2 - 19.70 = 0$$
$$0.019\ 2 = 0$$

$x = -0.64$:
$$2(-0.64)^2 - 5(-0.64) - 4 = 0$$
$$2(0.409\ 6) + 3.20 - 4 = 0$$
$$0.819\ 2 + 3.20 - 4 = 0$$
$$0.019\ 2 = 0$$

We cannot expect perfect balance since the roots were only accurate to two decimal places.

Answer: $x = 3.14$ or -0.64

2.6.3 SOLUTION BY FORMULA

A technician is someone who solves problems, generally of a routine nature, by methods which are well known. In the case of quadratic equations, he will be well served by the possession of a formula which he can use to solve *any* quadratic equation. Let us establish such a formula. It will be an extremely good example of how we use symbolic notation for the general case in order to develop a formula to be used for a particular case.

Any quadratic equation can be put into general form:

$$ax^2 + bx + c = 0$$

by ascribing suitable values to x, a, b and c. Let us solve this general form by the method of completing the square.

$$ax^2 + bx + c = 0$$

$$x^2 + \frac{b}{a}(x) + \frac{c}{a} = 0$$

$$x^2 + \frac{b}{a}(x) + \left(\frac{b}{2a}\right)^2 = -\frac{c}{a} + \left(\frac{b}{2a}\right)^2$$

$$\left(x + \frac{b}{2a}\right)^2 = \frac{-c}{a} + \frac{b^2}{4a^2} = \frac{b^2 - 4ac}{4a^2}$$

$$x + \frac{b}{2a} = \pm \sqrt{\frac{b^2 - 4ac}{4a^2}}$$

$$x + \frac{b}{2a} = \pm \frac{\sqrt{(b^2 - 4ac)}}{2a}$$

$$x = -\frac{b}{2a} \pm \frac{\sqrt{(b^2 - 4ac)}}{2a}$$

$$x = \frac{-b \pm \sqrt{(b^2 - 4ac)}}{2a}$$

We can now use the formula to solve any quadratic equation which has been put into the standard form of:

$$ax^2 + bx + c = 0$$

Before we do so, let us have a look at the character of the roots revealed by the formula:

$$x = \frac{-b \pm \sqrt{(b^2 - 4ac)}}{2a}$$

The significant portion of this formula is the expression $b^2 - 4ac$. There are three possibilities:

(a) If b^2 is greater than $4ac$, the roots can be determined, and they are unequal.

(b) If $b^2 = 4ac$, $b^2 - 4ac$ is zero. In this case the roots can be determined and they are equal.

(c) If b^2 is less than $4ac$, $b^2 - 4ac$ is negative. It will suffice at present to state that since the reader has not been introduced to a branch of mathematics in which we imagine there are roots to negative numbers, he must accept that the mathematician refers to such roots as imaginary roots. There will be no equation in his present studies which will produce imaginary roots.

If a quadratic equation cannot be solved by factors, the roots are usually numbers which, when substituted in the equation to prove their validity, lead to time-consuming calculations. We have already seen this when the equation $2x^2 - 5x - 4 = 0$ was solved by completing the square. Let us develop another method of checking the roots which may be to our advantage.

If $x = p$ and $x = q$ are the roots of a quadratic equation, then:

$$x - p = 0 \text{ and } x - q = 0$$
Hence
$$(x - p)(x - q) = 0$$
and
$$x^2 - px - qx + pq = 0$$
i.e.
$$x^2 - (p + q)x + pq = 0$$

The general form of quadratic equations is:

$$ax^2 + bx + c = 0$$
or
$$x^2 + \left(\frac{b}{a}\right)x + \frac{c}{a} = 0$$
Since
$$x^2 - (p + q)x + pq = 0$$

we observe that if p and q are the roots of a quadratic equation, $p + q = $ the sum of the roots $= \dfrac{-b}{a}$ and $pq = $ the product of the roots $= \dfrac{c}{a}$

Let us now solve a quadratic equation by formula and use this method of checking the roots. We will use the example which we solved by the method of completing the square, but in this case we will reword it to permit the use of a formula.

Example

Solve the quadratic equation:

$$2x^2 - 5x - 4 = 0$$

giving roots correct to two decimal places.

$$2x^2 - 5x - 4 = 0$$
Compare with
$$ax^2 + bx + c = 0$$
$$x = x, a = 2, b = -5, c = -4$$
(Note minus signs carefully)

$$x = \frac{-b \pm \sqrt{\{b^2 - 4ac\}}}{2a}$$

$$= \frac{-(-5) \pm \sqrt{\{(-5)^2 - 4(2)(-4)\}}}{2(2)}$$
(Note use of brackets to assist correct working)

$$= \frac{+5 \pm \sqrt{\{25 + 32\}}}{4}$$

$$= \frac{5 \pm \sqrt{57}}{4} = \frac{5 \pm 7 \cdot 550}{4}$$

$$= \frac{12 \cdot 55}{4} \text{ or } \frac{-2 \cdot 55}{4}$$

$$= 3 \cdot 14 \text{ or } -0 \cdot 64 \text{ (to two decimal places)}$$

Check: Sum of roots $= \dfrac{-b}{a}$

$$3 \cdot 14 + (-0 \cdot 64) = -\left(\frac{-5}{2}\right)$$

$$2 \cdot 5 = 2 \cdot 5$$

Product of roots $= \dfrac{c}{a}$

$$(3 \cdot 14)(-0 \cdot 64) = \frac{-4}{2}$$

$$-2 \cdot 009\ 6 = -2$$

(We cannot expect perfect agreement since the roots were only evaluated to two decimal places.)

Answer: $x = 3 \cdot 14$ or $-0 \cdot 64$

Problems 2.6

1. Solve the following quadratic equations:

(*a*) $x^2 - 8x + 15 = 0$ (*b*) $x^2 - x - 12 = 0$
(*c*) $x^2 = 9x$ (*d*) $6x^2 - x - 12 = 0$

(*e*) $x^2 + 10x = -25$ (*f*) $x + \dfrac{1}{x} = 2 \cdot 5$

(*g*) $\dfrac{x + 3}{x + 5} = \dfrac{4}{x}$ (*h*) $\dfrac{x - 3}{2x + 1} = \dfrac{x + 1}{5(x - 1)}$

2. Obtain the quadratic equations whose roots are:

(*a*) $x = 3$ and $x = 1$ (*b*) $x = -5$ and $x = 2$
(*c*) $x = 3\frac{1}{2}$ and $x = -\frac{2}{3}$ (*d*) $x = a$ and $x = b$

3. The resistance to motion R N of a particular wheeled vehicle is obtained from the formula:

$$R = \frac{V}{2} + \frac{V^2}{30}$$

V being the velocity in kilometres per hour. Find the velocity when the resistance is 45 N.

4. When a particular cable is freely suspended between two points at the same level whose distance apart is D, the length of the cable L produces a sag of magnitude S. The relationship between the variables is:

$$L = \frac{8S^2}{3D} + D$$

Find the value of the span D, so that a cable of length 25 m has a sag of 3 m.

5. When a plain cylindrical shell of diameter D and height H is formed by pressing from a blank of diameter D, a formula often used is:

$$B^2 = D^2 + 4DH$$

Find the diameter of the shell when a blank of diameter 60 mm is used to form a shell of depth 12·5 mm.

6. A parcel has square ends of length S. The length of the parcel is 50 mm longer than the side of the square. If the total surface area (i.e. two square ends plus four rectangular sides) is 33 600 mm², find the length of the square end.

7. A square tube of outer side L has a wall thickness t so that the bore is a square of side $L - 2t$. Find the value of t when $L = 40$ mm so that the cross-sectional area is 375 mm².

8. If a body is projected vertically upwards from a datum with a velocity of u, the height s with respect to the datum after a time of t is given approximately by the formula:

$$s = ut - 5t^2$$

In a particular circumstance the value of u was 20 m/s.

   (a) Find the values of s when $t = 2$ and $t = 4$.
   (b) Find the values of t when $s = 15$ m.
   (c) What is the significance of the two answers to (b)? (The answers to (a) should provide a guide.)

9. If $S = \dfrac{n}{2} \{2a + d(n - 1)\}$, find a positive value of n so that $S = 60$ when $a = 6$ and $d = 3$.

10. The sum S of the first n natural numbers is given by the formula:

$$S = \frac{n}{2}(n + 1)$$

How many numbers are required for the sum to total 45?

11. The third term in the expansion of $(1 + x)^n$ is $\dfrac{(n)(n - 1)x^2}{2}$. What are the values of n if the third term is $10x^2$?

12. A rectangular sheet has a length of 1·6 m and a width of 1·2 m. The width and length are each reduced by x m leaving a rectangle of area 1·17 m^2. Determine the value of x.

13. When a body is projected vertically upwards with a velocity of u, the distance h above the point of discharge after a time of t is given approximately by the formula:

$$h = ut - 5t^2$$

If $u = 30$ m/s, at what times is the body 40 m above the point of discharge? What is the significance of the two answers?

14. A vessel in the form of the frustum of a cone is to have a volume of 836 mm^3. The large radius R is to be 6 mm, and the height h is to be 10·5 mm. Determine the value of the smaller radius r. The volume is given by:

$$\frac{\pi h}{3} (R^2 + Rr + r^2)$$

and take π as $\frac{22}{7}$.

15. When a circular can with an open top having a diameter d and a height h is formed from a circular blank of diameter B, subject to certain conditions, the connection between B, d and h is given by the formula:

$$B^2 = d^2 + 4dh$$

15. What diameter of can is produced:
    (*a*) when $B = 80$ mm and $h = 30$ mm;
    (*b*) when $B = 50$ mm and $h = 10$ mm?

16. The total surface area of a solid cylinder of length 10 mm is 748 mm². Taking π as $\frac{22}{7}$, determine its radius.

17. A strip of metal of length 40 mm is bent to form a rectangle, the ends being butt-welded. Determine the length and width of the rectangle so that the area is:
    (*a*) 96 mm²;   (*b*) 50 mm².

18. If the lengths of the major and minor axes of an ellipse are *a* and *b*, the area of the ellipse is given by $\dfrac{\pi ab}{4}$. An ellipse has an area of 88 mm², the major axis being 6 mm longer than the minor axis. Taking π as $\frac{22}{7}$, find the lengths of the axes.

19. (*a*) Deduce a formula for the area *A* of the channel section shown in Figure 2.3 in terms of *B*, *D* and *T*.
    (*b*) Use the formula to find the value of *T* when $B = 16$ mm, $D = 7$ mm and the area is 28 mm².

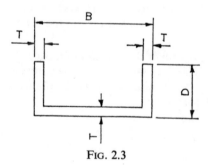

FIG. 2.3

20. If a segment of a circle has a radius *R*, a height *H*, and a length of chord *L*, then:

$$R = \frac{L^2}{8H} + \frac{H}{2}$$

Find the smallest value of *H* when $R = 13$ mm and $L = 10$ mm.

21. A solid roller has a length of 40 mm. If the roller has a diameter of d and a flat-bottomed hole of diameter $\dfrac{d}{2}$ is drilled co-axially to a depth of L, the distance $\bar{x}$ to the centre of gravity from the drilled end can be found from the equation:

$$\bar{x} = \frac{6\,400 - L^2}{320 - 2L}$$

If $\bar{x} = 21$ mm, show that:

$$L^2 - 42L + 320 = 0$$

and hence obtain two values of L corresponding to $\bar{x}$ being equal to 21 mm.

22. A rectangular hole is cut from a 25 mm × 20 mm rectangular plate. The distance x between the edge of the plate and the edge of the hole is the same on all sides. The hole reduces the area by 60%.

   (*a*) Show that:

$$2x^2 - 45x + 100 = 0$$

   (*b*) Solve this equation for x and hence determine the dimensions of the hole.

23. When a spherical cap of height h is cut from a sphere of radius r, the section reveals a circle of diameter d and:

$$d = 2\sqrt{\{h(2r - h)\}}$$

   (*a*) If $r = 7.5$ and $d = 9$, show that:

$$4h^2 - 60h + 81 = 0$$

   (*b*) Solve this equation to obtain the smallest value of h.
   (*c*) What does the other value of h represent?

24. A storage area is rectangular in shape, the dimensions being 60 m × 20 m. The length and breadth are each increased by a distance x metres so that the area is increased by 43%.

   (*a*) Show that the value of x can be obtained from the equation:

$$x^2 + 80x - 516 = 0$$

   (*b*) Solve this equation for x.

Answers to Problems 2.6

1. (a) $x = 5$ or $x = 3$ (b) $x = 4$ or $x = -3$
   (c) $x = 9$ or $x = 0$ (d) $x = 1\frac{1}{2}$ or $x = -1\frac{1}{3}$
   (e) $x = -5$ (twice)   (f) $x = 2$ or $x = \frac{1}{2}$
   (g) $x = 5$ or $x = -4$ (h) $x = 7$ or $x = \frac{2}{3}$
2. (a) $x^2 - 4x + 3 = 0$ (b) $x^2 + 3x - 10 = 0$
   (c) $6x^2 - 17x - 14 = 0$ (d) $x^2 - (a + b)x + ab = 0$
3. $V = 30$ km/h
4. $D = 24$ m
5. $D = 40$ mm
6. $S = 60$ mm
7. $t = 2 \cdot 5$ mm
8. (a) 20 m and zero
   (b) $t = 1$ second and $t = 3$ seconds
   (c) First value is when body is rising, second value when body is falling.
9. 5
10. 9
11. 5 or -4
12. $0 \cdot 3$ m
13. $t = 2$ s or $t = 4$ s
    First is when body is moving upward, second when it is moving downward.
14. 4 mm
15. (a) 40 mm   (b) $33 \cdot 8$ mm
16. 7 mm
17. (a) 12 mm × 8 mm
    (b) $17 \cdot 1$ mm × $2 \cdot 93$ mm
18. 14 mm and 8 mm
19. (a) $T(2D + B - 2T)$ (b) 1 mm
20. 1 mm
21. $\bar{x} = 32$ mm or 10 mm
22. (a) No numerical answer is required   (b) 20 mm × 15 mm
23. (a) No numerical answer is required   (b) $1 \cdot 5$ mm
    (c) The 'height' of the remaining portion of the sphere
24. 6 m

2.7 Transposition of Formulae

Formulae that are developed during the reader's studies are not always in a form suitable for direct use in answering a problem. For instance, the reader will soon meet a formula for the volume V

of a sphere in terms of the diameter D, this being $V = \dfrac{\pi D^3}{6}$.

This formula can be used directly if a problem states, 'Find the volume of a sphere of diameter 3 mm.' If a problem requires us to find the diameter of a sphere whose volume is 18 mm^3, what we require is a formula which gives the diameter in terms of the volume.

In the formula $V = \dfrac{\pi D^3}{6}$, V is called the subject of the formula.

What we have to do is to rearrange the equation $V = \dfrac{\pi D^3}{6}$ so that D becomes the subject instead of V. We reposition the symbols without disturbing the equality, the process being known as the *transposition of formulae.*

It must be emphasized that transposition of formulae is simply the solution of equations. The small difference when compared with previous work is that in the past most answers to equations have been numbers. In transposition of formulae the answer that is required usually consists of numbers and/or symbols.

A problem which states:

'If $V = \dfrac{\pi D^3}{6}$, make D the subject of the formula'

only means

'Solve the equation $V = \dfrac{\pi D^3}{6}$ for D.'

Consequently transposition of formulae within the scope for which this book was intended requires no further work beyond that already covered in this chapter on the solution of equations. Let us illustrate the above information by a series of typical examples, noting that in general we try to bring all the terms including the subject to one side of an equation. We will commence with formulae which equate two fractions, and we note that a single term can be made into a fraction by using a denominator of unity.

Example

If $V = \dfrac{\pi D^3}{6}$, make D the subject of the formula.

$$V = \frac{\pi D^3}{6} \qquad \frac{V}{1} = \frac{\pi D^3}{6}$$

By cross-multiplication
$$\frac{6V}{\pi} = \frac{D^3}{1}$$

Hence $$D^3 = \frac{6V}{\pi} \text{ and } D = \sqrt[3]{\frac{6V}{\pi}}$$

Having solved an equation, the validity of the solution should be checked. Transposition of formulae, it is repeated, is only the solution of equations, and hence the answer should be checked. This is best done by finding simple values which satisfy the original formula, and then seeing if the same values satisfy the answer.

Check: In the original formula, if $D = 6$, then $V = 36\pi$.

In the answer: $$D = \sqrt[3]{\frac{6 \times 36\pi}{\pi}} = \sqrt[3]{216} = 6$$

This is apparently correct, so we now conclude the exercise by stating the answer.

$$\textbf{Answer:} \ D = \sqrt[3]{\frac{6V}{\pi}}$$

Example

If $T = 2\pi \sqrt{\dfrac{GJ}{IL}}$, find a formula for G.

If a root sign appears it is advisable to move everything outside the root sign to the other side of the equation.

$$T = 2\pi \sqrt{\frac{GJ}{IL}}, \qquad \frac{T}{2\pi} = \sqrt{\frac{GJ}{IL}}$$

Now square both sides to eliminate the root sign:

$$\frac{T^2}{4\pi^2} = \frac{GJ}{IL}$$

and by cross-multiplication $\quad G = \dfrac{T^2 IL}{4\pi^2 J}$

In the original equation, if $I = 1$, $L = 2$, $J = \frac{1}{2}$ and $G = 16$, then $T = 2\pi\sqrt{4} = 4\pi$. In the final equation:

$$G = \frac{T^2 IL}{4\pi^2 J} = \frac{16\pi^2 \times 1 \times 2}{4\pi^2 \times \frac{1}{2}} = 16$$

$$\textbf{Answer:} \ G = \frac{T^2 IL}{4\pi^2 J}$$

Example

Make K the subject from the formula $E = \dfrac{9CK}{C + 3K}$.

We note that the line of a fraction can be interpreted as a pair of brackets.

$$\frac{E}{1} = \frac{9CK}{(C + 3K)}$$

By cross multiplication $E(C + 3K) = 9CK$
Remove brackets: $\quad EC + 3EK = 9CK$

Bring terms involving the unknown to one side:
$$EC = 9CK - 3EK$$

Factorize R.H.S.: $\quad\quad EC = K(9C - 3E)$

Hence $\quad\quad\quad \dfrac{EC}{(9C - 3E)} = K$

Check: In the original equation, if $C = 2$ and $K = 1$ then:
$$E = \frac{9 \times 2 \times 1}{2 + 3} = \frac{18}{5} = 3 \cdot 6$$

In the final equation:
$$K = \frac{EC}{9C - 3E} = \frac{3 \cdot 6 \times 2}{18 - 10 \cdot 8} = \frac{7 \cdot 2}{7 \cdot 2} = 1$$

Answer: $K = \dfrac{EC}{9C - 3E}$

Example

If $S = \dfrac{n\sqrt{Q}}{H^{3/4}}$, make Q the subject of the formula.

Write as two fractions: $\quad \dfrac{S}{1} = \dfrac{n\sqrt{Q}}{H^{3/4}}$

Leave root sign on one side by cross-multiplication:
$$\frac{SH^{3/4}}{n} = \frac{\sqrt{Q}}{1}$$

Square both sides: $\quad \left(\dfrac{SH^{3/4}}{n}\right)^2 = Q$

$$\therefore Q = \frac{S^2 H^{3/2}}{n^2}$$

Check: A convenient value of H must be chosen so that $H^{3/4}(= \sqrt[4]{H^3})$ can be evaluated. Let H be 2^4 ($= 16$), then $\sqrt[4]{H^3} = \sqrt[4]{(16 \times 16 \times 16)} = \sqrt[2]{(4 \times 4 \times 4)} = 2 \times 2 \times 2 = 8$. Let $Q = 4$ and $n = 3$:

then
$$S = \frac{3\sqrt{4}}{8} = \frac{3}{4}$$

Values which fit the original formula are $n = 3$, $Q = 4$, $H = 16$, and $S = \frac{3}{4}$. Let us see whether these values fit the answer.

Check: $Q = \dfrac{(\frac{3}{4})^2(16)^{3/2}}{3^2} = \dfrac{9 \times \sqrt[2]{16^3}}{16 \times 9} = \dfrac{9}{16} \times \dfrac{64}{9} = 4$

Example

Eliminate a from the simultaneous equations:

$$P = aL^2 + K$$
$$Q = 3aL^2 + K$$

and hence find an expression for P which does not contain a.

Multiply the first equation by 3: $\qquad 3P = 3aL^2 + 3K$
Rewrite the second equation: $\qquad\qquad Q = 3aL^2 + K$

Subtract:
$$3P - Q = \qquad\quad + 2K$$
$$3P = 2K \quad + \quad Q$$
$$\therefore P = \frac{2K + Q}{3}$$

Check: Let $a = 1$, $L = 2$, $K = 3$, then $P = 7$ and $Q = 12 + 3 = 15$

$$P = \frac{2K + Q}{3} = \frac{6 + 15}{3} = \frac{21}{3} = 7$$

Answer: $P = \dfrac{2K + Q}{3}$

Example

If $T = 2\pi \sqrt{\dfrac{k^2 + h^2}{gh}}$, make h the subject of the formula.

Leaving the root sign on one side:

$$\frac{T}{2\pi} = \sqrt{\frac{k^2 + h^2}{gh}}$$

Square both sides:
$$\frac{T^2}{4\pi^2} = \frac{k^2 + h^2}{gh}$$

Cross-multiply: $\quad ghT^2 = 4\pi^2(k^2 + h^2)$
Remove brackets: $\quad ghT^2 = 4\pi^2k^2 + 4\pi^2h^2$

This equation contains h^2 and h, and is therefore a quadratic in h. Rearrange in quadratic standard form:

$$4\pi^2h^2 - ghT^2 + 4\pi^2k^2 = 0$$

Compare with
$$ax^2 + bx + c = 0$$

$$x = h, \ a = 4\pi^2, \ b = -gT^2, \ c = 4\pi^2k^2$$

$$x = \frac{-b \pm \sqrt{(b^2 - 4ac)}}{2a}$$

$$\therefore h = \frac{-(-gT^2) \pm \sqrt{\{g^2T^4 - 4(4\pi^2)(4\pi^2k^2)\}}}{8\pi^2}$$

$$\therefore h = \frac{gT^2 \pm \sqrt{\{g^2T^4 - 64\pi^4k^2\}}}{8\pi^2}$$

Selection of simple values to make $\dfrac{k^2 + h^2}{gh}$ a simple number is not easy; but remember the 3, 4, 5 rule. Let $k = 3$ and $h = 4$, then $k^2 + h^2 = 25$. If we make $gh = 4$, then $g = 1$.

$$\sqrt{\frac{k^2 + h^2}{gh}} = \sqrt{\frac{25}{4}} = \frac{5}{2}$$

so therefore
$$T = 5\pi$$

Values which fit the original equation are $T = 5\pi$, $k = 3$, $h = 4$, and $g = 1$.

Check: $4 = \dfrac{1(5\pi)^2 \pm \sqrt{\{1(5\pi)^4 - 64\pi^4(9)\}}}{8\pi^2}$

$$= \frac{25\pi^2 \pm \sqrt{\{625\pi^4 - 576\pi^4\}}}{8\pi^2} = \frac{25\pi^2 \pm \sqrt{49\pi^4}}{8\pi^2}$$

$$= \frac{25\pi^2 \pm 7\pi^2}{8\pi^2} = \frac{32\pi^2 \text{ or } 18\pi^2}{8\pi^2} = 4 \text{ or } 2\cdot 5$$

E

123

(We have been able to check the one value we assumed, and since we had to solve a quadratic, we must expect two values. When we assumed $h = 4$ we automatically included another root whose value we did not know.)

$$\textbf{Answer:} \ h = \frac{gT^2 \pm \sqrt{(g^2T^4 - 64\pi^4k^2)}}{8\pi^2}$$

Problems 2.7

In questions 1 to 23 transpose the formulae to produce formulae for the symbol stated.

1. $I = \dfrac{BD^3}{12}$ for B

2. $W = \dfrac{mv^2}{2}$ for m

3. $V = \dfrac{\pi r^2 h}{3}$ for h

4. $A = \pi r^2$ for r

5. $V = \dfrac{\pi D^3}{6}$ for D

6. $F = \dfrac{mv^2}{r}$ for v

7. $t = \sqrt{\dfrac{2s}{g}}$ for s

8. $v = c\sqrt{(mi)}$ for i

9. $R = \sqrt[3]{\dfrac{3V}{4\pi}}$ for V

10. $s = ut - \frac{1}{2}at^2$ for a

11. $K = \dfrac{2c(m + 1)}{3(m - 2)}$ for m

12. $S = \dfrac{n}{2}\{2a + d(n - 1)\}$ for a

13. $R = \dfrac{2N}{N - n}$ for N

14. $\dfrac{1}{f} = \dfrac{1}{v} - \dfrac{1}{u}$ for v

15. $v^2 - u^2 = 2as$ for u

16. $T = 2\pi \sqrt{\dfrac{L}{g}}$ for g

17. $T = 2\pi \sqrt{\dfrac{k^2 + h^2}{gh}}$ for k

18. $N = \dfrac{1}{2L} \sqrt{\dfrac{T}{M}}$ for M

19. $\dfrac{1}{R} = \dfrac{1}{R_1} + \dfrac{1}{R_2}$ for R_1

20. $\dfrac{1}{R} = \dfrac{1}{R_1} + \dfrac{1}{R_2 + R_3}$ for R_2

21. $V = \sqrt{\dfrac{nP}{d}}$ for d

22. $A = P\left(1 + \dfrac{R}{100}\right)^n$ for R

23. $W = \dfrac{\pi LS}{4}(D^2 + d^2)$ for d

24. If $f = \dfrac{1}{2\pi\sqrt{(LC)}}$ find a formula expressing L in terms of f and C.

25. If $P = \dfrac{fa}{1 + r^2}$, express r in terms of f, a and P.

26. Make θ the subject of the formula $R = R_0(1 + \theta t)$.

27. If $A = g\left(\dfrac{1}{1-d}\right) - f$ express d in terms of A, g and f.

28. Make b the subject of the formula:
$$x = \frac{mb - ad}{a + b}$$

29. If $Z = \sqrt{\{R^2 + (X_1 - X_2)^2\}}$, rearrange the formula to obtain an expression for X_2.

30. If $V = \dfrac{\pi D^2 H}{12}$ and $A = \dfrac{\pi D^2}{4}$, find an expression for V in terms of A and H.

31. If $A = \dfrac{\pi D^2}{4}$ and $C = \pi D$, find an expression for A in terms of C.

32. If $H = \dfrac{4F}{\pi d^2}$ and $D = \dfrac{0.3HLd}{\sqrt{V}}$, express D in terms of F, L, d and V.

Answers to Problems 2.7

1. $B = \dfrac{12I}{D^3}$

2. $m = \dfrac{2W}{v^2}$

3. $h = \dfrac{3V}{\pi r^2}$

4. $r = \sqrt{\dfrac{A}{\pi}}$

5. $D = \sqrt[3]{\dfrac{6V}{\pi}}$

6. $v = \sqrt{\dfrac{Fr}{m}}$

7. $s = \dfrac{gt^2}{2}$

8. $i = \dfrac{v^2}{c^2 m}$

9. $V = \dfrac{4\pi R^3}{3}$

10. $a = \dfrac{2(ut - s)}{t^2}$

11. $m = \dfrac{6K + 2c}{3K - 2c}$

12. $a = \dfrac{S}{n} - \dfrac{d}{2}(n - 1)$

13. $N = \dfrac{nR}{R - 2}$

14. $v = \dfrac{uf}{u + f}$

15. $u = \sqrt{(v^2 - 2as)}$

16. $g = \dfrac{4\pi^2 L^2}{T^2}$

17. $k = \sqrt{\left(\dfrac{T^2 hg}{4\pi^2} - h^2\right)}$

18. $M = \dfrac{T}{4N^2 L^2}$

19. $R_1 = \dfrac{RR_2}{R_2 - R}$

20. $R_2 = \dfrac{RR_1}{R_1 - R} - R_3$ or $\dfrac{RR_1 + RR_3 - R_1 R_3}{R_1 - R}$

21. $d = \dfrac{nP}{V^2}$

22. $R = 100 \left\{ \sqrt[n]{\left(\dfrac{A}{P}\right)} - 1 \right\}$

23. $d = \sqrt{\left(\dfrac{4W}{\pi LS} - D^2\right)}$

24. $L = \dfrac{1}{4\pi^2 f^2 C}$

25. $r = \sqrt{\left(\dfrac{fa}{P} - 1\right)}$ or $\sqrt{\left(\dfrac{fa}{P} - P\right)}$

26. $\theta = \dfrac{R - R_0}{R_0 t}$

27. $d = 1 - \dfrac{g}{A + fg}$

28. $b = \dfrac{a(x + d)}{(m - x)}$

29. $X^2 = X_1 - \sqrt{(Z^2 - R_2)}$

30. $V = \dfrac{AH}{3}$

31. $A = \dfrac{C^2}{4\pi}$

32. $D = \dfrac{1 \cdot 2 FL}{\pi d \sqrt{v}}$

2.8 Variation

Let us imagine we had to deduce a formula for the volume of a cylinder. The dimensions that completely specify a cylinder are the diameter and the length; hence the volume can only depend upon the diameter and the length. If we had a container with a rectangular internal cross-section and partially filled it with water, we could find the volumes of cylinders by completely submerging them in the water. The volume of the cylinder would be the apparent increase in the volume of the water. In this particular case it would be the increase in the depth of the water multiplied by the cross-sectional area of the container.

A systematic approach would be to consider the effect of changing one variable at a time. Suppose we kept the diameter of several cylinders constant, and varied only the length. We should find that if we doubled the length, we should double the volume. If we halved the length, we should halve the volume. If we represent the cylinders by suffixes 1, 2, 3, etc. then:

$$\frac{V_1}{L_1} = \frac{V_2}{L_2} = \frac{V_3}{L_3} = \text{a constant value, say } k_1$$

In general $\qquad\qquad V = k_1 L$

We would say that the volume is proportional to the length. A mathematical way of writing this is $V \propto L$. The sign between the V and the L is known as the *variation sign* and we read that it *varies as* or *is proportional to*.

Since $V \propto L$ and $V = k_1L$, we note that we can replace the variation sign by an equals sign, provided we introduce a constant of correct magnitude.

Now let us keep the length of cylinders constant, but vary the diameter. We would find in this case that if we doubled the diameter the volume would be multiplied by four. Further experiments would show that:

$$\frac{V_1}{D_1{}^2} = \frac{V_2}{D_2{}^2} = \frac{V_3}{D_3{}^2} = \text{a constant value, say } k_2$$

In general $\hspace{2cm} V = k_2D^2$

Our formula for the volume of a cylinder must include V, D and L, and we know that our final formula must satisfy the conditions that $V = k_1L$ and $V = k_2D^2$. One way this can occur is when:

$$V = k_3D^2L \text{ where } k_3 = k_1k_2$$

This we can check by establishing that:

$$\frac{V_1}{D_1{}^2L_1} = \frac{V_2}{D_2{}^2L_2} = \frac{V^3}{D_3{}^2L_3} = \text{a constant value, say } k_3$$

Before we proceed further, let us note particularly that if $V \propto A$ and $V \propto B$:

then $\hspace{2cm} V \propto AB$

and $\hspace{2cm} V = \text{a suitable constant} \times AB$

Let us now return to our experiments concerning the volume of a cylinder, having thus far established that $V = k_3D^2L$, and proceed to determine the magnitude of the constant k_3. We now take a particular cylinder and find its volume. Suppose that a cylinder of diameter 7 mm and length 12 mm had a volume of 462 mm³.

$$V = k_3D^2L, \hspace{1cm} \therefore k_3 = \frac{V}{D^2L} = \frac{462 \text{ mm}^3}{49 \text{ mm}^2 \times 12 \text{ mm}} = \frac{11}{14}$$

We should note here that in this particular case the constant has no units; it is known as a *non-dimensional constant*.

We now have determined a formula for the volume of a cylinder:

$$V = \frac{11D^2L}{14}$$

$$\left(\text{If } \pi \text{ is taken as } \frac{22}{7}, \frac{11}{14} \text{ is } \frac{\pi}{4}, \text{ hence } V = \frac{\pi D^2L}{4} \right)$$

Thus far, we have met with one quantity being proportional to another, and one quantity being proportional to the square of another. The mathematicians say that these *vary directly*. In some investigations, we find that one quantity is proportional to the reciprocal of another quantity. In this case we say that one quantity *varies inversely with the other*.

For instance, if A varies inversely as B then:

$$A \propto \frac{1}{B}$$

and $\qquad A = $ a constant value $\times \dfrac{1}{B}$

Extending this further, if A varies inversely as the square of C, then:

$$A \propto \frac{1}{C^2}$$

and $\qquad A = \dfrac{1}{C^2} \times$ a constant value

Furthermore, by incorporating a point brought out earlier in this article:

if $\qquad A \propto \dfrac{1}{B}$ and $A \propto \dfrac{1}{C^2}$, then $A \propto \dfrac{1}{BC^2}$

and $\qquad A = $ a constant value $\times \dfrac{1}{BC^2}$

or $\qquad ABC^2 = $ a constant value

As a typical example of how scientific laws are deduced, let us consider the resistance R offered by circular wires made of a particular alloy, the temperature remaining constant. If the resistances are of the same material, the magnitude of the resistance can be changed by varying the diameter d and the length L. We should find that R *varies directly as* L and that R *varies inversely as the square of* d.

Hence $\qquad R \propto L$ and $R \propto \dfrac{1}{d^2}$

hence $\qquad R \propto \dfrac{L}{d^2}$ and $R = \dfrac{kL}{d^2}$

(We will repeat that this occurs if the temperature is constant.)

Let us now see whether this constant has a unit.

$$R = \frac{kL}{d^2}, \text{ then } k = \frac{Rd^2}{L}$$

the unit of R would be ohms
the unit of d would be metres
and   the unit of L would be metres

$$\text{Unit of } k = \frac{\text{unit of } R \times \text{unit of } d^2}{\text{unit of } L}$$

$$= \frac{\Omega \times m^2}{m} = \Omega m \text{ (ohm metres)}$$

In this case, the constant is dimensional; it not only has magnitude, it also has a unit.

Example

If a given quantity of gas is subjected to volume and temperature changes, its absolute pressure P (i.e. pressure in excess of a perfect vacuum) varies directly as the temperature in degrees celsius + 273, and inversely as the volume V.

A particular quantity of gas at 0.15 MN/m^2 absolute has a volume of 20 m^3 at 27°C. What will be its pressure at a volume of 10 m^3 and a temperature of 127°C?

$$P \propto (T + 273) \text{ and } P \propto \frac{1}{V}$$

$$\therefore P \propto (T + 273) \times \frac{1}{V}$$

or $$P \propto \frac{T + 273}{V}$$

$$\therefore P = \frac{k(T + 273)}{V}$$

or $$k = \frac{PV}{T + 273}$$

Hence $\dfrac{PV}{T + 273}$ is the same for each set of conditions.

Let suffix 1 denote the first set, and suffix 2 the second set.

$$\frac{P_1 V_1}{T_1 + 273} = \frac{P_2 V_2}{T_2 + 273}$$

$$\frac{0.15 \times 20}{27 + 273} = \frac{P_2 \times 10}{127 + 273}$$

$$\frac{3}{300} = \frac{P_2 \times 10}{400}$$

$$1\,200 = 3\,000\,P_2$$

$$P_2 = 0.4 \text{ (same unit as } P_1)$$

Answer: Final pressure = 0·4 MN/m²

Problems 2.7

1. The force F between two magnetic poles varies directly as the strengths m_1 and m_2 and inversely as the square of the distance apart d. Write down the formula with a constant k connecting F, m_1, m_2 and d. If $F = 4$ when $m_1 = 3$, $m_2 = 7$ and $d = 2.5$, find F when $m_1 = 4$, $m_2 = 9$ and $d = 3.5$.

2. The mass M of hexagonal bars of a free machining brass commonly used in the electrical industry varies directly as the length L and directly as the square of the distance across flats W. A hexagonal bar 20 mm across flats and 50 mm long has a mass of 0·147 2 kg. Calculate the mass, in kilogrammes, of a hexagonal bar 30 mm across flats and 2 metres long.

3. The power P that can be transmitted by a motor shaft made from a particular material varies directly as the rotational speed N and directly as the cube of the diameter d. If a shaft of diameter 20 mm can transmit 1 kW at 1 400 rev/min, what diameter shaft should be used to transmit 5 kW at 700 rev/min?

4. The mass M of a circular steel anchor ring varies directly as the mean diameter D and the square of the bar diameter d. A ring of mean diameter 80 mm made from bar of diameter 10 mm has a mass of 0·15 kg. Calculate the mass of a similar ring of mean diameter 100 mm made from bar of diameter 20 mm.

5. For a given quantity of gas, provided the temperature remains constant, the pressure P (in excess of zero) varies inversely as the volume V. A volume of 0·5 m³ of gas has a pressure of 0·104 MN/m². Determine the magnitude and unit of the constant of variation and the pressure when the volume changes to 0·4 m³ at constant temperature.

6. The power P transmitted by a particular vee-belt drive varies directly as the driving tension T and directly as the belt velocity v. A belt transmits 2 kW when the tension is 400 N and the velocity is 210 m/min. Find the power transmitted when the tension is 300 N and the belt velocity is 140 m/min.

7. The quantity of heat W generated by the passage of an electric current varies directly as the time t, directly as the square of the voltage V and inversely as the resistance R.

   (a) If $W = 500$ when $t = 2$, $V = 100$ and $R = 40$, establish the constant of variation and hence establish a formula giving W in terms of t, V and R.

   (b) Find W when $t = 0.5$, $V = 250$ and $R = 25$.

8. The intensity of illumination I provided at a point distant d from a particular light varies inversely as the square of d. The light source is originally 5 m from the point. How much nearer must the light be brought to the point to increase the intensity of illumination by $56\frac{1}{4}\%$?

9. The volume V of a particular solid varies directly as the height h and directly as the square of the base radius r. Such a solid has a base radius of 7 mm, a height of 30 mm and a volume of 1 540 mm^3. Taking π as $\frac{22}{7}$, deduce a formula for V in terms of π, r and h. Hence determine the volume of a similar solid whose base radius is 3.5 mm and whose height is 24 mm.

10. The voltage drop V in a conductor varies directly as the length L of the conductor and inversely as the square of its diameter d. If L is increased by 50% and d increased by 25%, find the resulting percentage change in V. State whether V increases or decreases.

11. The electric resistance R of a wire varies directly as its length L and inversely as its cross-sectional area A. If $R = 1\,340$ when $L = 20$ and $A = 0.02$, determine R when $L = 1.5$ and $A = 0.03$.

12. A quantity Q is proportional to $\dfrac{x \times y^{1/2}}{z^2}$. If $Q = 2$ when $x = 1\frac{1}{2}$, $y = \frac{1}{9}$ and $z = \frac{1}{2}$, calculate the constant of proportionality. If x, y and z are all doubled, what will be the new value of Q?

13. (*a*) The electrical resistance of a copper wire of circular cross-section varies directly as its length and inversely as the square of its diameter. If two copper wires have the same resistance but the diameter of one is twice that of the other, obtain the ratio of their lengths. Hence, show that the thicker wire is sixteen times as heavy as the thinner wire.

(*b*) A copper wire 10 metres long and 2 mm in diameter has a resistance of 0·054 ohms. Obtain the resistance of a second copper wire 40 metres long and 4 mm in diameter.

Answers to Problems 2.7

1. $F = \dfrac{km_1m_2}{d^2}$, $3\dfrac{171}{343}$
2. 13·2 kg
3. 43·1 mm
4. 0·75 kg
5. 52 000 Nm (= 0·052 MJ), 0·13 MN/m²
6. 1 kW
7. (*a*) $k = 1$, $W = \dfrac{V^2t}{R}$ (*b*) 1 250
8. 1 m
9. $V = \dfrac{\pi r^2h}{3}$, 308 mm³
10. V is decreased by 4%
11. $R = 67$
12. $k = 1$, $Q = 1·41$
13. (*a*) $\dfrac{L_2}{L_1} = 4$ (*b*) 0·054 ohm

Chapter Three

Graphs

3.1 The Pictorial Presentation of Data

3.1.1. CHARTS, DIAGRAMS AND GRAPHS

Let us imagine a situation in industry where a firm receives batches of mouldings in a plastics material for use on electrical switchgear. The mouldings, when received from the supplier, are sent to an inspection department. They are delivered in batches of 2 000, and the first task of the inspection department is to remove the mouldings which have unsatisfactory appearance due to surface defects. Each batch has an identification number. Let us suppose that the following table indicates the results of inspecting ten successive batches.

Batch no.	21	22	23	24	25	26	27	28	29	30
Rejections	10	12	6	11	5	9	8	4	7	6

Unless the reader had some experience in interpreting tabulated data, the table does not convey to him a great deal of significant information.

Suppose we now represent this data on a diagram. This can be done in a variety of ways, but the diagram shown in Figure 3.1 is how this would probably be done in industry. The diagram now rapidly conveys some significant information (see overleaf).

(a) The number of rejections per batch fluctuates.

(b) Although the number of rejections fluctuates, there is a tendency for that number to diminish.

(c) The average of the ten batches, i.e. the average height of the bars, is about 8.

Now let us simulate another industrial situation. An estimator, as part of his duties, has to determine masses. From a reference book he finds the following table, giving the mass per metre run of round steel bars of a certain specification.

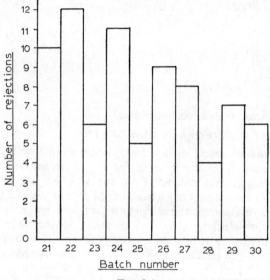

FIG. 3.1

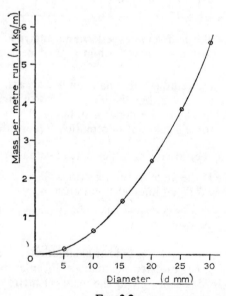

FIG. 3.2

Diameter (mm)	5	10	15	20	25	30
Mass per metre run (kg)	0·155	0·62	1·395	2·48	3·875	5·58

Once more, unless the reader has some skill in interpreting tabulated data, there is apparently little significant information.

Let us present this information pictorially. Fig 3.2 shows the usual manner by which this would be done.

The diagram now conveys some very interesting information not readily apparent from the tabulated data. A quite distinct trend is apparent. It is obvious that we are able to draw a continuous line which will enable us to determine the mass per metre run for other diameters not included in the table. The trend is not a directly proportional increase since the line is curved. If we double the diameter we more than double the mass per foot run.

Figures 3.1 and 3.2 are both pictorial representations of data, called *charts or diagrams*. For a pictorial representation to be a *graph* there must be some connexion, such as a formula, between the two quantities which are represented. This will be indicated by a line on the diagram.

Figure 3.1 is not a graph. For each of the two items represented, the values increase in definite steps. We cannot have such illogical values as '$5\frac{1}{4}$ rejections' or 'batch number 23·8'. The name of a diagram such as Figure 3.1 is a *histogram*. There is no formula which connects the number of defectives with the batch number.

If a graph is drawn, the variable quantities can take any value. In Figure 3.2, we could have a bar of diameter 23 mm, and we could have a bar with a mass of 4 kg/m run. There is a definite connexion between the mass per metre run in kilogrammes and the diameter in millimetres. It is actually

$$\text{Mass per metre run} = 0·006\ 2\ (\text{diameter})^2$$

We can therefore construct a graph by plotting points on a graphical field which satisfy a formula, and joining those points with a line. The line is normally continuous, and can be curved or straight. A discontinuity in the line may indicate that different formulae are applicable at different portions of the line.

3.1.2 PLOTTING OF GRAPHS

A common (but not the only) method of graphically illustrating a formula connecting two variables, say x and y, was invented by the

French mathematician Descartes. Two reference axes are positioned at right angles, it being conventional practice to position the *y*-axis vertically and the *x*-axis horizontally. These axes are the basis of *cartesian co-ordinates*, and the point where they intersect is the origin

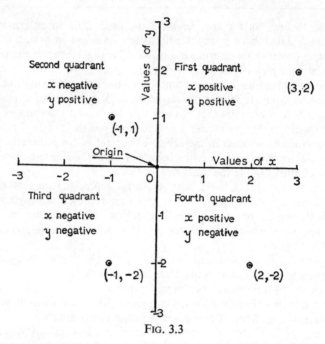

FIG. 3.3

of the co-ordinates, in short, the *origin*. A particular value of *x* is positioned horizontally from the origin to scale. A particular value of *y* is positioned vertically from the origin to scale, which need not necessarily be the same scale as that used for values of *x*. The point $x = 3$, $y = 7$ is indicated mathematically as (3,7), the horizontal distance being quoted first. The values of 3 and 7 are the *co-ordinates* of that particular point on the graphical field, the horizontal co-ordinate being the *abscissa* and the vertical co-ordinate being the *ordinate*.

It is conventional practice, using the origin as the starting point, to regard horizontal distances to the right as positive and horizontal distances to the left as negative. Vertical distances from the origin are positive above the origin, and negative below. Since the intersection of the *x*-axis and the *y*-axis produces four quadrants, it is useful to number them in sequence anticlockwise. The first quadrant

138

associates positive values of x with positive values of y. The second quadrant will associate negative values of x with positive values of y, and so on.

There are several methods of indicating points on a graphical field, none of which has yet been standardized. The reader should use any method to which he has been accustomed. Many people prefer to use a small cross, the intersection of the arms of the cross being the position of the point. Others prefer to use a dot, surrounded by a circle to bring it rapidly to attention. For the time being there are no especial considerations which support any particular method but one should be adopted and adhered to. In this textbook, we shall use the 'dot and circle' convention.

Until the reader has become accustomed to plotting, the following method of plotting points on a graphical field will be found useful.

1. Draw a short faint vertical line at the value of x, the line lying in the vicinity of the value of y.
2. Draw a short faint horizontal line at the value of y, to cross the line drawn previously.
3. Put a point at the intersection of these lines.
4. Draw a small circle around the point to bring it rapidly to notice.

Figure 3.3 shows the conventions employed when constructing graphs using cartesian co-ordinates. A point is indicated by a dot, but in order that its position is readily noticed, it is circled to bring it rapidly to attention. It is the dot which represents the point, not the circle. We use the circle merely for convenience in finding the point.

Some simple examples of the representation by formula on cartesian co-ordinates follow from the conventions used in Figure 3.3. Using cartesian co-ordinates:

(a) The x-axis represents the equation $y = 0$.
(b) The y-axis represents the equation $x = 0$.
(c) The equation $y = 3$ is represented by a horizontal line through the value of 3 on the y-axis.
(d) The equation $x = -4$ is represented by a vertical line through the value -4 on the x-axis.

3.1.3. PRESENTATION OF GRAPHS

In constructing graphs, students are advised:

(a) to label the axes;
(b) to indicate values on the axes;
(c) where appropriate, to indicate an answer on the graph;

    (*d*) if there is more than one line, to state the appropriate equation near each line.

Greatest accuracy is usually obtained when the greatest area is used for the plotting. *It is not essential to include the origin on every graph.* The usual area of a graphical field used in college work is that corresponding to what is known as the international A4 size of paper. There are light rulings at 2 mm intervals, and heavier rulings at 20 mm intervals. Bearing in mind the need for labelling the axes and indicating values on them, the graphical field available for actual plotting is about 200 mm × 160 mm, i.e. about 10 large squares × 8 large squares. If the data provided gave a minimum value for *y* of 42·7 and a maximum values for *y* of 86·9 then 40 to 90 would cover all values, a range of 50. Using the 200 mm dimension would prove most convenient using a scale of 1 large square = 5 units. One small square therefore represents 0·5 unit, and decimal values are then easy to plot. If the 8 large squares were used for a range of about 50, then either 1 large square to 6 or 1 large square to 6·25 could be used, but the choice of scales such as these would lead to difficulties in plotting. Whilst it is desirable to use the greatest area of the field which is available, it should never be selected so that the greater accuracy nominally available with the larger graphical field is lost due to difficulties of accurate plotting.

Many examiners assist students by indicating suitable scales in the questions, in which case it is relatively simple to deduce whether or not the graph paper should be used with the longer side vertical.

In general, graphs have three main uses:

    (*a*) to convey quickly to the observer how one variable changes with respect to another;

    (*b*) as a rapid method of obtaining values other than those of the original data;

    (*c*) as a means of solving equations.

The first two of these uses will now be demonstrated with appropriate examples.

Example

The mass of circular bars of deoxidized copper, in kilogrammes per metre length, varies with the diameter according to the following table.

Diameter d (mm)	10	20	30	40	50	60
Mass M (kg/m)	0·7	2·8	6·3	11·2	17·5	25·2

Illustrate this data graphically, using a horizontal scale for *d* of 20 mm = 10 mm, and a vertical scale for *M* of 20 mm = 5 kg/m. Use your graph to find the weight of a tube of deoxidized copper of outside diameter 44 mm, inside diameter 36 mm and length 80 mm.

The graph is shown in Figure 3.4. From the graph, a metre length of bar of diameter 44 mm has a mass of 13·6 kg, while a metre length of bar of diameter 36 mm has a mass of 9·1 kg.

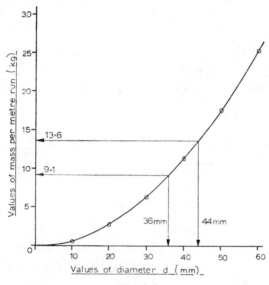

FIG. 3.4

A metre length of tube of outside diameter 44 mm and inside diameter 36 mm has a mass of 13·6 − 9·1 = 4·5 kg.

A tube of length 80 mm has a mass of $\dfrac{80}{1\,000} \times 4·5$ kg = 0·36 kg.

Answer: Mass of tube = 0·36 kg.

Example

The intensity of illumination *I* provided by a particular lamp when it is at a distance *d* from a light meter is given by the following data.

I (units)	270	120	67·5	43·2	30·0	16·9
d (m)	1·0	1·5	2·0	2·5	3	4

141

Illustrate this data on a graph, using a horizontal scale of 20 mm = 0·5 m for d and a vertical scale of 20 mm = 50 units for I.

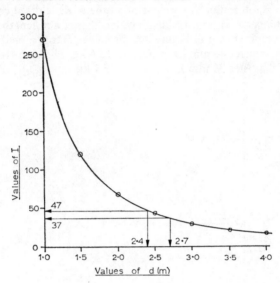

Fig. 3.5

Use your graph to determine:

(a) The value of I when $d = 2·4$ m
(b) The minimum number of lamps to provide a total value of I of 140 units when $d = 2·7$ m

The graph is shown in Figure 3.5. From the graph $I = 47$ when $d = 2·4$ and $I = 37$ when $d = 2·7$,

$$\text{Number of lamps} = \frac{140}{37} = \text{over 3 but less than 4}$$

Hence 4 lamps will be required.

Answers: (a) $I = 47$ units
(b) 4 lamps are required

3.1.4 THE GRAPHS OF QUADRATIC EXPRESSIONS

Figure 3.6 shows the graphs of five different quadratic expressions:

(a) $y = x^2$ and $y = x^2 + 20$
(b) $y = -25 + 10x - x^2$
(c) $y = x^2 - 7x + 10$
(d) $y = -20 + 5x - x^2$

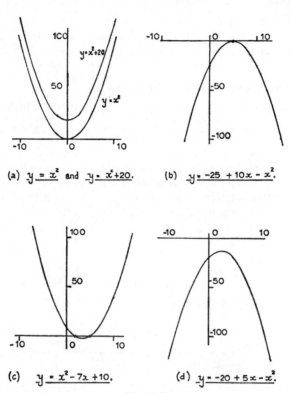

(a) $y = x^2$ and $y = x^2 + 20$. (b) $y = -25 + 10x - x^2$.

(c) $y = x^2 - 7x + 10$. (d) $y = -20 + 5x - x^2$.

FIG. 3.6

The following information can be obtained from the graphs.

1. The curves have similar characteristics, each having a 'nose' and each being symmetrical about an appropriate vertical centre line. The 'nose' is called the *vertex*. If the coefficient of x^2 is positive, the vertex is the lowest point on the curve. If the coefficient of x^2 is negative, the vertex is the highest point on the curve. The general name for the curve produced by a quadratic expression is a *parabola*.

2. If the expression contains x^2 terms or x^2 and constant terms only it is symmetrical about the y-axis. If the expression contains x terms it is displaced with reference to the y-axis.

3. It will be noticed that the graph of $y = -25 + 10x - x^2$ touches the y-axis, that the graph of $y = x^2 - 7x + 10$ cuts the y-axis at different points, and that the graph of $y = -20 + 5x - x^2$ does not cut or touch the x-axis at all. These graphs show a pictorial representation of the three types of solution to a quadratic equation:

143

    (b) $-25 + 10x - x^2 = 0$ has equal roots.
    (c) $x^2 - 7x + 10 = 0$ has two real unequal roots.
    (d) $-20 + 5x - x^2 = 0$ has imaginary roots.

3.1.6 THE GRAPH OF A HYPERBOLA

Let us consider the equation $xy = a$ *constant*, which can be rearranged to $y = \dfrac{a\ constant}{x}$. If x and the constant are positive, y will also be positive. As positive values of x diminish, y increases. As x becomes larger, y becomes smaller, approaching zero as x becomes very large. If x is negative, y will also be negative. If x is a large negative number, y is almost zero. If x is a small negative number, y is a large negative number.

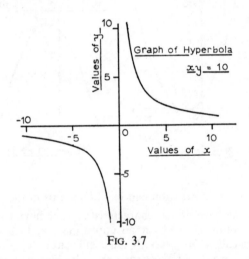

FIG. 3.7

The graphical representation of an equation of the type $xy = a$ *constant* is shown in Figure 3.7. The equation produces two separate curves on the graphical field; the curves are known as *hyperbolas*. Formulae of the type $xy = a$ *constant* occur commonly in engineering. A typical example is the connection between the spindle speed of a lathe and the diameter of work if the cutting speed is to be constant. If $S = \pi dn$, then $dn = \dfrac{S}{\pi}$. If S is constant, so is $\dfrac{S}{\pi}$. Hence the formula $dn = a$ *constant* results, the graphical representation of which is a hyperbola.

144

Problems 3.1

1. If $E = \dfrac{W}{20} + 10$, construct a graph that can be used to determine values of E for values of W between 0 and 100. Using the graph, obtain:

   (a) the value of E when $W = 72$;
   (b) the value of W when $E = 12 \cdot 8$.

2. Construct a graph which illustrates the law $y = x^2$, with values of x ranging from zero to 10. Using your graph read off values for

   (a) the square of $7 \cdot 3$;
   (b) the square root of 71.

3. Plot a graph to illustrate the equation $y = \sqrt[3]{x}$ as x varies from zero to 512. (You are advised to use values of x such as 1, 8, 27, 64, etc.) From the graph obtain the values of the cube of $7 \cdot 5$ and the cube root of 200.

4. If a hexagon has a width across flats of W, its area A is given by $0 \cdot 866 \, W^2$. Plot a graph of A against W as W varies from zero to 6 mm at intervals of 1 mm. Use the graph to find the width across flats of a hexagon whose area is 20 mm².

5. An electric current has variable magnitude I depending on a time t, according to the following table:

t (seconds)	0	0·001	0·002	0·003	0·004	0·005	0·006
I (amperes)	64·3	81·9	94·0	99·6	98·5	90·6	76·6

   Plot a graph of I against t, and from your graph determine:

   (a) the maximum value of I and the value of t at which this maximum occurs;
   (b) the first value of t for which $I = 90$ amperes.

6. A pipe of outside diameter 25 mm has a wall thickness of t so that its inside diameter is $(25 - 2t)$ mm. Plot a graph of the cross-sectional area against t as t varies from zero to 5 mm at intervals of 1 mm. Hence determine the value of t for a cross-sectional area of 225 mm².

7. The efficiency E of a lifting machine was determined for differing loads W, resulting in the following data:

W (N)	400	800	1 200	1 600	2 000
E (%)	25·0	33·3	37·5	40·0	41·7

Illustrate these values on a graph, and use the graph to determine the value of E when $W = 1\ 000$ N.

8. The price P of a particular type of hand tool depends upon the nominal size S according to the following table:

S (mm)	1	2	4	6	8	10
P (£)	0·30	0·45	1·05	2·05	3·45	5·25

If the firm decides to introduce a 3 mm and a 5 mm size, what prices can be expected for these two sizes?

9. A rectangular plate of length 30 mm and width 20 mm has square notches of side x cut out from each corner. The plate is then folded so as to form a rectangular tray of depth x. Show that the capacity C of the tray is given by the formula:

$$C = 4x^3 - 100x^2 + 600x$$

Plot a graph of C against x, as x varies from zero to 6 mm at intervals of 1 mm. Hence find the value of x when $C = 937\cdot5$ mm^3.

10. A cable suspended from two pylons 100 m apart takes the form of the curve $y = \dfrac{x^2}{100} + 45$, where:

y = height in metres of a point P on the cable above the ground
x = distance in metres of P from the lowest point on the cable

Plot the curve of x from -50 to 50. (Take intervals of 10.) From the graph, find:
(a) the clearance of the cable from the ground.
(b) the heights of the supports if the cable spans 60 m but takes the same form.

   (*c*) the distance between the supports to give a maximum sag of 5 m.

11. The work done per second, *W* joules, by an electric motor is given by:

$$W = IV - I^2R$$

where *I* is the current in amperes and *V* and *R* are constants. Plot a graph of *W* against *I* when *V* = 200 and *R* = 100, as the values of *I* range from zero to 2·4 at intervals of 0·4. From the graph determine:

   (*a*) the maximum value of *W* and the value of *I* at which this value occurs;

   (*b*) the values of *I* at which *W* is zero.

12. (*a*) If a cutting speed has to be kept constant at 66 m/min, take $\pi = \frac{22}{7}$ and show that the relationship between the spindle speed *n* rev/min and bar diameter *d* mm is *dn* = 21 000.

   (*b*) Plot a graph to illustrate this relationship, the values of *d* ranging from 20 mm to 70 mm.

   (*c*) Read off from the graph:

      (i) the value of *n* when *d* = 35 mm;

      (ii) the value of *d* when *n* = 500 rev/min.

Answers to Problems 3.1

1. (*a*) 13·6   (*b*) 56
2. (*a*) 53·3   (*b*) 8·43
3. 422, 5·85
4. 4·8 mm
5. (*a*) 100 amperes when *t* = 0·003 3 seconds
   (*b*) *t* = 0·001 6 seconds
6. 3·3 mm
7. 35·7%
8. £0·70 and £1·50
9. 2·5 mm
10. (*a*) 45 m   (*b*) 54 m   (*c*) 44·7 m
11. (*a*) *W* = 100 J when *I* = 1 ampere
   (*b*) *W* = 0 when *I* = 0 and when *I* = 2 amperes
12. (*a*) and (*b*) require no numerical answers
   (*c*) (i) 600 rev/min; (ii) 42 mm

3.2 The Straight Line Law

3.2.1 THE EQUATION OF A STRAIGHT LINE

The slope of a straight line on a graphical field is given by:

the difference in the values of y of two points on the line
$\overline{\text{the difference in the corresponding values of } x}$

Hence, if (x_1, y_1) and (x_2, y_2) are two points on the straight line, the slope is given by:

$$\frac{y_2 - y_1}{x_2 - x_1}$$

If the straight line slopes 'up to the right' it will have a positive slope, while if it slopes 'down to the right' it will have a negative slope. A horizontal line has zero slope since there is no difference in the values of y.

Let us consider the equation $y = ax + b$, where a and b are constants, and let two points on the line be (x_2, y_2) and (x_1, y_1).

If $\qquad\qquad y = ax + b$ always,
then $\qquad\qquad y_2 = ax_2 + b$
and $\qquad\qquad y_1 = ax_1 + b$

Subtracting these equations gives:

$$y_2 - y_1 = ax_2 - ax_1$$
$$\therefore y_2 - y_1 = a(x_2 - x_1)$$
and $\qquad\qquad a = \dfrac{y_2 - y_1}{x_2 - x_1}$

Now $\dfrac{y_2 - y_1}{x_2 - x_1}$ by definition is the slope of the line, while a is a constant. Hence the line which represents $y = ax + b$ has a constant slope of magnitude a. A line having a constant slope is a straight line.

The y-axis is the line $x = 0$. If we put $x = 0$ in the general equation $y = ax + b$, then $y = b$ when $x = 0$. This indicates that the line cuts the y-axis at the value of the constant b.

The representation of the equation $y = ax + b$ by cartesian co-ordinates on a graphical field is a straight line of slope a cutting the y-axis at b. The more formal way of describing where a line cuts an axis is to call it the *intercept* on that axis.

Since only two points are needed to draw a straight line, a graph of the type $y = ax + b$ can be drawn by plotting just two points and joining them by a straight line. However, the reader is recommended always to plot a third point to check the accuracy of the plotting. Conversely, the equation of a straight line can be determined if the co-ordinates of two points on the line are known. The equation is commonly referred to as the *law of the straight line*.

A straight line on a graphical field can also be specifically positioned by one point and the slope of the line. Hence the law of the straight line can be determined if the co-ordinates of one point and the slope of the line are known.

Example

Find the law of the straight line that passes through the points $(2, -3)$ and $(10, 21)$.

$$y = ax + b$$

Using $x = 2, y = -3$: $\quad -3 = 2a + b$
Using $x = 10, y = 21$: $\quad 21 = 10a + b$
By subtraction $\quad\quad \overline{-24 = -8a}$

$$\therefore a = \frac{-24}{-8} = 3$$

Substituting this value of a in the first equation:

$$-3 = 2(3) + b$$
$$-3 = 6 + b$$
$$-3 - 6 = b$$
$$b = -9$$

The law is $y = 3x - 9$

Check for $(2, -3)$: $\quad\quad -3 = 6 - 9$
$$-3 = -3$$

Check for $(10, 21)$: $\quad\quad 21 = 30 - 9$
$$21 = 21$$

Answer: Law is $y = 3x - 9$

Example

Find the law of the straight line of slope -2, passing through the point $(-2, 9)$.

$$y = ax + b$$

Since slope is -2 $\quad\quad a = -2$
$$\therefore y = -2x + b$$

149

Using $y = 9$, $x = -2$:

$$9 = (-2)(-2) + b$$
$$9 = 4 + b$$
$$9 - 4 = b$$
$$b = 5$$

The law is $y = -2x + 5$

or more conveniently $\qquad y = 5 - 2x$

Check for $(-2, 9)$: $\qquad 9 = 5 - 2(-2) = 5 + 4 = 9$

Answer: Law is $y = 5 - 2x$

3.2.2 DETERMINATION OF LAWS FROM EXPERIMENTAL DATA

If we conduct experiments and record values of two variables, say x and y, the results can be shown in graphical form. In many experiments in engineering, the points will be found to lie approximately on a straight line. A typical case would be the plotting of the length of a compression spring for various amounts of loading. It is most improbable that the points would lie *exactly* on a straight line. Although the load may be known precisely, inaccuracies of observation and defects in the apparatus and in the construction of the experiment may have disturbing effects on the value recorded for the length. If the length L were plotted against the load W, the values of L would be subject to error. In another experiment, we could record the resistance R offered by a particular conductor at various temperatures T. In this experiment both R and T have to be measured and in this case the values of R and of T would each be subject to error. We can average out the errors, either in one variable or in both variables, by drawing the *best straight line* to match a particular set of plottings. If a transparent rule is used, the line can be drawn so that the errors are equally distributed, which occurs in many circumstances when as many points lie above the line as lie below. Occasionally a point or points may lie on the line.

If such a graph of a particular experiment plots R vertically and T horizontally, we know from previous work that a straight line represents the relationship $R = aT + b$. Let us suppose that a first point on the line is (T_1, R_1) and a second point on the line is (T_2, R_2).

Since $\qquad\qquad\qquad R_2 = aT_2 + b$

and $\qquad\qquad\qquad R_1 = aT_1 + b$

by subtraction $\qquad R_2 - R_1 = aT_2 - aT_1$

$$= a(T_2 - T_1)$$

$$\therefore a = \frac{R_2 - R_1}{T_2 - T_1}$$

From a consideration of the above result, calculations will be eased if $T_2 - T_1$ is a convenient number for division, and greater accuracy will occur if $T_2 - T_1$ is as large as possible. Having found a value for a, the value of b can be found by substituting in the equation $R_1 = aT_1 + b$ or $R_2 = aT_2 + b$, whichever is the more convenient.

Consequently, the deduction of a straight line law of the type $y = ax + b$ can be made as follows:

1. Plot the values to the largest scales that the graph paper will allow. (*It is not necessary always to include the origin.*)
2. Draw the 'best straight line' to distribute the errors, usually by arranging as many points to lie above the line as below. Occasionally a point or points may lie on the line.
3. Select two points on the line, as far apart as possible but arranging that the distance between the x values will be a convenient divisor. This is best done by choosing the x values and then reading off the appropriate y values.
4. Substitution in $y = ax + b$ will give two simultaneous equations. By subtraction, b will be eliminated, and a can be determined. Substitution in an original equation will permit the evaluation of b.

In a few isolated circumstances the y-axis would appear, in which case the constant b can be determined immediately since it is the value of y at which the straight line crosses the y-axis. The value of a can be found by choosing one other point on the line and by substituting the (x, y) values of this point in $y = ax + b$. Since y, x and b are known, a can be determined. In order to give the greatest degree of accuracy the second point should be as far from the y-axis as possible, but allowing for a convenient value of x to simplify calculations.

Example

For a particular nickel-chrome steel the resulting percentage reduction in area R after tempering from a temperature of $T°C$ produced the following results:

T	200	300	400	500	600
R	47·0	50·3	54·0	57·7	61·0

Plot these values, T horizontally and R vertically. Draw the best straight line through the points, and hence deduce an approximate formula giving R in terms of T.

Presuming the A4 size of graph paper, a convenient area of field for plotting is 10 large squares by 8 large squares. (A large square is 20 mm × 20 mm.) Considering the values of T, which is to be plotted horizontally, the range is $600 - 200 = 400$. The use of 8 large squares suggests itself, with 20 mm = 50°C. Plottings then conveniently occur on every other heavy line. Proceeding to the values of R, they vary from 47 to 61, a range of 14. To use all the 10 large squares would produce a difficult scale for plotting. A scale of 1 large square = 2 units uses only 7 large squares. Although the full field is not used, the values will be easier to plot accurately. (Although in this case we shall use the longer side of the paper vertically, this is not essential.) Hence the scales will be:

> 20 mm = 50°C horizontally, ranging 200 to 600
> 20 mm = 2 units vertically, ranging from 46 to 62

The graph is shown in Figure 3.8. The best straight line has been drawn. Three points lie on the line. Of the other two, one lies above and one lies below, each being displaced by one small square. Two points on the line, a convenient distance apart, are (200, 47) and

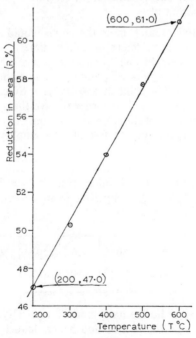

FIG. 3.8

(400, 61). It was pure coincidence that the two extreme points lay on the line, and are also a convenient distance apart horizontally. It should not be presumed that this always occurs.

Since $R = aT + b$
Using (600, 61): $61 = 600a + b$
Using (200, 47): $47 = 200a + b$
Subtracting: $14 = 400a$

$$a = \frac{14}{400} = 0{\cdot}003\ 5$$

Substituting this value in the first equation:

$$61 = 600\ (0{\cdot}003\ 5) + b$$
$$61 = 21 + b$$
$$b = 61 - 21 = 40$$

Answer: Approximate formula is $R = 0{\cdot}003\ 5T + 40$.

Problems 3.2

1. Determine the laws of straight lines that pass through the following pairs of points:

   (*a*) (2, 6) and (4, 8)   (*b*) (3, 6) and (−1, 22)
   (*c*) (−1, −7) and (3, 13)   (*d*) (0, 8) and (3, 17)
   (*e*) The origin and (3, 15)   (*f*) $(p, 4pq)$ and $(3p, -2pq)$

2. Determine the laws of the straight lines which pass through the points with the slopes as indicated below:

   (*a*) Through (0, 1) with unit slope.
   (*b*) Through the origin with slope 4.
   (*c*) Through (2, 6) with slope 0·5.
   (*d*) Through (6, 4) with slope $-\frac{2}{3}$.

3. An experiment was conducted to find the resistance R of a conductor at a temperature of $T°$C. The resulting graph was a straight line passing through the points (10°C, 52 ohms) and (40°C, 58 ohms). Determine the constants a and b in the equation $R = aT + b$, stating in each case the appropriate unit.

4. A spring was subjected to tensile loading, and the length L of the spring was plotted against the load W. The resulting graph was a straight line passing through the points (100 N, 65 mm) and (400 N, 80 mm). Find the 'free length' of the spring, i.e. the length L when $W = 0$.

5. An experiment was conducted on a lifting machine to find the effort E required to lift a load of W. It was found that the graph of E (vertical) against W (horizontal) was a straight line passing through the points (1 000 N, 100 N) and (1 800 N, 140 N). Determine the law of the machine in the form $E = aW + b$.

6. The speed N of a flywheel that was slowing down was measured at times of t seconds after a brake was applied. The following values were obtained:

t (seconds)	20	25	30	35	40
N (rev/min)	200	175	150	125	100

Show graphically that N and t are connected by a law of the type $N = ar + b$ and hence determine the speed of the flywheel when the brake was applied.

7. The following are details of a suggested relationship between the carbon content C and the ultimate tensile strength S of normalized plain carbon steels:

C (%)	0·2	0·3	0·4	0·5	0·6	0·7
S (MN/m²)	494	566	638	710	782	854

Find graphically the law from which these values were determined in the form $S = aC + b$.

8. A channel has a level bottom with straight sides tapering outward. The width W at the water level for various depths d of water flow is given by the following data:

d (m)	1	2	3	4	5
W (m)	7·75	8·70	9·65	10·60	11·55

Show graphically that W and d are related by a formula of the type $W = ad + b$, and determine this formula.

9. In an experiment on the compression of a closely coiled helical spring, the length of the spring L was measured when varying loads W were applied. The following results were obtained:

W (N)	400	500	600	700	800	900	1 000
L (mm)	66	63·8	61	58·5	56	53·2	51

Plot these values, W horizontally and L vertically. If $L = aW + b$, find appropriate values of a and b, and hence the nominal unloaded length of the spring.

10. The resistance, in ohms, of a pure resistor depends upon temperature following the law:

$$R = r(1 + kt)$$

where R is the resistance at t °C, r is the resistance at 0 °C, and k is a constant. A particular resistor has a resistance of 42·4 ohms at 15°C and 45·6 ohms at 35°C. Find by a graphical method the values of r and k.

11. During an experiment on a lifting tackle, the following values of the effort E to lift a load of W were recorded, the units of E and W being identical:

E	10	10·9	13	15·1	17
W	50	60	80	100	120

Plot these values, E vertically and W horizontally. Draw the best straight line for the plotting. If E and W are connected by a law of the type $E = aW + b$, determine graphically suitable values for the constants a and b.

12. The following information was obtained from the measurement of a set of lathe gears, N being the number of teeth and D being the outside diameter:

N	30	35	40	45	50
D (mm)	128	148	168	188	208

F

Plot these values, N horizontally and D vertically. If D and N are connected by a formula:

$$D = mN + c$$

find graphically the values of the constants m and c.

13. The following information has been extracted from a reference work, and indicates the tolerance T mm on the major diameter of a metric screw thread of pitch p mm:

Pitch p (mm)	1	1·5	2	2·5	3
Tolerance T(mm)	0·158	0·212	0·266	0·320	0·374

Plot these values, p horizontally and T vertically. Show that T and p are connected by a formula of the type $T = ap + b$. Determine the constants a and b, and hence calculate the tolerance on the major diameter of a thread of pitch 5 mm.

14. The resistance R of a length of copper wire was measured at various temperatures T, resulting in the following data:

R (ohms)	108	109·8	112·2	114	116	117·8	120·2
T (°C)	20	25	30	35	40	45	50

It was thought that R and T were connected by a formula of the type $R = aT + b$. By drawing a suitable graph find reasonable values for the constants a and b.

15. Steel samples were tested for hardness by two different methods, those being designated R and B. The values obtained were:

Sample nos.	1	2	3	4	5	6
B	382	393	402	412	421	432
R	39	40	41	42	43	44

Plot these values, R horizontally and B vertically. Show that, *over this particular range*, a law of the type $B = aR - b$ is approximately true and determine suitable values for the constants a and b.

Answers to Problems 3.2

1. (a) $y = x + 4$ (b) $y = 18 - 4x$
   (c) $y = 5x - 2$ (d) $y = 3x + 8$
   (e) $y = 5x$ (f) $y = 7pq - 3qx$
2. (a) $y = x + 1$ (b) $y = 4x$

   (c) $y = \dfrac{x}{2} + 5$ (d) $y = 8 - \dfrac{2x}{3}$

3. $a = 0\cdot2$ ohm/°C, $b = 50$ ohms
4. 60 mm
5. $E = 0\cdot005\ W + 50$ N
6. 300 rev/min, obtained from $N = 300 - 5t$
7. $S = 720\ C + 350$
8. $W = 0.95\ d + 6\cdot8$
9. $a = -0\cdot025,\ b = 76$; 76 mm
10. $r = 40,\ k = 0\cdot004$
11. $a = 0\cdot1,\ b = 5$
12. $m = 4,\ c = 8$
13. $a = 0\cdot108,\ b = 0\cdot05$; 0·59 mm
14. $a = 0\cdot4,\ b = 100$
15. $a = 10,\ b = 8$

3.3   Solution of Equations by Graphical Methods

3.3.1   GRAPHICAL SOLUTIONS

Many equations can be solved by recognizing the form of the equation, then applying operations suitable for that particular form. For instance, an equation could be recognized as a quadratic, for which a suitable method of solution would be an application of the formula for obtaining the roots of a quadratic equation.

There are other equations for which there is no formal operational method of solution, or for which the figures in the equation are perhaps such that formal mathematical methods are lengthy and involved. One general point in favour of using a graphical method for the solution of an equation is that *any equation can be solved by means of graph.* Graphical methods, however, depend upon the skill of the solver and upon the quality of the equipment being used. If a close degree of accuracy is required from a graphical solution, very rarely is an attempt made to obtain a final answer from the first graph. The first graph provides a *first approximation* to the root. This first approximation is then used to find a closer value to the root, that is, a *second approximation* is found. The second approximation can then be used to obtain a further closer value, and so on. The general name for a scheme which produces closer and closer values to the actual value of the desired root is an *iterative method*.

3.3.2 SOLUTION OF SIMULTANEOUS EQUATIONS BY GRAPHICAL MEANS

Consider the simultaneous equations:

$$2x + 3y = 13$$
$$3x - y = 3$$

The first equation can be rearranged as $3y = 13 - 2x$ or $y = \dfrac{13 - 2x}{3}$. This is the law of a straight line, and any point on the line will satisfy the law.

The second equation can be rearranged as $-y = 3 - 3x$, or $y = 3x - 3$. This is the law of another straight line, and any point on this second straight line satisfies the second law.

The only point which will satisfy both laws simultaneously is that at which the lines intersect. If the laws $y = \dfrac{13 - 2x}{3}$ and $y = 3x - 3$ are plotted on the same field, the lines will intersect at (2, 3), where $x = 2$, and $y = 3$.

Hence the solution of the simultaneous equations

$$2x + 3y = 13$$
and $$3x - y = 3$$
is $$x = 2, \quad y = 3$$

As with any solution to an equation, the answers should be checked by substitution in the original equations.

$$2x + 3y = 13, \quad 4 + 9 = 13, \quad 13 = 13$$
$$3x - y = 3, \quad 6 - 3 = 3, \quad 3 = 3$$

The steps in solving simultaneous equations by grahpical means are therefore as follows.

1. Rearrange the equations to the form of straight line laws.
2. Plot the two straight lines on the same graphical field.
3. The solution is given by the point of intersection of the straight lines.

Example

Solve the simultaneous equations:

$$y - 12x + 19 = 0$$
$$2y = 5x$$

by plotting values of x from 1 to 5.

The first equation can be adjusted to:

$$y = 12x - 19$$

and the second equation to $\quad y = \dfrac{5x}{2}$

Both of these equations are laws of straight lines. Since the values of x range from 1 to 5, points for straight lines will be determined for $x = 1$ and $x = 5$, with check points at $x = 3$.

x	1	3	5
$12x - 19$	−7	17	41
$\dfrac{5x}{2}$	2·5	7·5	12·5

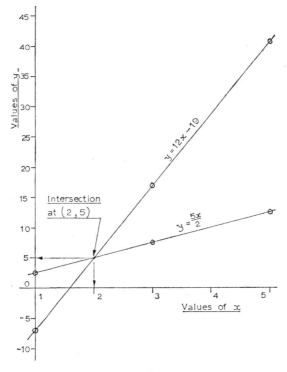

Fig. 3.9

The values of x range from 1 to 5, a range of 4. The values of y range from -7 to 41, a range of 48. Suitable scales on A4 paper, longer side vertical, are 20 mm $= 0.5$ for x and 20 mm $= 5$ for y.

The graphs are shown in Figure 3.9.

The intersection is at (2, 5).

$$Check:\ 5 - 24 + 19 = 0, 0 = 0$$
$$2 \times 5 = 5 \times 2, 10 = 10$$

Answer: $x = 2, y = 5$

3.3.3 THE SOLUTION OF QUADRATIC EQUATIONS BY GRAPHICAL METHODS

Let us now consider a typical quadratic equation in the conventional form, such as:

$$x^2 - 5x + 4 = 0$$

We can show on a graph the line:

$$y = x^2 - 5x + 4$$

The x-axis is the line which represents the equation:

$$y = 0$$

At the points where the line representing $y = x^2 - 5x + 4$ crosses the x-axis the values of y are identical.

Hence if $\qquad y = x^2 - 5x - 4$
and $\qquad y = 0$

are two lines on the same graphical field, the values of x at which the lines intersect satisfy the equation:

$$x^2 - 5x + 4 = 0$$

The lines $y = x^2 - 5x - 4$ and $y = 0$ are not the only lines whose intersections indicate the roots of $x^2 - 5x + 4 = 0$.

If $\qquad x^2 - 5x + 4 = 0$
then $\qquad x^2 = 5x - 4$

and the intersection of the lines $y = x^2$ and $y = 5x - 4$ also indicates the roots.

Also, since $x^2 - 5x = -4$ the intersection of $y = x^2 - 5x$ and $y = -4$ likewise indicates the roots.

The usual method adopted is to write the quadratic equation:

$$ax^2 + bx + c = 0$$

in the form

$$x^2 = \frac{-bx - c}{a}$$

and to plot the lines

$$y = x^2$$

and

$$y = \frac{-bx - c}{a}$$

The roots are the values of x at which the lines intersect. The curve of $y = x^2$ is one which can be drawn very rapidly, while $y = \dfrac{-bx - c}{a}$ is a straight line.

It is advisable to use three points to assist in drawing the straight line. Although only two are required, the third point checks the accuracy of the plotting. We will illustrate the two most popular methods of graphically solving a quadratic equation by a worked example.

Example

By drawing graphs within the limits of $x = -2$ and $x = 4$ solve the quadratic equation:

$$2x^2 - 3x = 9$$

First method:

Writing the equation as:

$$2x^2 - 3x - 9 = 0$$

the graphs of

$$y = 2x^2 - 3x - 9$$

and

$$y = 0 \text{ (the } x\text{-axis)}$$

are drawn on the same graphical field.

Calculations for plotting:

x	-2	-1	0	1	2	3	4
$2x^2$	8	2	0	2	8	18	32
$-3x$	6	3	0	-3	-6	-9	-12
-9	-9	-9	-9	-9	-9	-9	-9
$2x^2 - 3x - 9$	5	-4	-9	-10	-7	0	11

In Figure 3.10 the graphs of $y = 2x^2 - 3x - 9$ and $y = 0$ are shown plotted on the same graphical field.

161

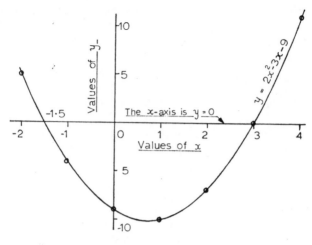

FIG. 3.10

The intersections occur at values $x = -1 \cdot 5$ and $x = 3$. Hence $x = -1 \cdot 5$ and $x = 3$ are the roots of the equation $2x^2 - 3x - 9 = 0$, i.e. the equation $2x^2 - 3x = 9$.

$$\textit{Check: } 2x^2 - 3x = 9$$

$$x = -1 \cdot 5: \qquad 2(-1 \cdot 5)^2 - 3(-1 \cdot 5) = 9$$
$$2(2 \cdot 25) + 4 \cdot 5 \qquad = 9$$
$$4 \cdot 5 + 4 \cdot 5 = 9$$
$$9 = 9$$
$$x = 3: \qquad 2(3)^2 - 3(3) \qquad = 9$$
$$2(9) - 9 = 9$$
$$18 - 9 = 9$$
$$9 = 9$$

Second method:

$$2x^2 - 3x = 9$$
$$2x^2 = 3x + 9$$
$$x^2 = \frac{3x + 9}{2}$$

The graphs of $y = x^2$ and $y = \dfrac{3x + 9}{2}$ are plotted on the same graphical field. Only three points need be determined for the straight line:

162

x	-2	-1	0	1	2	3	4
x^2	4	1	0	1	4	9	16
$3x$ $+9$	-6 9		0 9				12 9
$3x + 9$	3		9				21
$\dfrac{3x + 9}{2}$	1·5		4·5				10·5

The graphs of $y = x^2$ and $y = \dfrac{3x + 9}{2}$ are shown plotted on the same field in Figure 3.11.

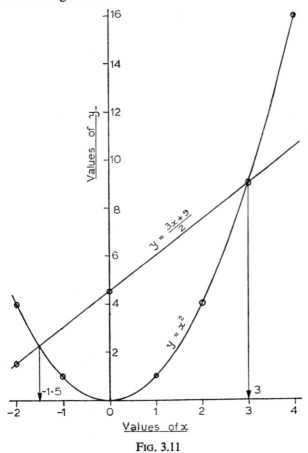

FIG. 3.11

The intersections occur at values of $x = -1.5$ and $x = 3$. Hence $x = -1.5$ and $x = 3$ are the roots of the equation. The validity of the roots has already been proved.

Example

(a) Draw the graph of $y = x^2 - 4x + 4$ between $x = 0$ and $x = 5$.

(b) With the same scales and on the same axes draw the line $y = x$.

(c) State the values of x at which the curve and the line intersect.

(d) Deduce the equation of which these values are the roots.

Calculations for plotting:

x	0	1	2	3	4	5
x^2	0	1	4	9	16	25
$-4x$	0	-4	-8	-12	-16	-20
$+4$	4	4	4	4	4	4
$x^2 - 4x + 4$	4	1	0	1	4	9

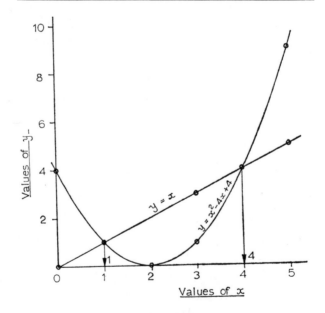

FIG. 3.12

The line $y = x$ is a straight line through the origin and points such as (3, 3) and (5, 5).

(*a*) and (*b*) The graphs are shown in Figure 3.12.

(*c*) The curve and the straight line intersect where $x = 1$ and $x = 4$.

(*d*) Since at intersection points the values of y are identical, and:

$$y = x^2 - 4x + 4 \text{ and } y = x$$

then
$$x^2 - 4x + 4 = x$$
$$x^2 - 4x - x + 4 = 0$$
$$x^2 - 5x + 4 = 0$$

$$\text{Check: } x^2 - 5x + 4 = 0$$
$$x = 1 \quad 1 - 5 + 4 = 0 \quad 0 = 0$$
$$x = 4 \quad 16 - 20 + 4 = 0 \quad 0 = 0$$

Answers: (*a*) and (*b*) The graphs are shown in Figure 3.12.
(*c*) Intersections are at $x = 1$ and $x = 4$.
(*d*) The equation is $x^2 - 5x + 4 = 0$.

3.3.4 CLOSER VALUE OF THE ROOT

It requires extremely careful work in order to obtain values of x which have greater accuracy than the amounts represented by plus or minus one small division of the graph paper on the x-axis. A closer value can be found by enlarging the areas of the graph in the vicinity of the intersection of the lines.

If we solve the equation $x^2 - x - 4 = 0$ graphically by plotting the graphs of $y = x^2$ and $y = x + 4$, a first approximation to the roots, from the intersections, gives $x = -1 \cdot 6$ and $x = 2 \cdot 6$. Let us enlarge the graphs in the ranges $x = -1 \cdot 7$ to $-1 \cdot 5$ and $x = 2 \cdot 5$ to $2 \cdot 7$. Although a parabola is a curve, the amount of curvature over such a small range is very little, and in the enlargement, for the sake of rapidity, we will approximate the curves to straight lines.

Tabulation of values to be used for 'enlarged graphs':

x	$-1 \cdot 7$	$-1 \cdot 5$	$2 \cdot 5$	$2 \cdot 7$
x^2	2·89	2·25	6·25	7·29
$x + 4$	2·3	2·5	6·5	6·7

Figure 3.13 shows graphs which are enlargements of the areas near the intersections, giving closer values of the roots of $-1 \cdot 56$ and $2 \cdot 56$.

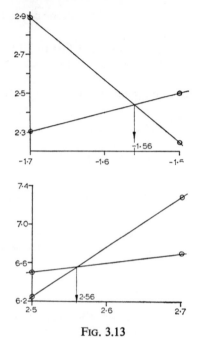

FIG. 3.13

If a closer accuracy is desired, we could now proceed to enlargements in the ranges $x = -1.57$ to $x = -1.55$ and $x = 2.55$ to 2.57.

$$\text{Check: } x^2 - x - 4 = 0$$

$x = -1.56$:
$$(-1.56)^2 - (-1.56) - 4 = 0$$
$$2.433\ 6 + 1.56 - 4 = 0$$
$$3.993\ 6 - 4 = 0$$
$$-0.006\ 4 = 0$$

$x = 2.56$:
$$(2.56)^2 - (2.56) - 4 = 0$$
$$6.553\ 6 - 2.56 - 4 = 0$$
$$6.553\ 6 - 6.56 = 0$$
$$-0.006\ 4 = 0$$

(We cannot expect perfect balance since the roots have only been evaluated to two decimal places.)

Answer: $x = -1.56$ or $x = 2.56$

Example

If a segment of a circle has a radius of R, and the chord subtends an angle of θ, the area A is given by the formula:

166

$$A = \frac{R^2}{2} (\theta - \sin \theta)$$

where θ is the angle in radians. Plot the values of (θ radians $-$ sin θ) for angles from 0° to 180°, and use the graph to find the angle subtended by a segment of radius 10 mm which has an area of 50 mm², to the nearest degree. By a suitable enlargement, find the angle θ to the nearest 10 minutes.

Using a base of 6 units, values of (θ radians $-$ sin θ) will be evaluated at intervals of 30°.

$$180° = \pi \text{ radians} = 3·141 \ 6 \text{ radians}$$

$$\theta \text{ radians} - \sin \theta = \frac{2A}{R^2} = \frac{100}{100} = 1$$

Tabulation:

$\theta°$	0	30°	60°	90°	120°	150°	180°
θ radians	0	0·523 6	1·047 2	1·570 8	2·094 4	2·618 0	3·141 6
sin θ	0	0·500 0	0·866 0	1·000 0	0·866 0	0·500 0	0·000 0
$\theta - \sin \theta$	0	0·023 6	0·181 2	0·570 8	1·228 4	2·118 0	3·141 6

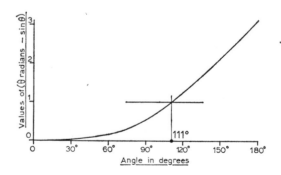

FIG. 3.14

Figure 3.14 shows the graph of θ against ($\theta - \sin \theta$).
The graph gives a first value of $\theta = 111°$ for ($\theta - \sin \theta$) = 1.
We will now calculate ($\theta - \sin \theta$) for 110° 30′ and 111° 30′.

167

Mathematics for Mechanical Technicians 1

$$90° = 1·570\ 8 \text{ rad} \qquad\qquad 90° = 1·570\ 8 \text{ rad}$$
$$20° 30' = 0·357\ 8 \text{ rad} \qquad\qquad 21° 30' = 0·375\ 2 \text{ rad}$$

$$110° 30' = 1·928\ 6 \text{ rad} \qquad\qquad 111° 30' = 1·946\ 0 \text{ rad}$$
$$\sin 110° 30' = 0·936\ 7 \qquad\qquad \sin 111° 30' = 0·930\ 4$$

$$\theta - \sin \theta = 0·991\ 9 \qquad\qquad \theta - \sin \theta = 1·015\ 6$$
$$\text{when} \qquad \theta = 110° 30' \qquad\qquad \text{when} \qquad \theta = 111° 30'$$

Figure 3.15 shows a straight line graph in the vicinity of $\theta = 111°$, giving a more accurate answer of $\theta = 110·85°(110° 51')$.

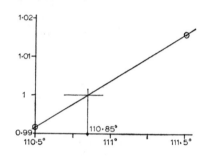

Fig. 3.15

$$\textit{Check:} \quad 90° \qquad = 1·570\ 8 \text{ rad}$$
$$20° 51' = 0·363\ 9 \text{ rad}$$

$$110° 51' = 1·934\ 7 \text{ rad}$$
$$\sin 110° 51' = 0·934\ 5$$

$$\theta - \sin \theta = 1·000\ 2$$

Answer: $\theta = 111°$ to nearest degree
$\theta = 110° 50'$ to nearest 10 minutes

Problems 3.3

1. Plot on the same graphical field, with values of x ranging from $x = 0$ to $x = 5$, the graphs of $y = x + 1$ and $y = 2x - 2$. Using your graph solve the simultaneous equations:

$$x - y = -1$$
$$2x - y = 2$$

168

2. Plot, on the same graphical field, the values of x ranging from $x = -6$ to $x = 0$, the graphs of $y = x + 8$ and $y = \dfrac{x + 13}{2}$.

Using your graph solve the simultaneous equations:
$$x - y = -8$$
$$x - 2y = -13$$

3. By drawing suitable graphs within the range $x = 0$ to $x = 6$, solve the simultaneous equations:
$$3x - y = 9$$
$$x + 2y = 10$$

4. By drawing suitable graphs within the range $x = -4$ to $x = 2$, solve the simultaneous equations:
$$3x + 2y = 4$$
$$5x - 3y = -15 \cdot 5$$

5. By drawing suitable graphs within the range $x = -1$ to $x = 5$, solve the simultaneous equations:
$$3x - 4y - 19 = 0$$
$$\frac{x + 7}{2} = \frac{y + 16}{3}$$

6. Plot the graph of $y = x^2 - 6x + 5$ with values of x ranging from $x = 0$ to $x = 6$, and use your graph to solve the quadratic equation:
$$x^2 - 6x + 5 = 0$$

7. Plot the graph of $y = 9 - 16x - 4x^2$ with values of x ranging from $x = -5$ to $x = 1$ and use your graph to solve the quadratic equation:
$$9 - 16x - 4x^2 = 0$$

8. Plot the graph of $y = x^2 + 2x - 8$ within the range of $x = -4$ to $x = 2$. Use the graph to solve the quadratic equations:

(a) $x^2 + 2x - 8 = 0$ (b) $x^2 + 2x - 3 = 0$
(c) $x^2 + 2x = 0$ (d) $x^2 + 2x + 1 = 0$

9. Plot the graph of $y = x^2$ with values of x ranging from $x = -3$ to $x = 3$. On the same graphical field plot the graph of $y = \dfrac{x + 6}{2}$.

9. Obtain the values of x at which the straight line cuts the curve. Find the equation for which these values of x are the roots.

10. (a) Draw the graph $y = x^2 - 5x + 7$ between $x = 0$ and $x = 8$.
    (b) With the same scales and on the same axes draw the line $y = x$.
    (c) Write down the values of x where (a) and (b) intersect, and the equation of which these values are roots.
    (d) and (e) Repeat (b) and (c) with the line $y = -2x + 5$ instead of the line $y = x$.

11. Plot the graphs of $y = x^2$ and $y = 6x - 6$ with values of x ranging from 0 to 6. Hence show that a first approximation to the roots of the quadratic equation:

$$x^2 - 6x + 6 = 0$$

is $x = 4 \cdot 7$ or $1 \cdot 3$. By suitable enlargements of the graph in the vicinities of these values of x, find more accurate values of the roots to two places of decimals.

12. The total cost of producing a batch of x articles consists of a fixed charge of £100 plus 25p per article. The articles are sold at a price of 75p each. Show on a graph lines which represent total cost and the income from sales and hence determine:
    (a) the number of articles for which total cost = income from sales,
    (b) the number of articles for which the profit is £50.
    (A suitable range of values of x is from 0 to 400.)

13. Two stations A and B are 5 km apart. Trains travelling in the same direction pass A and B at the same time. The train passing A is travelling at 60 km/h, while the train passing B is travelling at 30 km/h. Assuming that the trains maintain constant speeds, how far are they from A when they pass? (The faster train passes A in the direction of B.)

14. A production engineer estimates that by using tooling equipment costing £40 the cost of machining a component is $12\frac{1}{2}$p each. If more expensive tooling equipment costing £90 is used, the cost of machining can be reduced to 10p each. Determine graphically the minimum of articles to be produced before the second method becomes the cheaper. (A range of 0 to 2 500 articles will prove suitable.)

15. When solving a problem dealing with the geometry of a segment, the following equation occurred

    Angle A in radians − the sine of angle $A = 0.15$

    (*a*) Find the values of A (radians) − sin A as the angle A varies from 30° to 70° at intervals of 10°.

    (*b*) Plot these values, draw a smooth curve through the points, and find the angle A, to the nearest degree, when:

    $$A \text{ (radians)} - \sin A = 0.15$$

16. When the life of a particular machine is N years, its value V has been intentionally depreciated so that $VN = £750$. The annual running cost F at a given time is $£(100 + 10\ N)$. By plotting values of V and F vertically, and N horizontally, with values of N ranging from 0 to 6, determine the value of N when the value of the machine tool is equal to the annual running cost.

Answers to Problems 3.3

1. $x = 3$, $y = 4$
2. $x = -3$, $y = 5$
3. $x = 4$, $y = 3$
4. $x = -1$, $y = 3.5$
5. $x = 1$, $y = -4$
6. $x = 1$ or $x = 5$
7. $x = 0.5$ or $x = -4.5$
8. (*a*) $x = -4$ or $x = 2$ (*b*) $x = -3$ or $x = 1$
   (*c*) $x = -2$ or $x = 0$ (*d*) $x = -1$ (twice)
9. $x = -1.5$ or $x = 2$; $2x^2 - x - 6 = 0$
10. (*a*) requires no numerical solution
    (*b*) $x = 1$ and $x = 7$ (*c*) $x^2 - 6x + 7 = 0$
    (*d*) $x = 1$ and $x = 2$ (*e*) $x^2 - 3x + 2 = 0$
11. $x = 4.73$ or $x = 1.27$
12. (*a*) 200   (*b*) 300
13. 10 km
14. 2 001
15. (*a*) 0.023 6, 0.055 3, 0.106 7, 0.181 2, 0.282 0
    (*b*) 56°
16. 5 years

Chapter Four

Geometry and Trigonometry

4.1 The Measurement of Angles

4.1.1 SEXAGESIMAL MEASURE OF ANGLES

An *angle* is a measurement of an amount of turning. In article 3.1.1, dealing with graphs, the reader was introduced to the convention of two axes intersecting at right angles at the origin. Figure 4.1(*a*) shows axes XOX_1 and YOY_1, with the quadrants indicated.

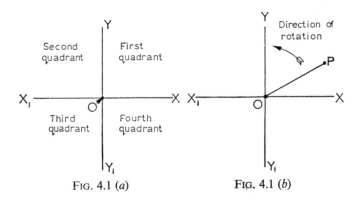

FIG. 4.1 (*a*)   FIG. 4.1 (*b*)

Now let us suppose we have a line *OP*, and it turns in an anti-clockwise direction, the end *O* always being coincident with the origin, as shown in Figure 4.1(*b*). If the arm turns so that the end *P* moves through the four quadrants in numerical sequence and eventually coincides with *OX*, the arm has rotated through one revolution. There is no reason at all why the arm should cease turning, and consequently there is no limit to the magnitude of an angle. The basic unit is one revolution. Just as we can take a metre as the basic unit of length and subdivide it for convenience, so we can take one revolution and subdivide it into smaller quantities. One way of doing this, but not the only way, is to divide one revolution into 360 equal parts called degrees. Each of these degrees can be divided into 60 equal parts called minutes, and a minute can be further subdivided into 60 equal parts called seconds. An angle of thirty-nine degrees, twenty-seven minutes and fourteen seconds is indicated mathematically as 39° 27′ 14″.

This particular dividing is called *sexagesimal measure*. Another way of subdividing a revolution is to divide it into 2π equal angles. This at first may seem a little strange, but at a further stage of our studies we shall find that this *circular measure* of angles proves to be very useful indeed.

If the arm OP moves anticlockwise from OX until it becomes coincident with OY it will have turned through one quarter of a revolution, i.e. 90°, in which case OP is perpendicular to OX and the angle POX of 90° is termed a *right angle*. If the arm OP turns from OX to any angle between zero and 90°, P will lie on the first quadrant. An angle between zero and 90° is called an *acute angle*. If arm OP rotates a further 90° it will be coincident with OX_1. POX is now a straight line, and naturally enough an angle of 180° is called a *straight angle*. An angle of between 90° and 180° is known as an *obtuse angle*. If OP rotates from OX by an obtuse angle, P will then fall in the second quadrant. An angle of between 180° and 360° is called a *reflex angle*; hence if OP rotates from OX through a reflex angle, P will fall in the third quadrant if the angle is between 180° and 270°, and in the fourth quadrant if the angle is between 270° and 360°.

Angles which total 90° are known as *complementary angles*; for example 43° is the complementary angle of 47°. Angles which total 180° are *supplementary angles*; for example, the supplementary angle of 45° is 135°.

We have tacitly assumed a convention that the anticlockwise direction of rotation from OX results in a positive angle. Consequently we must accept the implication that a clockwise rotation of OP from OX results in a negative angle. Hence an angle of 330° could, if we so wished, be regarded as $-30°$.

A convenient method of indicating a direction is to state the nearest cardinal point (either north, east, south and west) followed by the angular deviation toward one of the adjacent cardinal points. Typical examples are N 25° W and S 10° W. Let us now assume the cardinal points to be superimposed upon our four-quadrant convention. North becomes 90°, west 180°, south 270° and east 0°. If we consider the bearing N 25° W, north is 90° and a westerly deviation from north is in the anticlockwise or positive direction. N 25° W can therefore be drawn as $90° + 25° = 115°$ in our four-quadrant convention. In a similar manner, for the bearing S 10° W, south is 270°, a westerly deviation from south is in the clockwise or negative direction, hence S 10° W can be represented as $270° - 10° = 260°$. An illustration of directional bearings is given in Figure 4.2 overleaf.

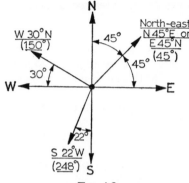

FIG. 4.2

4.1.2 CIRCULAR MEASURE OF ANGLES

As our knowledge of mathematics develops, we shall find that while the degree is a very convenient unit for the magnitude of an angle when trigonometric and similar calculations are to be applied, there are branches of mathematics where a different unit is more convenient than the degree. In the *circular measure of angles* we divide one revolution of 360° into 2π equal divisions called *radians*.

One radian is therefore equal to $\dfrac{360°}{2\pi}$. This value cannot be expressed precisely in decimal notation but is very nearly equal to 57·3°. A geometrical appreciation of a radian can be obtained by drawing a figure composed of a circular arc and two radii, the arc being equal in length to the radius, as shown in Figure 4.3. (A little later we shall

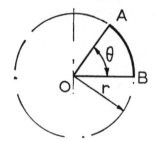

When length of arc AB is equal to radius r, angle θ is 1 radian

FIG. 4.3

find that a shape bounded by any two radii and a circular arc is called a *sector* of a circle. In this case the figure is a sector of rather special proportions.)

Since a radius can be spaced along the circumference 2π times, the angle included by the two radii is $\dfrac{360°}{2\pi}$ or one radian. If the magnitude of an angle shows no indication of degrees and/or minutes and/or seconds, being given by values such as $\dfrac{\pi}{4}$, $\dfrac{2\pi}{3}$ or 0·4, it is assumed that the unit is the radian. Since 2π radians are equal to 360°, to convert radians to degrees we multiply by $\dfrac{360°}{2\pi}$. Conversely, to convert degrees to radians, we multiply by $\dfrac{2\pi}{360°}$.

As examples:

$$\frac{\pi}{3} = \frac{\pi}{3} \times \frac{360°}{2\pi} = 60°$$

$$\frac{\pi}{4} = \frac{\pi}{4} \times \frac{360°}{2\pi} = 45°$$

and
$$180° = 180° \times \frac{2\pi}{360°} = \pi \text{ radians}$$

Conversions can also be made using the tables on pages 32 and 33 of Castle's *Four-figure Mathematical Tables*. Values are given for intervals of one minute from zero to 89° 59′ $\left(90° \text{ is } \dfrac{\pi}{2} = 1·570\ 8\right)$. It should be noted that since the magnitude of an angle in radians is directly proportional to its magnitude in degrees, the rows of mean differences in the end columns are constant, irrespective of the angle. Furthermore, the mean differences have to be added. For angles in excess of 90°, $\dfrac{\pi}{4}$ or 1·570 8 is added for every interval of 90°. The reader should now check that:

$$51° = 0·890\ 1 \text{ radians}$$
$$80° 36′ = 1·406\ 7 \text{ radians}$$
$$68° 53′ = 1·202\ 3 \text{ radians}$$

while 1·309 0 radians = 75°
   0·524 5 radians = 30° 3′
   0·500 0 radians = 28° 39′ (as accurately as tables allow)

For angles in the range 90° to 360° the following procedure is normally adopted.

Example

Convert an angle of 323° 46′ to circular measurement.

$$323° \ 46′$$

Nearest whole
multiple of 90°
below value given $= \underline{270°} \qquad = 3 \times 1{\cdot}570\ 8 = 4{\cdot}712\ 4$
$$\overline{53° \ 46′} \qquad\qquad\qquad\qquad = \underline{0{\cdot}938\ 4} \text{ from tables)}$$
$$\text{Add} \quad \overline{5{\cdot}650\ 8}$$

Answer: 323° 46′ = 5·650 8 radians

Example

Convert 2·753 7 radians to sexagesimal measure to the nearest minute.

$$2{\cdot}753\ 7$$

Nearest whole number
multiple of
1·570 8 below value given $= 1{\cdot}570\ 8 = 90°$
$$\overline{1{\cdot}182\ 9} = \underline{67° \ 46′} \text{ (from tables)}$$
$$\text{Add} \quad \overline{157° \ 46′}$$

Answer: 2·753 7 radians = 157° 46′

The above procedure should normally be adopted within the range of zero to 360°. For very large amounts of turning, the conversion factor:

$$360° = 2\pi \text{ radians}$$

should be used, with a number of places of decimals selected for π as accuracy demands. For interest, π to ten decimal places is 3·141 592 653 6.

In certain restricted cases, when an angle is given in radians to an accuracy of two decimal places and does not exceed $\dfrac{\pi}{2}$, a very convenient table appears on page 34 of Castle's *Four-figure Mathematical Tables*. For example, 0·48 radians is given directly as 27° 30′.

Problems 4.1

1. What angle, to the nearest second, corresponds to an amount of turning of $2\frac{1}{7}$ revolutions?

2. State whether the following angles are acute, obtuse or reflex:

   (*a*) 57°   (*b*) 125°   (*c*) 5°   (*d*) 284°   (*e*) 343°   (*f*) 179°

3. *OP* is an arm which rotates about the origin *O* of cartesian co-ordinates. The arm is originally coincident with the *x*-axis and rotates in an anticlockwise direction. State in which quadrant *P* falls when the arm rotates:

   (*a*) 60°   (*b*) 80°   (*c*) 120°
   (*d*) 170°   (*e*) 330°   (*f*) 365°
   (*g*) 530°   (*h*) 780°   (*j*) 4·3 revolutions

4. State which angles, in the four-quadrant convention, correspond to the following bearings:

   (*a*) west   (*b*) south-east   (*c*) N 10° W
   (*d*) W 10° N   (*e*) S 16° W   (*f*) W 20° S

5. State which bearings correspond to the following angles in the four-quadrant convention:

   (*a*) 25°   (*b*) 65°   (*c*) 171°   (*d*) 240°

6. Convert:

   (*a*) 1·77 radians to degrees and minutes
   (*b*) 50° to radians

7. Convert the following to degrees:

   (*a*) $\dfrac{2\cdot5\pi}{12}$ radians   (*b*) 5·515 2 radians

8. (*a*) Using mathematical tables convert the following to radians:
     (i) 69° 23′   (ii) 270°

   (*b*) Using mathematical tables convert the following to degrees:

     (i) $\dfrac{5\pi}{12}$ radians   (ii) 2·775 radians

9. Evaluate $\left(100\pi t - \dfrac{\pi}{4}\right)$ when $t = 0\cdot01$, giving the answer:

   (*a*) in radians, as a multiple of π;   (*b*) in degrees.

10. Convert:

   (*a*) 2 100 rev/min to rad/s   (*b*) 44 rad/s to rev/min
   (Take π as $\frac{22}{7}$)

Answers to Problems 4.1

1. 771° 25′ 43″
2. (*a*) Acute   (*b*) Obtuse   (*c*) Acute
    (*d*) Reflex   (*e*) Reflex   (*f*) Obtuse
3. (*a*) First   (*b*) First   (*c*) Second
    (*d*) Second   (*e*) Fourth   (*f*) First
    (*g*) Second   (*h*) First   (*j*) Second
4. (*a*) 180°   (*b*) 315°   (*c*) 100°
    (*d*) 170°   (*e*) 254°   (*f*) 200°
5. (*a*) E 25° N   (*b*) N 25° E   (*c*) W 9° N   (*d*) S 30° W
6. (*a*) 101° 25′   (*b*) 0·872 7
7. (*a*) 37° 30′   (*b*) 316°
8. (*a*) (i) 1·211 0; (ii) 4·712 4   (*b*) (i) 75°; (ii) 159°
9. (*a*) $\dfrac{3\pi}{4}$ (*b*) 135°
10. (*a*) 220 rad/s   (*b*) 420 rev/min

4.2 Some Important Theorems in Geometry

The theorems in geometry introduced in this article are submitted without proof.

4.2.1 PROPERTIES OF INTERSECTING STRAIGHT LINES

When two straight lines interesect, four angles are formed. If the lines do not intersect at right angles, two of the angles are acute, the other two are obtuse. The two acute angles are equal to each other and the two obtuse angles are equal to each other. The usual way of expressing this fact is to state that *if two straight lines interesect, vertically opposite angles are equal.*

If a straight line crosses parallel straight lines, that straight line is called a *transversal*. A transversal crossing two parallel straight lines is shown in Figure 4.4. We have already stated:

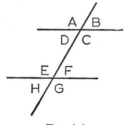

FIG. 4.4

$$\angle A = \angle C \qquad \angle B = \angle D$$
$$\angle E = \angle G \qquad \angle F = \angle H$$

In addition
$$\angle A = \angle E \qquad \angle B = \angle F$$
$$\angle C = \angle G \qquad \angle D = \angle H$$

these being known as *corresponding angles on the same side of the transversal*.

Furthermore $\qquad \angle D = \angle F$ while $\angle C = \angle E$

these being known as *alternate angles*.

Summarizing the above:

If a transversal crosses a pair of parallel straight lines:

(a) *Vertically opposite angles are equal.*

(b) *Corresponding angles on the same side of the transversal are equal.*

(c) *Alternate angles are equal.*

Hence, referring back to Figure 4.4:

$$\angle A = \angle C = \angle E = \angle G$$
and
$$\angle B = \angle D = \angle F = \angle H$$

4.2.2 PROPERTIES OF CIRCLES AND CHORDS

A *chord* of a circle is a straight line which divides the circle into two parts. The end of the chord touch the circumference at two different points. The chord divides the area of circle into two *segments*. The segment of larger area is the major segment, the other being the minor segment. If we erect a triangle in a segment, one side being a chord, the apex opposite that chord lying on the circumference, the angle opposite that chord is said to be the *angle in a segment*, and is the angle at the circumference subtended by a chord. If we draw radii from the ends of a chord, those radii contain the *angle subtended at the centre*.

The foregoing are the necessary definitions to understand a very important theorem, which once more is presented without proof.

The angle subtended at the centre of the circle is twice the angle subtended at the circumference, and all angles subtended at the circumference by the same chord are equal in magnitude.

The theorem is illustrated in Figures 4.5(a) and 4.5(b) overleaf.

In Figure 4.5(a), obtuse angle AOC = twice acute angle ABC

In Figure 4.5(b), reflex angle AOB = twice obtuse angle ADB

179

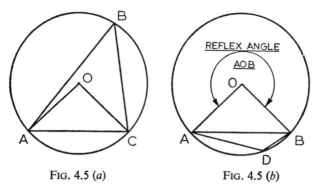

FIG. 4.5 (*a*)   FIG. 4.5 (*b*)

Let us proceed to two very important results of this theorem. The first is that if the chord is a diameter, the angle at the centre is a straight angle of 180°. The angle at the circumference is therefore one half of this, i.e. 90°, or a right angle. All angles in the same segment are equal, *hence the angle in a semicircle is a right angle.* In Figure 4.6, all the angles marked *B* are right angles.

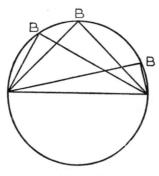

FIG. 4.6

A cyclic quadrilateral is a figure bounded by four straight sides, the four corners lying on the circumference of a circle. A diagonal joining opposite corners forms a chord of the circle. If we join the ends of the chord to the centre, we can reason that since the two angles subtended at the centre total 360°, the sum of the two angles subtended at the circumference is 180°. *Hence, opposite angles of a cyclic quadrilateral total* 180°, *i.e. they are supplementary.*

A *tangent* to a circle is a line which touches the circumference at one point, but does not cut the circumference when extended. The tangent lies at right angles to a radius drawn to the point of contact.

Let us conclude this article on geometrical theorems with some important properties of intersecting chords.

If two chords of a circle intersect, either within or without the circle, the product of the two segments of one chord is equal to the product of the two segments of the other chord.

Figure 4.7 shows at (*a*) the chords intersecting inside a circle, at (*b*) the chords intersecting outside a circle and at (*c*) the special case of one chord just touching a circle so that the chord is a tangent.

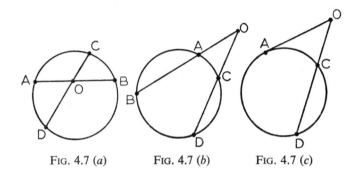

FIG. 4.7 (*a*)   FIG. 4.7 (*b*)   FIG. 4.7 (*c*)

In Figure 4.7(*a*) and 4.7(*b*): $OA \times OB = OC \times OD$.

In Figure 4.7(*c*) $(OA)^2 = OC \times OD$.

An important application occurs when one chord is the diameter of the circle, the other chord intersecting the diameter at right angles within the circle, as shown in Figure 4.8.

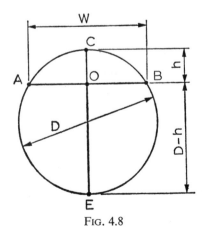

FIG. 4.8

The chord AB is bisected and $AO = OB$.

Let D = diameter of circle,

W = length of chord AB, and h = height of smaller segment.

$$AO \times OB = OE \times OC$$

$$\therefore \frac{W}{2} \times \frac{W}{2} = (D - h)h$$

and
$$\frac{W^2}{4} = Dh - h^2$$

$$\therefore W^2 = 4(Dh - h^2)$$
and
$$W = 2\sqrt{(Dh - h^2)}$$

If D is required, using
$$\frac{W^2}{4} = Dh - h^2$$

$$Dh = \frac{W^2}{4} + h^2$$

$$D = \frac{W^2}{4h} + h$$

If h is required, using
$$\frac{W^2}{4} = Dh - h^2$$

$$h^2 - Dh + \frac{W^2}{4} = 0$$

This is a quadratic in h, which can be solved by formula or by factors, depending upon the values of D and W. It will be noticed that two values of h will be obtained; these will be the heights of the major and minor segments, that is, the values of h and $D - h$.

Example

A flat of width 30 mm is machined on a bar of diameter 34 mm. Calculate the depth of cut, measured from the outside of the bar.

Figure 4.8 can be used for the problem.

$$OC = \text{depth of cut} = h$$
$$OE = \text{diameter} - h = 34 - h$$
$$AO = OB = \text{half width of flat} = 15$$
$$AO \times OB = OC \times OE$$
$$h \times (34 - h) = 15 \times 15$$
$$34h - h^2 = 225$$
$$h^2 - 34h + 225 = 0$$
$$(h - 9)(h - 25) = 0$$

Either
$$h - 9 = 0, h = 9$$
or
$$h - 25 = 0, h = 25$$

The first of these answers is the particular value requested (the other is the distance from the flat to the other side of the bar).

Answer: Depth of cut = 9 mm

4.2.3 THE PROPERTIES OF TRIANGLES

A *triangle* is a plane figure bounded by three straight lines. A triangle therefore contains three angles. The conventional way of indicating a triangle is to give each corner a capital letter.

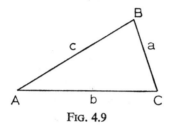

FIG. 4.9

A side is given a small letter, the same character as the opposite angle. Side a is opposite angle A, side p is opposite angle P, and so on. The convention is shown in Fig. 4.9. The longest side is opposite the largest angle and the smallest side is opposite the smallest angle.

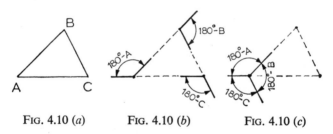

FIG. 4.10 (*a*)   FIG. 4.10 (*b*)   FIG. 4.10 (*c*)

Figure 4.10(*a*) shows a triangle lettered conventionally. In Figure 4.10(*b*) the sides have been extended, giving the three angles indicated. Now if we slide these angles along the sides indicated until B and C are coincident with A, as shown in Figure 4.10(*c*), we note that:

$$(180° - A) + (180° - B) + (180° - C) = 360°$$
$$180° - A + 180° - B + 180° - C = 360°$$
$$180° + 180° + 180° - 360° = A + B + C$$
$$180° = A + B + C$$

Hence the sum of the angles in a triangle is 180°.

In our study of angles, we noted that we were able to classify angles into groups. The same thing occurs with triangles. An *equilateral* triangle is a triangle with equal sides and equal angles.

An *isosceles triangle* is a triangle having two of its sides of equal length. The angles opposite these sides are also equal.

A *scalene triangle* has three sides of differing lengths and the three angles differ in magnitude.

A *right-angled triangle* contains one angle of 90°. Such a triangle could be a scalene triangle. It could be an isosceles triangle, in which case the sides containing the right angle would be of equal length and the other two angles would each be 45°. A right-angled triangle cannot possibly be equilateral.

Congruent triangles are equal in all respects. The three individual angles of one triangle are equal to the three corresponding individual angles of the other triangle, and furthermore, the three individual sides of one triangle are equal to the three individual sides of the other. Congruent triangles also have equal areas.

Similar triangles are triangles in which only the three angles of one are equal to the three angles of the other. It should be noted that while congruent triangles are equal in area, *similar triangles are not*. There is a very important property of similar triangles which must be remembered. This property is that the ratio of corresponding sides is constant.

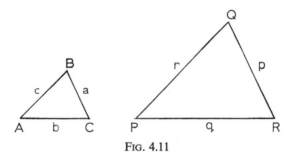

Fig. 4.11

Figure 4.11 shows two similar triangles, *ABC* and *PQR*. In the magnitude of the angles:

$$A = P, B = Q \text{ and } C = R$$

while

$$\frac{a}{p} = \frac{b}{q} = \frac{c}{r}$$

Example

Calculate the distance X on the template shown in Figure 4.12(*a*).

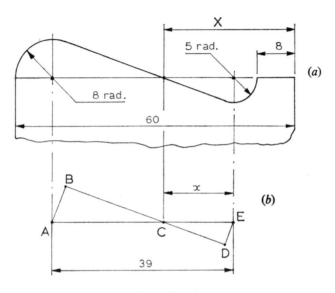

Fig. 4.12

Figure 4.12(*b*) shows information extracted from the drawing, identifying letters having been added to describe the triangles.

Considering triangles ABC and CDE:

1. Angle B = angle D = 90°, since a radius is at right angles to a tangent at a point of contact.
2. Angle C in triangle ABC is equal to angle C in triangle CDE, being vertically opposite angles.
3. From the two statements above

$$\text{Angle } A = \text{angle } E = (90° - C)$$

The three angles in triangle ABC are equal to the three angles in triangle CDE, hence triangles ABC and CDE are similar, and ratios of corresponding sides are equal.

$$\text{Let } CE = x, \text{ so that } AC = 39 - x$$
$$DE = 5 \text{ and } AB = 8$$
$$\frac{DE}{CE} = \frac{AB}{AC}$$

185

$$\frac{5}{x} = \frac{8}{39 - x}$$
$$5(39 - x) = 8x$$
$$195 - 5x = 8x$$
$$195 = 8x + 5x = 13x$$
$$x = \frac{195}{13} = 15$$
$$X = 8 + 5 + x = 28$$

Answer: $X = 28$ mm

Problems 4.2

1. AB is the diameter of a circle, of length 100 mm. C is a point on the diameter so that $AC = 70$ mm. Calculate the length of the chord which is at right angles to the diameter and passes through the point C.

2. A segment of a circle has a chord of length 8 mm and a height of 2 mm. Calculate the radius of the circle.

3. A circular bar has a diameter of 34 mm. A cut is taken across the bar to produce a flat of width 30 mm. Calculate the depth of the cut.

4. Use the theorem of intersecting chords to find the dimension x of the layout shown in Figure 4.13.

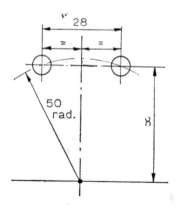

Fig. 4.13

5. A circle has a diameter of 70 mm. *P* is a point 125 mm from the centre of the circle. Use the theorem of intersecting chords (for the special case of a tangent) to find the length of the tangent to the circle.

6. A keyway of width 9 mm is cut in a bar of diameter 41 mm. The depth at the side of the keyway is 4 mm. Calculate its nominal depth at the centre.

7. A triangle has sides of length 15, 24 and 36 mm. The length of the shortest side of a similar triangle is 20 mm. Calculate the lengths of the other two sides.

8. A cone has a diameter of 48 mm and a vertical height of 60 mm. From this cone is removed a smaller cone, of vertical height 20 mm. Calculate the diameter of the smaller cone.

9. A symmetrical wedge has a length from base to apex of 100 mm, the base having a width of 20 mm. If it is placed in an aperture of width 8 mm, what length of the wedge projects from the aperture?

10. A crossed belt drive connects pulleys of diameters 100 mm and 240 mm whose centres are 400 mm apart. Calculate the distance to where the belt lines cross, measured from the centre of the larger pulley.

11. Calculate the distances *x* and *y* in Figure 4.14.

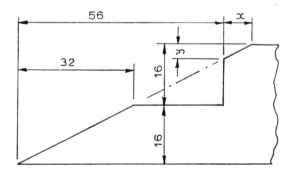

Fɪɢ. 4.14

Answers to Problems 4.2

1. 91·7 mm
2. 5 mm
3. 9 mm
4. 48 mm
5. 120 mm
6. 4·5 mm
7. 32 mm and 48 mm
8. 16 mm
9. 60 mm
10. 282 mm
11. $x = 8$ mm, $y = 4$ mm

4.3 The Theorem of Pythagoras

In Figure 4.15, *ABC* is a right-angled triangle, with a square erected on the longest side (called the *hypotenuse*). A larger square has been erected on continuations of sides *a* and *b*. The extension of side *a* is of length *b*, and the extension of side *b* is of length *a*. We now have four congruent triangles of sides *a*, *b* and *c*, surrounding a square of side *c*.

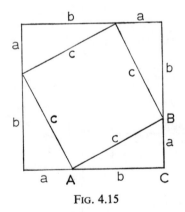

FIG. 4.15

$$\text{Area of large square} = (a + b)^2$$
$$= a^2 + 2ab + b^2$$

Area of square on hypotenuse

= area of large square − area of four triangles

$$\therefore c^2 = a^2 + 2ab + b^2 - 4\left(\frac{ab}{2}\right)$$
$$c^2 = a^2 + 2ab + b^2 - 2ab$$
$$c^2 = a^2 + b^2$$

The above equation is an algebraic form of the *Theorem of Pythagoras*. This states that in a right-angled triangle the square on the hypotenuse is equal to the sum of the squares on the other two sides.

There are certain sets of whole numbers for sides of triangles whose proportionalities produce right-angled triangles. The most well known set is 3 : 4 : 5, but some others are:

5 : 12 : 13	9 : 40 : 41
7 : 24 : 25	11 : 60 : 61
8 : 15 : 17	12 : 35 : 37

Before we proceed to examples which include the Theorem of Pythagoras, let us particularly note that the Theorem only applies to right-angled triangles, *not to all triangles*.

Example

Show that a triangle having sides of length 13 mm, 85 mm and 84 mm is right-angled.

Let c be the longest side (i.e. the hypotenuse), with a and b the other two sides. If the triangle is right-angled, using the Theorem of Pythagoras:

$$c^2 = a^2 + b^2$$

Substituting the values, working in mm units:

$$85^2 = 13^2 + 84^2$$
$$7\,225 = 169 + 7\,056 \text{ (values from tables)}$$
$$7\,225 = 7\,225$$

Answer: The square on the hypotenuse is equal to the sum of the squares on the other two sides, hence the triangle is right-angled.

Example

The hypotenuse of a right-angled triangle has a length of 34 mm. The other two sides differ in length by 14 mm. Find the length of the shortest side.

Let $\quad x$ = length of shortest side, and work in mm units
then $\quad x + 14$ = the other of the sides containing the right angle
and $\qquad 34$ = hypotenuse

Applying the Theorem of Pythagoras:

$$34^2 = (x)^2 + (x + 14)^2$$
$$1\,156 = x^2 + x^2 + 28x + 196$$
$$0 = x^2 + x^2 + 28x + 196 - 1\,156$$
$$0 = 2x^2 + 28x - 960$$
$$x^2 + 14x - 480 = 0$$
$$(x - 16)(x + 30) = 0$$

Either $\qquad\qquad\qquad x - 16 = 0, x = 16$
or $\qquad\qquad\qquad\quad x + 30 = 0, x = -30$

The negative root is inadmissible, hence $x = 16$.
Length of other side $= 16 + 14 = 30$.

Check: Sides are 16 mm, 30 mm, and 34 mm long:

$$34^2 = 16^2 + 30^2$$
$$1\,156 = 256 + 900 \qquad \text{(values from tables)}$$
$$1\,156 = 1\,156$$

Answer: Shortest side is 16 mm long

Example

Figure 4.16 shows a cable drum of diameter 2·5 m resting on two

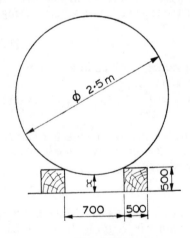

Fig. 4.16

baulks of timber of 500 mm square cross-section. The distance between the baulks is 700 mm. Calculate the ground clearance x, in millimetres.

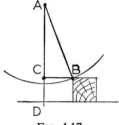

FIG. 4.17

Referring to Figure 4.17, *ABC* is a right-angled triangle. Working in millimetres:

$$AC = AD - DC = (1\ 250 + x) - 500 = 750 + x$$
$$BC = \text{half distance between baulks} \quad = 350$$
$$AB = \text{half diameter of drum} \quad\quad\quad = 1\ 250$$

Applying the Theorem of Pythagoras:

$$(AB)^2 = (AC)^2 + (BC)^2$$
$$1\ 250^2 = (750 + x)^2 + 350^2$$
$$1\ 562\ 500 = 562\ 500 + 1\ 500x + x^2 + 122\ 500$$
$$x^2 + 1\ 500x - 1\ 562\ 500 + 562\ 500 + 122\ 500 = 0$$
$$x^2 + 1\ 500x - 877\ 500 = 0$$
$$(x + 1\ 950)(x - 450) = 0$$

Either $x + 1\ 950 = 0$, $x = -1\ 950$ (not admissible)
or $x - 450 = 0$, $x = 450$

Answer: Ground clearance $= 450$ mm

This problem illustrates very clearly the large numbers which can occasionally result when the conventional engineering unit of the millimetre applies to dimensions. Sometimes it eases calculations to work in larger units, or work to a scale. Supposing for instance, we worked in centimetres (1 cm = 10 mm). In that case:

$$AC = 75 + x, \ BC = 35, \text{ and } AB = 125$$

and the equation would have been:

$$x^2 + 150x + 8\ 775 = 0, \text{ from which } x = 45 \text{ cm} = 450 \text{ mm}$$

191

Example

Figure 4.18 shows a link *AB* of length 160 mm, the rollers *A* and *B* moving in guides at right angles. Originally the centre of *B* was

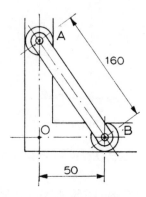

Fɪɢ. 4.18

50 mm from *O*. If roller *B* moves 10 mm nearer to *O*, how far does the centre of roller *A* move?

Let us work this example in centimetres; 160 mm = 16 cm and 50 mm = 5 cm.

According to Pythagoras:

$$(AB)^2 = (OB)^2 + (OA)^2$$
$$16^2 = (OB)^2 + (OA)^2$$
$$16^2 - (OB)^2 = (OA)^2$$
$$(OA)^2 = 256 - (OB)^2$$

When *B* is 5 cm from *O*:

$$(OA)^2 = 256 - 5^2 = 256 - 25 = 231$$
$$OA = \sqrt{231} = 15\cdot20$$

If *B* moves 1 cm nearer *O*, *OB* will be **4 cm**:

$$(OA)^2 = 256 - 4^2 = 256 - 16 = 240$$
$$OA = \sqrt{240} = 15\cdot49$$

Difference in *OA* values = 15·49 cm − 15·20 cm
= 0·29 cm = 2·9 mm

Answer: Roller *A* moves 2·9 mm upwards

Example

Figure 4.19 shows a method of determining a large radius on a template. Show, by applying the Theorem of Pythagoras to triangle *EFG*, that $R = \dfrac{c^2}{8d}$

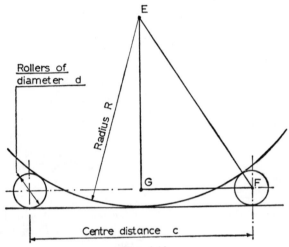

Fig. 4.19

In the right-angled triangle *EFG*:

$$GF = \frac{c}{2}, \quad FE = R + \frac{d}{2}, \quad EG = R - \frac{d}{2}$$

Applying the Theorem of Pythagoras:

$$(FE)^2 = (GF)^2 + (EG)^2$$

$$\therefore \left(R + \frac{d}{2}\right)^2 = \left(\frac{c}{2}\right)^2 + \left(R - \frac{d}{2}\right)^2$$

$$R^2 + Rd + \frac{d^2}{4} = \frac{c^2}{4} + R^2 - Rd + \frac{d^2}{4}$$

$$2Rd = \frac{c^2}{4}$$

whence $$R = \frac{c^2}{8d}$$

193

Example

Figure 4.20 shows another method of determining a large radius. In this case, rollers of diameter d are fixed at a centre distance of C,

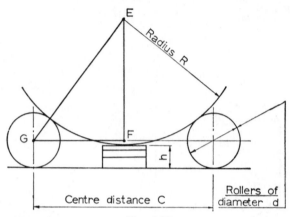

FIG. 4.20

and the height h checked with a slip gauge pile. If the height of the slip gauge pile is h, find an expression for the value of R. Find R when $C = 50$ mm, $d = 10$ mm and $h = 5$ mm.

In the right-angled triangle, *EFG*:

$$GF = \frac{C}{2}, \quad FE = R + h - \frac{d}{2}, \quad EG = R + \frac{d}{2}$$

Applying the Theorem of Pythagoras:

$$(EG)^2 = (FE)^2 + (GF)^2$$

$$\therefore \left(R + \frac{d}{2} \right)^2 = \left(R - \frac{d}{2} + h \right)^2 + \frac{C^2}{4}$$

$$\therefore \left(R + \frac{d}{2} \right)^2 - \left(R - \frac{d}{2} + h \right)^2 = \frac{C^2}{4}$$

Factorizing the difference of two squares on the left-hand side:

$$\left(R + \frac{d}{2} + R - \frac{d}{2} + h \right) \left(R + \frac{d}{2} - R + \frac{d}{2} - h \right) = \frac{C^2}{4}$$

$$(2R + h)(d - h) = \frac{C^2}{4}$$

$$2R + h = \frac{C^2}{4(d - h)}$$

$$2R = \frac{C^2}{4(d - h)} - h$$

$$R = \frac{C^2}{8(d - h)} - \frac{h}{2}$$

Working in centimetres:

When $C = 5$, $d = 1$, and $h = 0.5$

$$R = \frac{5^2}{8(1 - 0.5)} - \frac{0.5}{2}$$

$$= 6.25 - 0.25 = 6 \text{ cm} = 60 \text{ mm}$$

Answer: (a) $R = \dfrac{C^2}{8(d - h)} - \dfrac{h}{2}$

(b) $R = 60$ mm

Problems 4.3

1. The sides containing the right angle of a right-angled triangle have lengths of 12 mm and 35 mm. Calculate the length of the hypotenus.e

2. The hypotenuse of a right-angled triangle has a length of 100 mm. The other two sides are in the ratio of five to one. Determine the length of the shortest side, to three significant figures.

3. An isosceles triangle has a base of length 16 mm. Each of the other two sides has a length of 17 mm. Find the perpendicular height of the triangle.

4. The hypotenuse of a right-angled triangle has a length of 39 mm. The other two sides differ in length by 21 mm. Determine the length of the shortest side.

5. Discs of diameter 27 mm are stamped out in alternate rows of five and four so that there is 3 mm between edges of adjacent holes. Determine the distance between the centre lines of parallel rows of discs, to three significant figures.

6. The profile shown in Figure 4.21 has no straight portions. Determine the smallest width of the profile, *W*.

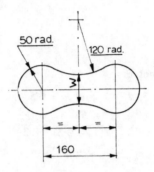

Fig. 4.21

7. *A* and *B* represent the centres of two switches on the front panel of a receiver. Measured in millimetres, the co-ordinates of *A* and *B* are (36, 71) and (60, 116) respectively. Calculate the distance, in millimetres, between the centres of *A* and *B*.

8. A field is rectangular in shape, the length being twice the breadth. The field has an area of 1 hectare.
   (*a*) Determine the length and breadth.
   (*b*) *A* and *B* represent two diagonally opposite corners. If a wire runs direct from *A* to *B* instead of along around the perimeter, determine the saving of wire, in metres (1 hectare = 10^4 m²).

9. Figure 4.22 shows three cables passing through a circular aperture. If the cables have an outside diameter of 8 mm, determine the smallest possible diameter *D* of the aperture. Give the answer to the nearest half-millimetre above theoretical size.

10. Figure 4.23 shows a cable strung between three pylons.
   (*a*) Calculate the height of the pylon at *B* so that the angle of inclination remains constant.
   (*b*) Calculate the straight length of cable required from pylon *A* to pylon *C*.
   (*c*) If $3\frac{3}{4}\%$ of the theoretical length must be provided for sagging, contraction, etc. calculate the actual length of cable used.

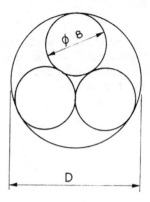

FIG. 4.22

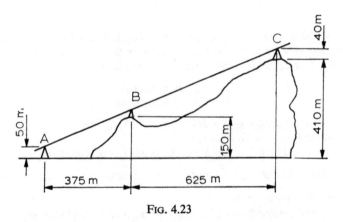

FIG. 4.23

Answers 4.3

1. 37 mm
2. 19·6 mm
3. 15 mm
4. 15 mm
5. 26·0 mm
6. 60 mm
7. 51 mm
8. (a) 70·7 m × 141 m   (b) 54·0 m
9. 17·5 mm
10. (a) 50 m   (b) 1 080 m   (c) 1 120 m

4.4 Basic Trigonometry

4.4.1 BASIC TRIGONOMETRICAL RATIOS

Trigonometry literally means the measurement of triangles. Our first excursion into trigonometry will be confined to right-angled triangles. Consider two similar right-angled triangles lettered conventionally, as shown in Figure 4.24.

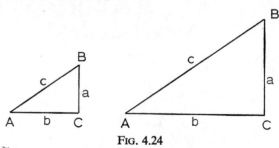

Fig. 4.24

The longest side of a right-angled triangle is the hypotenuse. We can also give names to the other sides with reference to the acute angles. For example, with reference to angle A:

side a is the 'side opposite A'
and   side b is the 'side adjacent A'

(There are actually two sides adjacent to A, but we have already nominated one as the hypotenuse.)

Since the triangles are similar, the ratios of corresponding sides are constant. The ratios $\dfrac{a}{c}$, $\dfrac{b}{c}$ and $\dfrac{a}{b}$ are the same for all similar right-angled triangles.

In a right-angled triangle, *and only in a right-angled triangle*, the ratio:

$$\frac{\text{side opposite an angle}}{\text{hypotenuse}}$$

is called the *sine* of that angle. We abbreviate sine to sin but read it as sine.

Hence $\sin A = \dfrac{\text{side opposite } A}{\text{hypotenuse}} = \dfrac{a}{c}$

In a similar fashion, in a right-angled triangle, the ratio:

$$\frac{\text{side adjacent an angle}}{\text{hypotenuse}}$$

is called the *cosine* of that angle. We abbreviate cosine to cos.

Hence $$\cos A = \frac{\text{side adjacent to } A}{\text{hypotenuse}} = \frac{b}{c}$$

Finally, in a right-angled triangle, the ratio:

$$\frac{\text{side opposite an angle}}{\text{side adjacent that angle}}$$

is called the *tangent* of that angle. We abbreviate tangent to tan.

Hence $$\tan A = \frac{\text{side opposite } A}{\text{side adjacent to } A} = \frac{a}{b}$$

Let us now investigate how the values of the sine, the cosine and the tangent vary with the magnitude of the angle A. We will return to the indication of an amount of turning by rotating an arm about

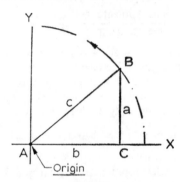

FIG. 4.25

the origin of cartesian co-ordinates. In particular, the arm will be of unit length, and we shall confine the rotation of the arm to within the first quadrant, as shown in Figure 4.25.

In the right-angled triangle ABC, in terms of cartesian co-ordinates:

$$a = y, \quad b = x \quad \text{and} \quad c = 1$$

In the first quadrant all these values are positive, and therefore ratios of these values will be positive. Hence if A lies between zero and 90°, the ratios of $\sin A$, $\cos A$ and $\tan A$ are all positive values.

The sine of angle A is:

$$\frac{\text{side opposite } A}{\text{hypotenuse}} = \frac{a}{c} = \frac{y}{1} = y$$

When A is zero, y is zero and $\sin 0° = 0$. As the angle A increases, y increases but not in direct proportion. y reaches its maximum value when $A = 90°$, when $y = 1$, hence $\sin 90° = 1$.

The cosine of angle A is:

$$\frac{\text{side adjacent } A}{\text{hypotenuse}} = \frac{b}{c} = \frac{x}{1} = x$$

When A is zero, x is unity and $\cos 0° = 1$. As the angle A increases, x decreases, but not in direct proportion. x reaches its minimum value of zero when $A = 90°$, hence $\cos 90° = 0$.

It should be particularly noted that since y or x can never exceed unity, the value of the sine or the cosine can never exceed unity. When the magnitude of angle A lies between zero and 90°, the range of the sine is from zero to unity, and that of the cosine is from unity to zero.

The tangent of angle A is:

$$\frac{\text{side opposite } A}{\text{side adjacent } A} = \frac{a}{b} = \frac{y}{x}$$

When the magnitude of angle A is zero, $y = 0$ and $x = 1$, hence $\tan 0° = 0$. As the angle A increases, y increases but x decreases. Hence as the angle increases, the tangent increases, but not in direct proportion. When $A = 45°$, $x = y = 1$, hence $\tan 45° = 1$. As A nears 90°, y is increasing only slightly, but x is diminishing very rapidly. At the value of 90°, $y = 1$ and $x = 0$, whence $\tan 90° = \frac{1}{0}$, a value of infinite magnitude.

Let us pause in our development of basic trigonometry to recapitulate the basic trigonometrical ratios.

$$\sin A = \frac{\text{side opposite } A}{\text{hypotenuse}}$$

$$\cos A = \frac{\text{side adjacent } A}{\text{hypotenuse}}$$

$$\tan A = \frac{\text{side opposite } A}{\text{side adjacent } A}$$

We have already considered how these values vary as the angle increases. Let us now be more precise by calculating specific values, and plotting them on a graph. We have already calculated values of the ratios for 0° and 90°. Let us proceed by determining the values for 30°, 45° and 90°, since triangles containing these angles are simple to construct.

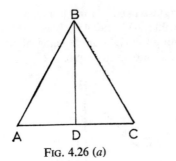

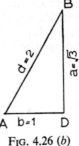

FIG. 4.26 (*a*)   FIG. 4.26 (*b*)

Figure 4.26(*a*) shows an equilateral triangle *ABC* with angle *B* bisected.

In the triangle *ABD*:

$$A = 60°, B = 30°$$

hence $D = 180° - (60° + 30°) = 90°$

ABD is therefore a right-angled triangle, and is repeated for convenience in Figure 4.26. If each side of the original equilateral triangle had a length of 2 units, since *ABD* and *BDC* are congruent triangles, $AD = DC = 1$ unit. Using the Theorem of Pythagoras, $(BD)^2 = (AB)^2 - (AD)^2 = 4 - 1 = 3$. Hence $BD = \sqrt{3}$ units long.

Thus in the right-angled triangle *ABD*:

$$
\begin{array}{llll}
A = 60° & a = \sqrt{3} & \text{(side opposite to } A) \\
B = 30° & b = 1 & \text{(side adjacent to } A) \\
D = 90° & d = 2 & \text{(hypotenuse)}
\end{array}
$$

$$\sin 60° = \sin A = \frac{\text{side opposite to } A}{\text{hypotenuse}} = \frac{\sqrt{3}}{2} = 0.866\,0$$

$$\cos 60° = \cos A = \frac{\text{side adjacent to } A}{\text{hypotenuse}} = \frac{1}{2} = 0.500\,0$$

$$\tan 60° = \tan A = \frac{\text{side opposite to } A}{\text{side adjacent to } A} = \frac{\sqrt{3}}{1} = 1.732\,1$$

$$\sin 30° = \sin B = \frac{\text{side opposite to } B}{\text{hypotenuse}} = \frac{1}{2} = 0.500\,0$$

$$\cos 30° = \cos B = \frac{\text{side adjacent to } B}{\text{hypotenuse}} = \frac{\sqrt{3}}{2} = 0.866\,0$$

$$\tan 30° = \tan B = \frac{\text{side opposite to } B}{\text{side adjacent to } B} = \frac{1}{\sqrt{3}} = 0.577\,4$$

201

Now let us construct a right-angled triangle containing an angle of 45°. The angles must be 90°, 45° and 45°, hence the triangle is isosceles, the sides containing the right angle being of equal length.

Let this length be unity, as shown in Figure 4.27.

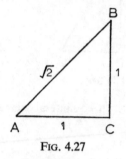

FIG. 4.27

Using the Theorem of Pythagoras:

$$c^2 = a^2 + b^2 = 1 + 1 = 2 \qquad \therefore c = \sqrt{2}$$

$$\sin 45° = \sin A = \frac{\text{side opposite to } A}{\text{hypotenuse}} = \frac{1}{\sqrt{2}} = 0\cdot707\,1$$

$$\cos 45° = \cos A = \frac{\text{side adjacent to } A}{\text{hypotenuse}} = \frac{1}{\sqrt{2}} = 0\cdot707\,1$$

$$\tan 45° = \tan A = \frac{\text{side opposite to } A}{\text{hypotenuse}} = \frac{1}{1} = 1\cdot000\,0$$

Let us now collect all our information, and show graphically how the basic trigonometrical ratios change as the angle increases from zero to 90°.

Angle	0°	30°	45°	60°	90°
sin	0	0·500 0	0·707 1	0·866 0	1·000 0
cos	1·000 0	0·866 0	0·707 1	0·500 0	0
tan	0	0·577 4	1·000 0	1·732 1	Infinite

The final graph is shown in Figure 4.28. The graph is actually incomplete, since as the angle approaches 90° the tangent of an angle approaches a value of infinite magnitude.

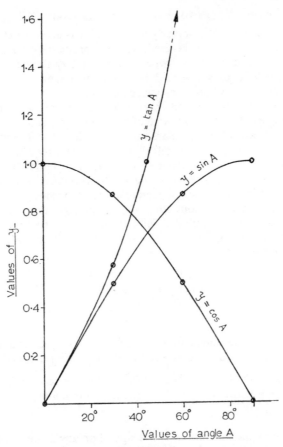

FIG. 4.28

In a right-angled triangle, the two angles other than the right angle total 90°. Angles which total 90° are said to be complementary to each other. Referring back to Figure 4.24:

$$\sin A = \frac{\text{side opposite to } A}{\text{hypotenuse}} = \frac{\text{side adjacent to } B}{\text{hypotenuse}} = \cos B$$

Hence the sine of an angle is the cosine of its complementary angle, and vice versa. For example:

$$\sin 60° = \cos 30°$$
$$\sin 80° = \cos 10°$$
$$\cos 25° = \sin 65°$$

4.4.2 TABLES OF TRIGONOMETRICAL RATIOS

The technician does not study mathematics as an abstract subject. Mathematics is a tool to be used, where appropriate, to accomplish tasks. Let us put our knowledge of trigonometry to such practical usage. In order to do so, we shall have to know the magnitudes of the trigonometrical ratios of sine, cosine and tangent for angles between zero and 90°. We have already been able to calculate these values for certain angles. As our knowledge of mathematics increases, we shall see how it is possible to calculate values for other specific angles, and eventually for any angle. The information which we require at present has been worked out and collected in the form of tables. The reader should now open Castle's *Four-figure Mathematical Tables* at the page marked 'natural sines'. The magnitude of the sine of an angle is obtained in a manner somewhat similar to logarithms. It will be noticed that values are quoted fully at intervals of six minutes, and increments are given for intervals of one minute. The reader should now check that:

$$\sin 17° = 0.292\ 4$$
$$\sin 17°\ 12' = 0.295\ 7$$
$$\sin 61° = 0.874\ 6$$
$$\sin 87°\ 42' = 0.999\ 2$$

If we require the sine of an angle such as 21° 38', we cannot obtain this by direct reading. We proceed in the following manner:

$$\sin 21°\ 36' = 0.368\ 1 \quad \text{(nearest direct reading below)}$$
$$\text{increment for } 2' = \quad\quad 5 \quad \text{(from end columns)}$$
$$\overline{\sin 21°\ 38' = 0.368\ 6}$$

If we know the magnitude of the sine of an angle, we can find the angle by using the table of sines in a reverse manner to the method previously described. The mathematical way of abbreviating 'the angle whose sine is' is to write *arcsin*. The question 'find the angle whose sine is 0·75' can be written 'find arcsin 0·75' and the answer will be an angle. The reader may have been used to representing 'the angle whose sine is' by sin⁻¹. This is now considered to be a non-standard notation.

Hence   arcsin 0·374 6 = 22°
and   arcsin 0·938 5 = 69° 48'

both these values being obtained directly.

For the case of arcsin 0·511 3, this value is not obtained directly. We proceed as follows:

nearest direct value below = 0·510 5 = sin 30° 42'
addition required = 8 = increment for 3'

0·511 3 = sin 30° 45'

One of the most common sources of error is in reading the wrong table. The reader is advised to write in large capitals SIN, in red, at the top of each page of the table of sines. He should now turn over to the table of cosines and write COS in large capitals, in red, at the top of each table of cosines, and then to turn over to the table of tangents and write, at the top of each table of tangents TAN, in large capitals, in red. We are now looking at our table of tangents, which are read in a similar manner to sines. The reader should check the following values:

$$\tan 23° = 0·424\ 5$$
$$\tan 32°\ 18' = 0·632\ 2$$
$$\tan 67°\ 46' = 2·446\ 2$$

$$\arctan 0·649\ 4 = 33°$$
$$\arctan 1·118\ 4 = 48°\ 12'$$
$$\arctan 1·748\ 5 = 60°\ 14'$$

With sines and tangents, as the angle increases, their magnitude increases, and hence the differences for extra minutes must be added. With the cosine, as the angle increases, the cosine decreases. Consequently, for extra minutes the values have to be subtracted. Returning to the table of cosines, the reader is advised now to write plainly in red, at the top of each table, SUBTRACT MEAN DIFFERENCES.

If the angle is a multiple of six minutes, the value can be read directly. For example:

$$\cos 23° = 0·920\ 5$$
$$\cos 48°\ 24' = 0·663\ 9$$

while in reverse $$\arccos 0·358\ 4 = 69°$$
$$\arccos 0·925\ 2 = 22°\ 18'$$

For values which cannot be read directly, noting carefully that mean differences have to be subtracted, we proceed as follows:
To find cos 37° 52':

cos 37° 48' = 0·790 2
decrement for 4' = 7   (to be subtracted)

cos 37° 52' = 0·789 5

To find arccos 0·418 4:

$$
\begin{array}{rl}
\text{nearest direct value above} = & 0{\cdot}419\ 5 = \cos 65°\ 12' \\
\text{decrement required} = & 1\ 1 = \qquad\qquad 4' \\
\hline
& 0{\cdot}418\ 4 = \cos 65°\ 16'
\end{array}
$$

4.4.3 PRACTICAL APPLICATIONS OF TRIGONOMETRY

We will proceed to use our knowledge of trigonometry to solve problems. The reader is advised wherever possible to use scale diagrams to check whether or not the answer is reasonable. A useful method of approach is for the reader to ask himself certain questions.

(a) Is there a right-angled triangle (if not, can one be formed)?

(b) By what ratio must I multiply the known side to obtain the unknown side, i.e. what is the ratio $\dfrac{\text{unknown side}}{\text{known side}}$?

Example

A guy-rope of length 30 m runs from a vertical telegraph pole to the horizontal ground level. The guy-rope makes an angle of 41° to the horizontal. How far is it from the base of the pole to the ground attachment?

The details are illustrated in Figure 4.29. We are told that the pole is vertical and the ground is horizontal, hence C is 90°. We therefore have a right-angled triangle.

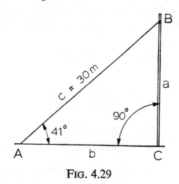

FIG. 4.29

We are told that angle A is 41° and that $c = 30$ m; this is the known side. b is the unknown side.

$$\text{Required multiplier is } \frac{\text{unknown side}}{\text{known side}}$$

$$= \frac{b}{c} = \frac{\text{side adjacent to } A}{\text{hypotenuse}} = \cos A = \cos 41°$$
$$\therefore b = \text{known side} \times \cos 41°$$
$$= 30 \text{ m} \times 0.754\ 7$$
$$= 22.641 \text{ m}$$

Measuring the diagram shows that the answer is reasonable.

Answer: Distance is 22·6 m

Example

Five holes lie equally spaced on a pitch circle diameter of 80 mm. Determine the chordal distance between two adjacent holes.

Figure 4.30 shows the details, P being the centre of the circle, and A and B being two adjacent holes. We have no right-angled triangle

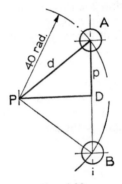

FIG. 4.30

thus far, but PAB is an isosceles triangle. We know that if we bisect the angle contained by the two equal sides we can form two congruent right-angled triangles. These are the triangles PAD and PDB, D being the mid-point of AB.

$$d = \text{pitch circle radius} = \frac{80 \text{ mm}}{2} = 40 \text{ mm}$$

In triangle PAB:

$$\text{angle } P = \frac{360°}{5} = 72°$$

Now triangle PAD is right-angled. In triangle PAD:

$$\text{angle } P = \frac{72°}{2} = 36°$$

and
$$p = \frac{AB}{2} = \text{unknown side}$$

$$\text{Required multiplier} = \frac{\text{unknown side}}{\text{known side}} = \frac{\text{side opposite } P}{\text{hypotenuse}}$$

$$= \sin P = \sin 36°$$
$$\therefore AD = 40 \text{ mm} \times \sin 36° = 40 \text{ mm} \times 0\cdot587\,8$$
$$= 23\cdot512 \text{ mm}$$
$$AB = \text{twice } AD = 47\cdot024 \text{ mm}$$

Scaling the diagram shows the value to be reasonable.

Answer: Chordal distance = 47·0 mm

The reasoning in the above problem has been given in detail. As skill is acquired, the reader will proceed, having sketched the diagram, to an expression such as $p = d \sin P$. In many cases a general idea of the trend of the magnitude of trigonometrical ratios will often indicate which of the ratios is correct.

Example

A telegraph pole is erected on level ground. An observer notes that the angle of elevation from the ground to the top of the pole is 32°. From a point 15 m nearer the base of the pole, the angle of elevation is 45°. Calculate the height of the pole.

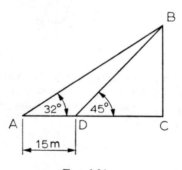

Fig. 4.31

Referring to Figure 4.31, the pole is represented by BC.

$$\frac{BC}{DC} = \tan 45° = 1$$
$$\therefore BC = DC$$

In the triangle ABC:

$$\frac{BC}{AC} = \tan 32°$$

$$AC = AD + DC = 15 + BC, \text{ since } BC = DC$$

$$\therefore \frac{BC}{15 + BC} = \tan 32°, \ BC = (15 + BC) \tan 32°$$

$$BC = (15 + BC)\,0·624\,9, \ BC = 9·373\,5 + 0·624\,9\,BC$$

$$BC - 0·624\,9\,BC = 9·373\,5, \quad 0·375\,1\,BC = 9·373\,5$$

$$BC = \frac{9·373\,5}{0·375\,1} = 25·00$$

No.	Log
9·373 5	0·971 9
0·975 1	$\bar{1}$·574 1
25·00	1·397 8

Rough check:

$$\frac{9\frac{3}{8}}{\frac{3}{8}} = \frac{75}{8} \times \frac{8}{3} = 25$$

Answer: Height of pole = 25·0 m

4.4.4 INVERSE TRIGONOMETRICAL RATIOS

It has been suggested earlier that a wise procedure to adopt when solving trigonometrical problems where an unknown side had to be determined is:

(a) to draw a scale diagram to roughly check the validity of the answer;

(b) to find the ratio by which the known side must be multiplied in order to determine the unknown side, i.e. the ratio

$$\frac{\text{unknown side}}{\text{known side}}.$$

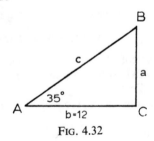

FIG. 4.32

Figure 4.32 shows a right-angled triangle ABC where $b = 12$ and angle $A = 35°$.

209

If we wished to determine side a, we would reason that the ratio:

$$\frac{\text{unknown side}}{\text{known side}} = \frac{a}{b} = \tan 35°, \text{ and } a = b \tan 35°$$

If, on the other hand, we had to determine side c, the ratio would be

$$\frac{\text{unknown side}}{\text{known side}} = \frac{c}{b} = \frac{1}{\sin 35°}, \text{ and } c = b \times \frac{1}{\sin 35°}$$

This would normally cause us to use logarithms, even if b were a simple value. There are many similar occasions in trigonometry where we find it either convenient or necessary to deal with the reciprocals of the sine, the cosine and the tangent, and consequently we find it useful to give the reciprocals special names and provide numerical values in tables. The names of the reciprocal ratios are:

$$\frac{1}{\sin A} = \text{cosecant } A$$

$$\frac{1}{\cos A} = \text{secant } A$$

$$\frac{1}{\tan A} = \text{cotangent } A$$

Their abbreviations are cosec, sec and cot respectively.

A general idea of their values as an angle varies from zero to 90° can be considered from the reciprocals of the values of sin, cos and tan. Cosec 0° $\left(= \dfrac{1}{\sin 0°} \right)$ is infinitely large; the cosecant decreases as the angle approaches 90°, taking the value of 2 for cosec 30° and unity for cosec 90°. The cosecant of the angle is always unity or greater. Secant 0° $\left(= \dfrac{1}{\cos 0°} \right)$ is unity. The secant is unity or greater; it increases as the angle increases; sec 60° = 2 and sec 90° is infinitely large. Cot 0° $\left(= \dfrac{1}{\tan 0°} \right)$ is infinitely large. The cotangent decreases as the angle increases; cot 45° = 1, and cot 90° = 0.

The reader is now advised to open his mathematical tables to the tables of cosecants and cotangents and to write plainly in red across the top of each of the four pages, the words SUBTRACT MEAN DIFFERENCES.

From our previous studies we should be aware that if ABC is a triangle with a right angle at C:

$\sin A = \cos B$, i.e. $\cos (90° - A)$

In a similar manner, for the reciprocal ratios:

$$\tan A = \cot B, \text{ i.e. } \cot (90° - A)$$
$$\sec A = \operatorname{cosec} B, \text{ i.e. } \operatorname{cosec} (90° - A)$$

For some occasions when trigonometry is used in calculations, in order to avoid looking up a trigonometrical ratio and then its logarithm, Castle's *Four-figure Mathematical Tables* include logarithms of the trigonometrical ratios. The logarithms are obtained in a similar manner to ordinary trigonometrical ratios, but special care has to be taken with characteristics. We will adopt our usual procedure of writing in red, very plainly, across the top of the six pages dealing with the logarithms of cosines, the logarithms of cosecants and the logarithms of cotangents, the words SUBTRACT MEAN DIFFERENCES.

There are certain values, either at the beginning or the end of tables of tangents, secants, cosecants and cotangents, for which the mean differences cease to be sufficiently accurate, and hence no values of mean differences are quoted. In every case of tables of logarithms of trigonometrical ratios, at either the beginning or the end, the mean differences are again insufficiently accurate. If mean differences are not quoted, intermediary values should be obtained between quoted values by using simple proportion.

Example

Find tan 86° 50′.

$$\tan 86° 54' = 18 \cdot 46$$
$$\tan 86° 48' = 17 \cdot 89$$
$$\overline{\text{increment for } 6' = 0 \cdot 57}$$

$$\text{increment for } 2' = \frac{2}{6} \times 0 \cdot 57 = 0 \cdot 19$$

$$\tan 86° 50' = 17 \cdot 89 + 0 \cdot 19 = 18 \cdot 08$$

Answer: tan 86° 50′ = 18·08

Example

Find log cosec 2° 33′.

$$\log \operatorname{cosec} 2° 30' = 1 \cdot 360\ 3$$
$$\log \operatorname{cosec} 2° 36' = 1 \cdot 343\ 3$$
$$\overline{\text{decrement for } 6' = 0 \cdot 017\ 0}$$

$$\text{decrement for } 3' = \frac{3}{6} \times 0\cdot017\ 0 = 0\cdot008\ 5$$

$$\log \operatorname{cosec} 2° 33' = 1\cdot360\ 3 - 0\cdot008\ 5 = 1\cdot351\ 8$$

Answer: $\log \operatorname{cosec} 2° 33' = 1\cdot351\ 8$

4.4.5 MEASUREMENT PROBLEMS INVOLVING TRIGONOMETRY
Screw threads

A *helix* is the path of a point which moves on the curved surface of a cylinder so that the distance it moves parallel to the axis of the cylinder is proportional to the angular rotation of the cylinder.

A particular application of a helix is a screw thread. If the cylinder rotates one revolution, the distance moved parallel to the axis is the *lead* of the helix. The pitch of a screw thread is the distance between the centre lines of adjacent thread forms. If the helix is single-start,

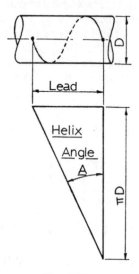

FIG. 4.33

the pitch is equal to the lead. If the thread is multi-start, having n starts of pitch p, then the lead of the thread $= np$. If the helix is developed, as shown in Figure 4.33, the helix angle is given by arctan $\dfrac{\text{lead}}{\pi D}$. It should be noted that for a constant value of the lead, the value of the helix angle depends upon the value of D. Unless specifically stated to the contrary, all threads are assumed to be single-start, and the helix angle of a screw thread is assumed to correspond with the effective diameter. The reader should note that with some threads the effective diameter lies at half the thread depth. This is not true of all threads, however, particularly those of SI form.

Example

The M16 metric thread has an outside diameter of 16 mm and a pitch of 2 mm. The effective diameter of a metric thread is given by the outside diameter minus 0·65 times the pitch. Calculate the helix angle of an M16 metric thread.

$$\text{Lead} = \text{pitch} = 2 \text{ mm}$$
$$\text{Effective diameter} = 16 - 2(0·65) = 16 - 1·3 = 14·7$$

$$\text{Helix angle} = \arctan\left(\frac{\text{lead}}{\pi \times \text{eff. dia.}}\right) = \arctan\left(\frac{2}{\pi \times 14·7}\right)$$
$$= \arctan 0·043\ 3 = 2°\ 29'$$

No.	Log
π 14·7	0·497 2 1·167 3
Denom.	1·664 5
2 Denom.	0·301 0 1·664 5
0·043 3	$\bar{2}$·636 5

Rough check: $\dfrac{2}{50} = 0·04$

Answer: Helix angle = 2° 29′

(It should be noted that the table of the logarithms of tangents were not used because for very small angles the mean differences are insufficiently accurate.)

Tapers

The nominal dimension of a taper can be indicated either by stating its included angle or the reduction in diameter per distance of axial travel. Typical examples are 'included angle of 15°' or 'taper of 7/24'.

With the use of Figure 4.34 the connection between the two systems can be deduced (see diagram overleaf).

$$\tan \tfrac{1}{2} \text{ (included angle } \theta) = \frac{BC}{AB} = \frac{\tfrac{1}{2} \text{ reduction in diameter}}{L}$$
$$\therefore \tan \frac{\theta}{2} = \frac{\text{reduction in diameter}}{2L}$$

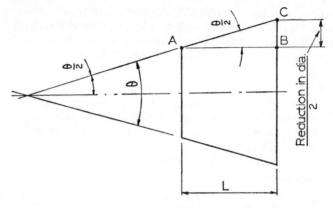

FIG. 4.34

Example

Find the included angle corresponding to a taper of 1/8.

$$\tan \left(\frac{\text{included angle}}{2} \right) = \frac{1}{2 \times 8} = \frac{1}{16} = \text{arctan } 3° \, 34'$$

$$\therefore \text{ included angle} = 3° \, 34' \times 2 = 7° \, 8'$$

Answer: Included angle $= 7° \, 8'$

Use of rollers and spheres in measurement

Consider the male dovetail slide, dimensioned in millimetres and drawn theoretically in Figure 4.35(*a*). In order to machine this profile an undercut would be necessary; an enlargement of this portion of the slide is shown in Figure 4.35(*b*).

It is not possible to measure the 30 mm dimension directly, since this dimension is between two imaginary lines in space. Problems similar to this occur repeatedly in measurement, the difficulty being

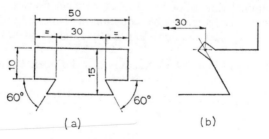

FIG. 4.35

214

overcome by measuring the 30 mm dimension indirectly. Rollers are placed in the vees and a measurement made across rollers. By the use of trigonometry the theoretical dimension of 30 mm can be checked. If the surface is internal and conical, balls are used instead of rollers.

There are two fundamental principles to remember in solving problems involving rollers (or balls) in tapers and/or vees:

1. If a roller (or ball) is placed against a flat surface, a line from the centre of the roller (or ball) to the point of contact is at right-angles to the surface and its length is equal to the radius of the roller (or ball).

2. A line from the centre of the roller (or ball) to the apex of the vee (or taper) bisects the angle of the vee (or taper).

It cannot be emphasized too much that calculations of this type invariably deal with half the included angle of the taper or vee.

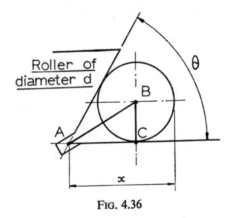

FIG. 4.36

Case 1: Roller in a vee (Figure 4.36)

Triangle ABC is right-angled, $\angle A = \dfrac{\theta}{2}$

$$AC = \frac{d}{2} \cot \frac{\theta}{2}$$

$$\therefore x = \frac{d}{2} + \frac{d}{2} \cot \frac{\theta}{2}$$

whence

$$x = \frac{d}{2} \left(1 + \cot \frac{\theta}{2} \right)$$

215

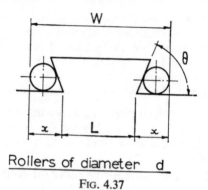

Rollers of diameter d

FIG. 4.37

In the symmetrical dovetail slide shown in Figure 4.37:

$$W = L + 2x = L + 2\left(\frac{d}{2}\right)\left(1 + \cot\frac{\theta}{2}\right)$$

$$= L + d\left(1 + \cot\frac{\theta}{2}\right)$$

This formula should not be applied to an asymmetrical dovetail slot. If the slot is not symmetrical, each side of the dovetail should be considered separately, as demonstrated in the example which follows.

Example

Calculate the dimensions x and y and hence determine the checking dimension W for the asymmetrical dovetail slot shown in Figure 4.38.

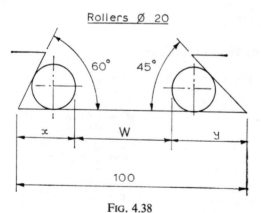

FIG. 4.38

$$x = \frac{d}{2}\left(1 + \cot\frac{\theta}{2}\right) = 10\,(1 + \cot 30°)$$

$$= 10\,(1 + 1\cdot732\ 1) = 10\,(2\cdot732\ 1) = 27\cdot321$$

$$y = \frac{d}{2}\left(1 + \cot\frac{\theta}{2}\right) = 10\,(1 + \cot 22°\ 30')$$

$$= 10\,(1 + 2\cdot414\ 2) = 10\,(3\cdot414\ 2) = 34\cdot142$$
$$W = 100 - (x + y) = 100 - (27\cdot321 + 34\cdot142)$$
$$= 100 - 61\cdot463 = 38\cdot537$$

Answer: Checking distance $= 38\cdot5$ mm

Case 2: Included angle of external taper

Referring to Figure 4.39, two dimensions over rollers W_1 and W_2

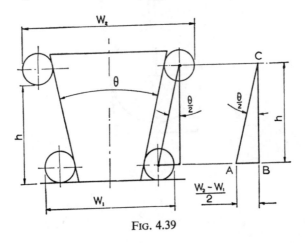

Fig. 4.39

are taken, the measurements being made at different heights and the separation being h.

Consider triangle ABC: $\quad AB = \dfrac{W_2 - W_1}{2}$

$$BC = h$$

If θ is the included angle:

$$\tan\frac{\theta}{2} = \frac{W_2 - W_1}{2h}$$

217

Case 3: Included angle of an internal taper

Referring to Figure 4.40, balls of diameters D and d are placed in the taper and, by the use of measurements from some datum surface, the separation of their centres h is determined.

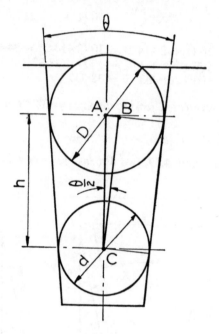

Fig. 4.40

Consider triangle ABC: $\quad AB = \dfrac{D - d}{2} \qquad AC = h$

If θ is the included angle:

$$\operatorname{cosec} \frac{\theta}{2} = \frac{2h}{D - d}$$

Example

Figure 4.41 shows dimensions obtained when measuring a taper plug gauge. Determine the included angle of the gauge and the diameter at the small end.

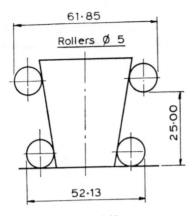

FIG. 4.41

$$\tan \frac{\theta}{2} = \frac{W_2 - W_1}{2h} = \frac{61 \cdot 85 - 52 \cdot 13}{2 \times 25}$$

$$= \frac{9 \cdot 72}{50} = 0 \cdot 194\,4 = \arctan 11°$$

included angle $= 2(11°) = 22°$

The diameter at the small end can be found from an application of the dovetail formula, as shown in Figure 4.36.

$$W = 52 \cdot 13, \quad d = 5, \quad \theta = 90° - 11° = 79°$$

$$W = L + d \left(1 + \cot \frac{\theta}{2} \right), \; \theta \text{ being the vee angle}$$

$$\therefore L = W - d \left(1 + \cot \frac{\theta}{2} \right)$$

$$= 52 \cdot 13 - 5(1 + \cot 39° \, 30')$$
$$= 52 \cdot 13 - 5(1 + 1 \cdot 213\,1)$$
$$= 52 \cdot 13 - 11 \cdot 066 = 41 \cdot 064$$

Answer: Included angle $= 22°$

Diameter at small end $= 41 \cdot 06$ mm

219

H

Example

Figure 4.42 shows dimensions obtained when checking an internal taper feature. Find the included angle of the taper and the diameter at the large end.

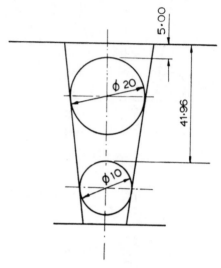

Fig. 4.42

Separation $h = (41\cdot96 + 5\cdot00) - (5\cdot00 + 10\cdot00)$
$ = 46\cdot96 - 15\cdot00 = 31\cdot96$

$$\operatorname{cosec} \frac{\theta}{2} = \frac{2h}{D - d} = \frac{2 \times 31\cdot96}{20 - 10} = \frac{63\cdot92}{10} = 6\cdot392$$

$$\therefore \frac{\theta}{2} = 9°, \quad \theta = 18°$$

Figure 4.43 shows the condition at the top of the taper.

$AB = 10 \sec 9° = 10 \times 1\cdot012\,5 = 10\cdot125$
$CB = 5\cdot00 + 10\cdot00 = 15\cdot00$
$CD = CB \tan 9° = 15 \times 0\cdot158\,4 = 2\cdot376$
$OD = OC + CD = AB + CD = 10\cdot125 + 2\cdot376$
$ = 12\cdot501$

Diameter at top of hole $= 2(12\cdot501) = 25\cdot002$.

Answer: Included angle $= 18°$
Diameter at large end $= 25\cdot0$ mm

220

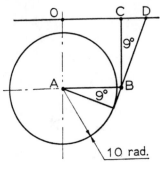

FIG. 4.43

The Sine-Bar

The sine-bar consists of two rollers of equal diameter whose centres are accurately positioned on a body. In use the sine-bar is tilted, either by resting on slip gauge piles as shown in Figure 4.44(*a*) or by being placed on an angular surface as shown in Figure 4.44(*b*).

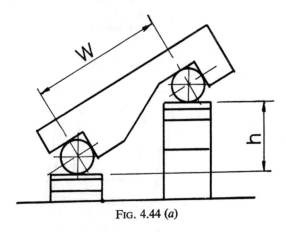

FIG. 4.44 (*a*)

In either case, the distance *h* is equal to the difference in height between the centres of the rollers.

If W = centre distance of rollers
and θ = angle of tilt of sine-bar
then $h = W \sin \theta$

221

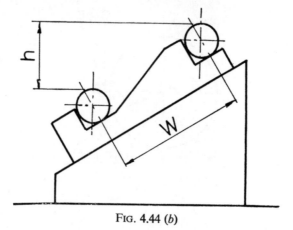

FIG. 4.44 (*b*)

To facilitate calculations, *W* is specifically made a convenient distance, such as 100 mm or 200 mm.

As the angle of tilt approaches 90°, the increment for a small difference of angle becomes less. Hence if an angle near 90° is to be checked or set using a sine-bar, greater accuracy can be obtained if use is made of a square with the sine-bar, so that the angle determined by the sine-bar is small (see Figure 4.44(*c*)).

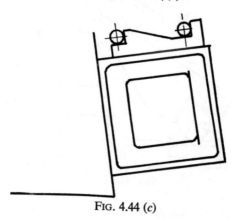

FIG. 4.44 (*c*)

Problems 4.4

1. Find the values of:

    (*a*) sin 22°   (*b*) sin 67°   (*c*) sin 8° 12′
    (*d*) sin 81° 18′   (*e*) sin 29° 53′   (*f*) sin 62° 3′

2. Find the values of:

   (*a*) cos 14° (*b*) cos 53° (*c*) cos 62° 48'
   (*d*) cos 8° 30' (*e*) cos 0° 50' (*f*) cos 69° 9'

3. Find the values of:

   (*a*) tan 81° (*b*) tan 16° (*c*) tan 0° 48'
   (*d*) tan 52° 30' (*e*) tan 9° 51' (*f*) tan 62° 20'

4. Find the values, where the angle lies between 0° and 90°, of:

   (*a*) arcsin 0·927 2 (*b*) arcsin 0·374 6 (*c*) arcsin 0·504 5
   (*d*) arcsin 0·917 8 (*e*) arcsin 0·750 0 (*f*) arcsin 0·380 6

5. Find the values, where the angle lies between 0° and 90°, of:

   (*a*) arccos 0·515 0 (*b*) arccos 0·970 3 (*c*) arccos 0·863 4
   (*d*) arccos 0·400 3 (*e*) arccos 0·449 6 (*f*) arccos 0·699 9

6. Find the values, where the angle lies between 0° and 90°, of:

   (*a*) arctan 3·270 9 (*b*) arctan 0·900 4 (*c*) arctan 2·808 3
   (*d*) arctan 0·240 1 (*e*) arctan 2·001 4 (*f*) arctan 0·520 2

7. In the following question, each answer should state one value only, but if two answers are equally appropriate from four-figure tables, take the even value. If three answers seem equally appropriate, take the central value. If there are four, take the even value of the central two, and so on. The angles lie between 0° and 90°.

   Find the values of:

   (*a*) arcsin 0·261 4 (*b*) arccos 0·307 8 (*c*) arctan 1·590 2
   (*d*) arcsin 0·763 2 (*e*) arcsin 0·987 2 (*f*) arccos 0·342 7
   (*g*) arccos 0·990 6 (*h*) arccos 0·999 0 (*j*) arccos 0·996 0

8. In a right-angled triangle, the hypotenuse has a length of 15 mm and the shortest side a length of 9 mm. Find the length of the other side and the magnitudes of the two acute angles.

9. The distance from a point *P* to the centre of a circle of diameter 36 mm is 42 mm. Determine the angle between the two tangents drawn from *P* to the circle.

10. A drill point has an included angle of 118°. A hole of diameter 20 mm has to be drilled so that the depth of full diameter is 48 mm. Calculate the depth to which the point of the drill has to be fed.

11. A spindle is tapered, and two measurements taken axially 160 mm apart indicate diameters of 88 mm and 64 mm. Calculate the included angle of the taper.

12. A pendulum has a length of 320 mm. The maximum swing from the centre is 18° 25′. What is the vertical distance between the maximum and minimum heights of the moving end of the pendulum?

13. Figure 4.45 shows the details of a groove in a pulley for a vee-belt drive. Calculate the distance x.

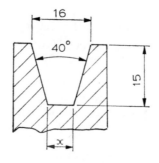

Fig. 4.45

14. Nine holes lie equally spaced on a pitch circle diameter. The direct distance between the centres of two adjacent holes is 51·3 mm. Calculate the pitch circle diameter.

15. An open belt connects two pulleys of diameters 380 mm and 200 mm, the centre distance of the pulleys being 410 mm. Calculate the included angle between the straight portions of the belt.

16. Figure 4.46 shows a corner in which a radius has to be drawn so as to be tangential at points P. Determine the magnitude of this radius, and the shortest distance x from the curve to the sharp corner.

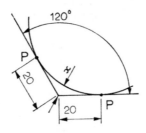

FIG. 4.46

17. Calculate the co-ordinate distances x and y of the centre of the hole shown in Figure 4.47.

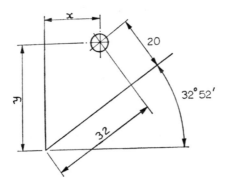

FIG. 4.47

18. Two guy-ropes are attached to a vertical pole, each guy-rope being 20 m long. In plan, the guy-ropes are at right angles. Each meets the ground at an angle of 70° to the horizontal. Determine the distance between their ground attachments.

19. Calculate the distance across corners of a hexagon which measures 64 mm across flats.

20. Calculate the setting for a 200 mm sine-bar to measure an angle of 8° 43′.

21. Ten holes lie equally spaced on a pitch circle diameter of 80 mm. Calculate the chordal distance between two adjacent holes.

225

22. Calculate the nominal pitch circle diameter of a sprocket wheel having 36 teeth suitable for a chain of pitch 20 mm.

23. Calculate the included vertical angle and the slant height of a cone having a base diameter of 80 mm and a vertical height of 120 mm.

24. The profile of a cam consists of circles of radii 10 mm and 30 mm lying at a centre distance of 60 mm. The radii are joined by tangents. Calculate the angle between the tangents.

25. Calculate the angle A on the template shown in Figure 4.48.

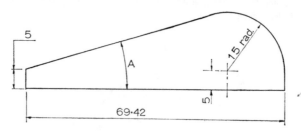

FIG. 4.48

26. Calculate the checking distance W for the dovetail slot shown in Figure 4.49.

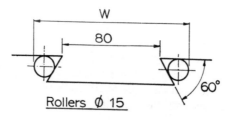

FIG. 4.49

27. Calculate the included angle of the taper of a standard milling machine spindle nose. It is designated 7/24, i.e. the diameter reduces by 7 mm for every 24 mm of axial travel.

28. Calculate the taper on diameter, in millimetres per metre of axial travel, that corresponds to an included angle of 5°.

29. Calculate the helix angle of an M36 metric thread which has an outside diameter of 36 mm and a pitch of 4 mm. The effective diameter is equal to the outside diameter minus 0·65 of the pitch.

30. A bar tapers from a distance of 80 mm to a diameter of 40 mm over a length of 40 mm. If all of these sizes are subjected to limits of ± 0·5 mm, calculate the maximum and minimum possible included angles of the taper.

31. Figure 4.50 shows a 20 mm square boring tool correctly set. The cutting rake and clearance angles are both equal to 8°.

    (*a*) Determine the minimum diameter of hole that can be cut.

    (*b*) If the tool is maintained in a horizontal position but the top edge is 5 mm below centre, calculate the effective cutting rake and clearance angles when cutting a diameter of 200 mm.

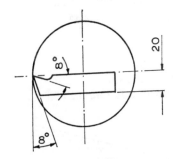

Fig. 4.50

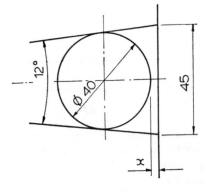

Fig. 4.51

32. Figure 4.51 shows a taper feature being checked with the aid of a disc of diameter 40 mm. Calculate the distance x.

33. Calculate the checking distance W of the asymmetrical dovetail slot shown in Figure 4.52.

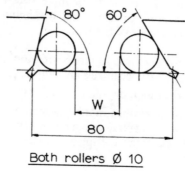

Both rollers Ø 10

FIG. 4.52

34. Calculate:
    (a) the included angle,
    (b) the setting for a 100 mm sine bar,
    for the wedge shown in Figure 4.53.

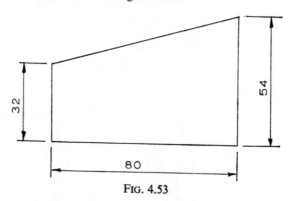

FIG. 4.53

35. Figure 4.54 shows a portion of a gusset plate. P represents the centre of a drilled hole which has a diameter of 20 mm. Calculate:
    (a) the angle AOP;
    (b) the distance OP;
    (c) the thickness of metal x.

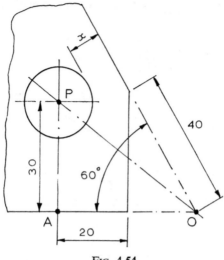

FIG. 4.54

36. A vee-groove is cut in a circular shaft of diameter 40 mm; the width at the top of the groove is 20 mm and the distance from the apex of the vee to the outside of the shaft is 30 mm. Calculate the included angle of the vee.

37. Calculate, with reference to axes OY and OX, the co-ordinates of the holes A, B and C shown in Figure 4.55.

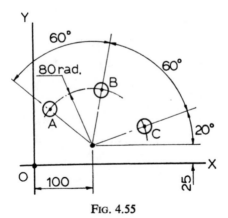

FIG. 4.55

229

38. Calculate the co-ordinates *A*, *B*, *C* and *D* of the gusset corner shown in Figure 4.56.

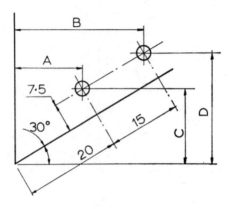

FIG. 4.56

39. (*a*) From the information contained on the template in Figure 4.57 obtain two different expressions for the height *H* in terms of *x*.

(*b*) Equate these expressions and solve the equation for *x*.

(*c*) Use the value of *x* found in (*b*) to determine *H*.

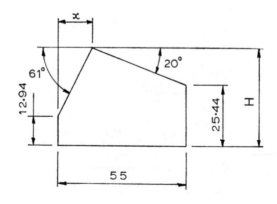

FIG. 4.57

40. A crossed-belt drive connects pulleys of diameter 200 mm and 480 mm at a centre distance of 600 mm. Calculate:

    (*a*) the point at which the straight portions cross measured from the centre of the smaller pulley;

    (*b*) the included acute angle of the straight portions of the belt drive.

41. Calculate the co-ordinates *A*, *B*, *C* and *D* of the holes shown in Figure 4.58.

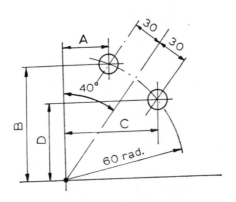

FIG. 4.58

42. Calculate the included angle θ and the dimension *x* of the layout shown in Figure 4.59.

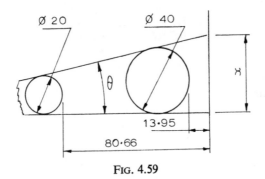

FIG. 4.59

43. Calculate the checking dimensions W_1 and W_2 for the taper plug gauge shown in Figure 4.60.

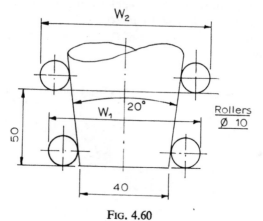

Fig. 4.60

Answers 4.4

1. (a) 0·374 6   (b) 0·920 5   (c) 0·142 6
    (d) 0·988 5   (e) 0·498 3   (f) 0·883 3
2. (a) 0·970 3   (b) 0·601 8   (c) 0·457 1
    (d) 0·989 0   (e) 0·999 9   (f) 0·355 9
3. (a) 6·313 8   (b) 0·286 7   (c) 0·014 0
    (d) 1·303 2   (e) 0·173 6   (f) 1·907 4
4. (a) 68°   (b) 22°   (c) 30° 18′
    (d) 66° 36′   (e) 48° 35′   (f) 22° 22′
5. (a) 59°   (b) 14°   (c) 30° 18′
    (d) 66° 24′   (e) 63° 17′   (f) 45° 35′
6. (a) 73°   (b) 42°   (c) 70° 24′
    (d) 13° 30′   (e) 63° 27′   (f) 27° 29′
7. (a) 15° 9′   (b) 72° 4′   (c) 57° 50′
    (d) 49° 44′   (e) 80° 50′   (f) 69° 58′
    (g) 7° 50′   (h) 2° 34′   (j) 5° 6′
8. 12 mm, 36° 52′, 53° 8′
9. 50° 44′
10. 54·0 mm
11. 8° 34′
12. 16·4 mm
13. 5·08 mm
14. 150 mm
15. 25° 22′

16. 34·6 mm, 5·4 mm
17. $x = 16·0$ mm, $y = 34·2$ mm
18. 9·67 m
19. 73·9 mm
20. 30·3 mm
21. 24·7 mm
22. 229 mm
23. 36° 52′, 126 mm
24. 38° 56′
25. 16° 0′
26. 121 mm
27. 16° 36′
28. 87·4 mm
29. 2° 11′
30. 54° 52′ and 51° 25′
31. (*a*) 145 mm   (*b*) 10° 52′ and 5° 8′
32. 2·74 mm
33. 55·4 mm
34. (*a*) 15° 22′   (*b*) 26·5 mm
35. (*a*) 36° 52′   (*b*) 50 mm   (*c*) 9·64 mm
36. 107° 36′
37. $A = (38·7$ mm, 76·4 mm) $B = (114$ mm, 104 mm)
    $C = (175$ mm, 52·4 mm)
38. $A = 13·6$ mm $B = 26·6$ mm $C = 16·5$ mm
    $D = 24·0$ mm
39. (*a*) $12·94 + 1·804 x$ and $45·46 − 0·364 x$
    (*b*) $x = 15·0$ mm   (*c*) $H = 40·0$ mm
40. (*a*) 176 mm   (*b*) 69° 2′
41. $A = 10·4$ mm $B = 59·1$ mm $C = 56·4$ mm
    $D = 20·5$ mm
42. $\theta = 20°$ 0′, $x = 53·6$ mm
43. $W_1 = 61·9$ mm $W_2 = 79·5$ mm

4.5   Trigonometrical Ratios of Angles Greater than 90°

Article 4.1 was introduced by stating that there is no limit to the magnitude of an angle. We have already considered the trigonometrical ratios of angles up to and including 90° and we shall proceed to the trigonometrical ratios of angles greater than 90°, commencing with the basic ratios of sine, cosine and tangent. The reader will recall that we represented an angle by considering a rotating arm *OP*, the end *O* being coincident with the origin of cartesian coordinates, as shown in Figure 4.61 overleaf.

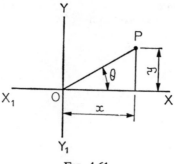

FIG. 4.61

The arm OP was made of unit length, hence:

$$\sin \theta = \frac{\text{side opposite } \theta}{\text{hypotenuse } \theta} = \frac{y}{1} = y$$

$$\cos \theta = \frac{\text{side adjacent } \theta}{\text{hypotenuse } \theta} = \frac{x}{1} = x$$

$$\tan \theta = \frac{\text{side opposite } \theta}{\text{side adjacent } \theta} = \frac{y}{x}$$

When θ is acute, P lies in the first quadrant. In this quadrant values of x and of y are positive. Hence, when θ is acute, $\sin \theta$, $\cos \theta$ and $\tan \theta$ are all positive ratios.

When θ is greater than 90°, we still take the values of y, x and $\frac{y}{x}$ as the sine, cosine and tangent respectively. By considering the quadrants in turn we can deduce the following table for the arithmetical sign of the basic trigonometric ratios:

Quadrant	sine = y	cosine = x	tangent = y/x
First	positive	positive	positive
Second	positive	negative	negative
Third	negative	negative	positive
Fourth	negative	positive	negative

This information can be presented in a different manner by indicating in the appropriate quadrant only the positive values which occur. They are, in the sequence of the quadrants, 'all, sin, tan, cos' as shown in Figure 4.62.

FIG. 4.62

Having established the arithmetical sign for the sine, the cosine, and the tangent of an angle, we now have to determine the magnitude discounting the sign. If we nominate a 'principal' angle of θ, we observe that the numerical values of y and x, if the signs are discounted, are the same for $(180° - \theta)$, $(180° + \theta)$ and $(360° - \theta)$.

The steps in determining the sine, or the cosine, or the tangent of an angle between 90° and 360° are therefore as follows:

1. Determine the arithmetical sign from the four-quadrant series of positive values, 'all, sin, tan, cos'.
2. Determine a principal value by establishing a difference from 180° or 360°. This difference will lie between zero and 90°.
3. Establish the desired ratio of the principal value.
4. Couple the arithmetical sign with the numerical value.

In setting out the working, the reader will find the use of straight brackets to be of assistance. A pair of straight brackets indicates *the numerical value neglecting the arithmetical sign*. Thus $|\cos 172°|$ means 'the cosine of 172° neglecting its arithmetical sign'.

Example

Determine the values of:

    (a) sin 168° 23'   (b) cos 247° 32'   (c) tan 315°

(a) 168° 23' falls in the second quadrant. Sign of sin is positive.
    Principal value $= 180° - 168° 23' = 11° 37'$
    $|\sin 168° 23'|\ = \sin 11° 37'\ \ \ = 0{\cdot}201\ 4$
    $\sin 168° 23'\ \ \ = +0{\cdot}201\ 4$

(b) 247° 32' falls in the third quadrant. Sign of cos is negative.
    Principal value $= 247° 32' - 180° = 67° 32'$
    $\cos 247° 32'|\ = \cos 67° 32'\ \ \ = 0{\cdot}382\ 2$
    $\cos 247° 32'\ \ \ = -0{\cdot}382\ 2$

(c) 315° falls in the fourth quadrant. Sign of tan is negative.
    Principal value $= 360° - 315°$ $= 45°$
    $|\tan 315°|$ $= \tan 45°$ $= 1$
    $\tan 315°$ $= -1$

         Answer: (a) $\sin 168° 23' = 0·201\ 4$
                  (b) $\cos 247° 32' = -0·382\ 2$
                  (c) $\tan 315°$ $= -1$

If we are given a trigonometric value, and asked for the angle or angles, we use a 'shorthand' manner of indicating the question. 'Find arctan 0·577 4' means 'find the angle whose tangent is 0·577 4'. Had we been asked this question during our previous studies we would have stated only the principal value of 30°. We now realize that a tangent is positive in the third quadrant as well as in the first. Consequently, there is a second value which answers the question, i.e. $180° + 30°$ or $210°$. The reader should appreciate that if a logical numerical value is given, there are two valid angles within the range of zero and 360°.

(*There are, in fact, a multiplicity of angles, being these two angles plus whole number multiples of* 360°.

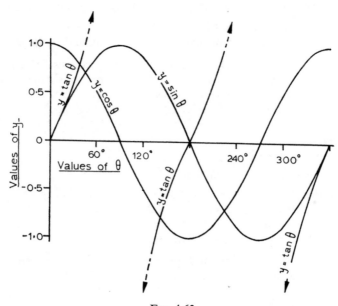

Fig. 4.63

arctan 0·577 4 is 30°, **390°**, **750°**, **1 110°**, etc.

and   210°, 570°, 930°, etc.

Unless stated to the contrary, it is assumed that only values in the range zero to 360° are desired.)

Before we proceed to numerical examples of trigonometrical ratios of angles greater than 90°, let us illustrate graphically how the ratios of sine, cosine and tangent change within the range of zero to 360°. The waves for the sine and the cosine repeat themselves at intervals of 360°, while the curve for the tangent repeats itself at intervals of 180°, as shown in Figure 4.63.

Example

In each of the following cases, find two angles between zero and 360°, such that:

    (*a*) $\sin A = 0{\cdot}611\ 5$ (*b*) $\cos B = 0{\cdot}432\ 1$ (*c*) $\tan C = -1{\cdot}732\ 1$

  (*a*)   Sin is positive in first and second quadrants
       Principal value $= \arcsin 0{\cdot}611\ 5 = 37°\ 42'$
       First value of A is 37° 42′
       Second value of A is $(180° - 37°\ 42') = 142°\ 18'$

  (*b*)   cos is positive in first and fourth quadrants
       Principal value $= \arccos 0{\cdot}432\ 1 = 64°\ 24'$
       First value of B is 64° 24′
       Second value of B is $(360° - 64°\ 24') = 295°\ 36'$

  (*c*)   tan is negative in second and fourth quadrants
       Principal value $= \arctan 1{\cdot}732\ 1 = 60°$
       First value of C is $(180° - 60°) = 120°$
       Second value of C is $(360° - 60°) = 300°$

            Answers: (*a*) $A = 37°\ 42'$ or 142° 18′
                   (*b*) $B = 64°\ 24'$ or 295° 36′
                   (*c*) $C = 120°$ or 300°

Example

Find the value of θ between zero and 360° which satisfies both equations:

$$\tan \theta = -0{\cdot}466\ 3 \qquad \cos \theta = -0{\cdot}906\ 3$$

tan is negative in second and fourth quadrants
Principal value $= \arctan 0{\cdot}466\ 3 = \quad 25°$
First value of θ is $(180° - 25°)\quad = 155°$
Second value of θ is $(360° - 25°) = 335°$

cos is negative in second and third quadrants
Principal value = arccos 0·906 3 = 25°
First value of θ is (180° − 25°) = 155°
Second value of θ is (180° + 25°) = 205°
arctan (−0·466 3) = 155° or 335°, arccos (−0·906 3) = 155° or
205°
The value of θ which satisfies both is 155°

Answer: $\theta = 155°$

The trigonometrical ratios of angles greater than 90° now have to
be extended to the reciprocal ratios of cosecant, secant and cotangent.
We have already stated that:

$$\text{cosec } \theta = \frac{1}{\sin \theta}, \text{ sec } \theta = \frac{1}{\cos \theta}, \text{ cot } \theta = \frac{1}{\tan \theta}$$

The pattern of signs is therefore identical with the ratios for sin,
cos and tan since positive divided by positive produces a positive
result and positive divided by negative produces a negative result.

We can therefore produce a second diagram, similar to Figure 4.62
which indicates in appropriate quadrants which ratios are positive.
This diagram is shown in Figure 4.64.

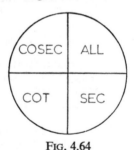

Fig. 4.64

The evaluation of ratios and angles follows the method for sin, cos
and tan.

Example

Find the values of:

    (*a*) cot 123° 51'   (*b*) sec 341° 17'   (*c*) cosec 263° 26'

(*a*)   cot is the reciprocal of tan
          123° 51' falls in the second quadrant
          Sign of tan (and cot) is negative

Principal value $= 180° - 123° 51' = 56° 9'$
$\cot 56° 9' = 0·670\ 7$
$\cot 123° 51' = -0·670\ 7$

(b)   sec is the reciprocal of cos
341° 17′ falls in the fourth quadrant
Sign of cos (and sec) is positive
Principal value $= 360° - 341° 17' = 18° 43'$
$\sec 18° 43' = 1·055\ 8$
$\sec 341° 17' = +1·055\ 8$

(c)   cosec is the reciprocal of sin
263° 26′ falls in the third quadrant
Sign of sin (and cosec) is negative
Principal value $= 263° 26' - 180° = 83° 26'$
$\operatorname{cosec} 83° 26' = 1·006\ 6$
$\operatorname{cosec} 263° 26' = -1·006\ 6$

Answers: (a) $\cot 123° 51'\quad = -0·670\ 7$
(b) $\sec 341° 17'\quad = 1·055\ 8$
(c) $\operatorname{cosec} 263° 26' = -1·006\ 6$

Example

Find two angles between zero and 360° for:

(a) arccot (0·600 9)   (b) arccosec (−1·045 4)
(c) arcsec (−1·496 7)

(a) cot is the reciprocal of tan
tan (and cot) is positive in the first and third quadrants
Principal value $=$ arccot $(0·600\ 9) = 59°$
First value is 59°
Second value is $(180° + 59°) = 239°$

(b) cosec is the reciprocal of sin
sin (and cosec) is negative in the third and fourth quadrants
Principal value $=$ arccosec $(1·045\ 4) = 73° 3'$ or $73° 4'$
Round off by rule to even value of 73° 4′
First value is $180° + 73° 4' = 253° 4'$
Second value is $360° - 73° 4' = 286° 56'$

(c) sec is the reciprocal of cos
cos (and sec) is negative in second and third quadrants
Principal value $=$ arcsec $(1·496\ 7) = 48° 4'$ (to nearest minute)
First value is $180° - 48° 4' = 131° 56'$
Second value is $180° + 48° 4' = 228° 4'$

Answers: (a) arccot (0·600 9) = 59° or 239°
(b) arccosec (−1·045 4) = 253° 4′ or 286° 56′
(c) arcsec (−1·496 7) = 131° 56′ or 288° 4′

Problems 4.5

1. Determine the values of:
   (a) sin 147° 34′   (b) cos 236° 22′   (c) tan 250°

2. Using tables, find the values of:
   sin 156° 4′   cos 157°   tan 258°

3. In each of the following cases, find two angles between 0° and 360° such that:
   (a) sin A = 0·461 2   (b) cos B = 0·704 0   (c) tan C = −1

4. Evaluate using tables:
   (a) sin 560°   (b) cos $\left(\dfrac{5\pi}{6}\right)$ (c) tan (−160°)

5. Find the values of θ between 0° and 360° which satisfy:
   (a) sin θ = −0·898 8   (b) cos θ = −0·438 4
   Which value of θ satisfies both (a) and (b)?

6. Find the value of θ between 0° and 360° which satisfies both the equations:
   sin θ = 0·882 9   cos θ = −0·469 5

7. If A is an acute angle and tan A = $\dfrac{5}{12}$, calculate, without tables, the value of cos A sin (180° − A).

8. Find the values of:
   (a) sin 153° 40′   (b) tan 240°   (c) cos 0·6 radians

9. Find the values of:
   (a) sin 253° 28′   (b) cos 63° 46′   (c) tan $\dfrac{\pi}{6}$

10. Find the values of:
    (a) sin 2·5 radians   (b) cos 126° 14′
    (c) the angles less than 360° whose tangent is 1·324 6

11. Find the value, correct to three significant figures, of
$$2 \tan 2\theta - 3 \cos 3\theta$$
when $\theta = 47° 45'$

12. (*a*) State the values of:

   (i) $\tan 143° 35'$ (ii) $\sin \left(\dfrac{11}{18} \pi \text{ radians} \right)$

   (*b*) If $I = 70·7 \sin \left(100\pi t + \dfrac{\pi}{4} \right)$, calculate the value of I when $t = 0·01$.

13. Draw on the same axes, graphs of $\sin \theta$ and $\cos \theta$ for values of θ from 0° to 360°. From your graphs find the values of θ for which the sine and cosine are equal.

14. Plot the graph of $y = \sin 2\theta$ for values of θ between 0° and 360°. From your graph, read off the values of to the nearest degree when:

   (*a*) $y = +0·5$ (*b*) $y = -0·5$

15. Draw the graphs of $y = 3 \cos x$ and $y = 4 \sin x$ on the same axes at intervals of 30° from $x = 0$ to $x = 180°$. Use these two graphs to sketch the graph of $y = 3 \cos x + 4 \sin x$ and estimate the value of x to satisfy the equation:
$$3 \cos x + 4 \sin x = 0$$

16. Draw the graph of $y = 3 \cos 2x + 8 \cos x$ between the values of $x = 0°$ and $x = 90°$. Hence determine approximately an acute angle x such that:
$$3 \cos 2x + 8 \cos x = 5$$

17. Compile a table to show the values of:

   (*a*) $y = 3 \sin (\theta + 60°)$ (*b*) $y = \cos 2\theta$
   and hence (*c*) $y = 3 \sin (\theta + 60°) + \cos 2\theta$

   for values of θ at intervals of 10° between $\theta = 0°$ to $\theta = 90°$. Plot the graph of $y = 3 \sin (\theta + 60°) + \cos 2\theta$ between $\theta = 0°$ and $\theta = 90°$ and determine the value of θ within this range for which:
$$3 \sin (\theta + 60°) + \cos 2\theta = 3$$

Answers to Problems 4.5

1. (*a*) 0·536 3   (*b*) −0·553 8   (*c*) 2·747 5
2. 0·405 6, −0·920 5, 4·704 6
3. (*a*) $A = 27° 28'$ or $152° 32'$ (*b*) $B = 45° 15'$ or $314° 45'$
   (*c*) $C = 135°$ or $315°$
4. (*a*) −0·342 0   (*b*) −0·866 0   (*c*) 0·364 0
5. (*a*) $\theta = 244°$ or $296°$ (*b*) $116°$ or $244°$
   $\theta = 244°$ satisfies both
6. 118°
7. $\dfrac{60}{169}$
8. (*a*) 0·443 6   (*b*) 1·732 1   (*c*) 0·825 3
9. (*a*) −0·958 6   (*b*) 0·442 1   (*c*) 0·577 4
10. (*a*) 0·598 5   (*b*) −0·591 1   (*c*) $52° 57'$ or $232° 57'$
11. −20·78 + 2·403 9 = 18·4 to three significant figures
12. (*a*) (i) −0·737 8; (ii) 0·939 7   (*b*) −50·0
13. 45° and 225°
14. (*a*) 15°, 75°, 195° and 255°
    (*b*) 105°, 165°, 285° and 345°
15. 143°
16. 48°
17. 43°

4.6 The Sine Rule and the Cosine Rule

4.6.1 THE SINE RULE

Let us consider a triangle *ABC* which has an acute angle at *A* and an obtuse angle at *B*, as shown in Figure 4.65(*a*).

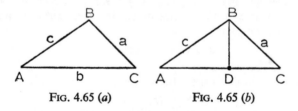

FIG. 4.65 (*a*)   FIG. 4.65 (*b*)

The triangle has been repeated in Figure 4.65(*b*) with a perpendicular dropped from *B* on to side *AC* at *D*.

Length of perpendicular $BD = c \sin A = a \sin C$

hence
$$\frac{a}{\sin A} = \frac{c}{\sin C}$$

For ease of presentation, let us rotate the triangle so that c becomes the base, as shown in Figure 4.66(*a*).

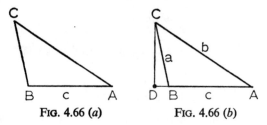

FIG. 4.66 (*a*)   FIG. 4.66 (*b*)

This triangle has been repeated in Figure 4.66(*b*) with a perpendicular dropped from C on to a continuation of side c at D.

Length of perpendicular $CD = b \sin A = a \sin (180° - B)$
$$\sin (180° - B) = \sin B$$
$$\therefore b \sin A = a \sin B$$

and
$$\frac{a}{\sin A} = \frac{b}{\sin B}$$

Since
$$\frac{a}{\sin A} = \frac{b}{\sin B}$$

and
$$\frac{a}{\sin A} = \frac{c}{\sin C}$$

we can write
$$\frac{a}{\sin A} = \frac{b}{\sin B} = \frac{c}{\sin C}$$

The previous deduction considered a triangle with an obtuse angle. We would have repeated the first part of the deduction for the second angle of a triangle with three acute angles. The relationship is true both for a triangle with an obtuse angle and two acute angles, or a triangle with three acute angles.

In Figure 4.67, *ABC* is a right-angled triangle.

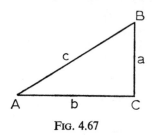

FIG. 4.67

Now
$$\frac{a}{c} = \sin A, \quad c = \frac{a}{\sin A}$$

and
$$\frac{b}{c} = \sin B, \quad c = \frac{b}{\sin B}$$

and
$$c = \frac{c}{\sin C} \text{ since } \sin C = \sin 90° = 1$$

Hence, once more $\dfrac{a}{\sin A} = \dfrac{b}{\sin B} = \dfrac{c}{\sin C}$

This relationship is therefore true for *any* triangle, whether it be right-angled or not.

In Figure 4.68, *ABC* is a triangle with a circumscribed circle.

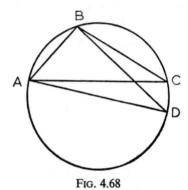

Fɪɢ. 4.68

AD is a diameter of the circumscribed circle. *ABD* is a right-angled triangle, *B* being the angle in a semicircle.

We will let the radius of the circumscribed circle be *r*. In triangle *ABD*, $AB = 2r \sin D$

Now angle D = angle C, being angles subtended at the circumference of a circle by the same chord. Hence:

$$AB = 2r \sin C,$$

and
$$2r = \frac{AB}{\sin C} = \frac{c}{\sin C} \text{ in triangle } ABC$$

In triangle *ABC*:

$$\frac{a}{\sin A} = \frac{b}{\sin B} = \frac{c}{\sin C}$$

and we now know that $\dfrac{c}{\sin C} = 2r$

hence finally we can say that:

In any triangle *ABC*, whether it be right-angled or not

$$\frac{a}{\sin A} = \frac{b}{\sin B} = \frac{c}{\sin C} = D$$

where *D* is the diameter of the circumscribing circle.

This relationship shows that in *any* triangle, the ratio of the length of a side to the sine of the angle opposite that side is constant, being equal to the diameter of the circumscribing circle. The relationship is commonly referred to as the *sine rule*.

The reader has already been advised when solving questions involving trigonometry to use scale diagrams to check the accuracy of working. This is particularly true when using the sine rule. A step may occur where he has to establish arcsin θ. He must note carefully that there are two angles in the range zero to 180° for θ (excluding the unusual case of $\theta = 90°$). If the angle is reasonably larger or smaller than 90°, a scale diagram will generally indicate which value of θ is logical. In certain circumstances both values of θ may be logical. (A worked example which follows illustrates this point.) If only one value is logical, the reader is reminded that if all three angles in a triangle are determined, they total 180°. This fact will often help to eliminate illogical values. The use of the sine rule when one angle in the triangle is obtuse can result in an ambiguity. The circumstances are referred to mathematically as the 'ambiguous case'.

Example

In Figure 4.69(*a*), from a point *A* on the roof of a workshop the angle of elevation to the top of a chimney *EC* is 32°, and from *B* on

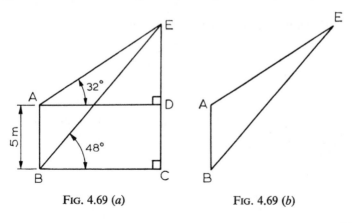

FIG. 4.69 (*a*)   FIG. 4.69 (*b*)

the ground 5 m vertically below *A* it is 48°. Show that $\angle AEB$ is 16°. Apply the sine rule to triangle *AEB* to find the distance *BE* and hence calculate the height of the chimney *EC*.

Figure 4.69(*b*) shows triangle *AEB* extracted from the original diagram.

$$B = 90° - 48° = 42° \qquad A = 90° + 32° = 122°$$
$$A + B + E = 180°$$
$$\angle AEB = E = 180° - (A + B) = 180° - (122° + 42°)$$
$$= 180° - 164° \qquad = 16° \qquad \text{(Q.E.D.)}$$

In triangle *ABE*:

$$\frac{AB}{\sin E} = \frac{BE}{\sin A}$$

$$\therefore BE = \frac{AB \sin A}{\sin E} = \frac{5 \sin 122°}{\sin 16°}$$

$$= \frac{5 \sin 58°}{\sin 16°} \text{ since } \sin 122° = \sin (180° - 122°)$$

$$= 15 \cdot 38$$

No.	Log
5 sin 58°	0·699 0 $\bar{1}$·928 4
sin 16°	0·627 4 $\bar{1}$·440 3
15·38	1·187 1

Rough check: $\dfrac{5 \times 0 \cdot 84}{0 \cdot 28} = 15$

Referring back to Figure 4.69(*a*), in triangle *BCE*:

$$CE = BE \sin 48°$$
$$= 15 \cdot 38 \sin 48°$$
$$= 11 \cdot 44$$

No.	Log
15·38 sin 48°	1·187 1 $\bar{1}$·871 1
11·44	1·058 2

Rough check: $16 \times 0 \cdot 75 = 12$

Answer: Height of chimney = 11·4 m

Example

A, B and C are the centres of three holes on the front of an instrument panel, these holes lying on a pitch circle. If a triangle ABC is constructed, $AB = 118·2$ mm, $A = 65°$ and $B = 63°$. Obtain the pitch circle diameter and the distances BC and CA.

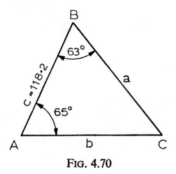

FIG. 4.70

The triangle is shown in Figure 4.70.

$$A + B + C = 180°$$
$$C = 180° - A - B$$
$$= 180° - 65° - 63°$$
$$= 52°$$

$$\frac{AB}{\sin C} = \frac{BC}{\text{si } A} = \frac{CA}{\sin B} = D$$

where D is the diameter of the circumscribing circle, which is the pitch circle diameter.

$$D = \frac{AB}{\sin C} = \frac{118·2}{\sin 52°} = 150·0$$

No.	Log
118·2	2·072 6
sin 52°	$\bar{1}$·896 5
150·0	2·176 1

Rough check: $\dfrac{120}{0·8} = 150$

$$\frac{BC}{\sin A} = \frac{AB}{\sin C} = \frac{CA}{\sin B} = 150·0$$

247

$$BC = 150 \sin A \quad = 150 \sin 65°$$
$$= 150 \times 0.906\,3 = 135.945$$
$$CA = 150 \sin B \quad = 150 \sin 63°$$
$$= 150 \times 0.891\,0 = 133.65$$

Answers: Pitch circle diameter = 150 mm
$$BC = 136 \text{ mm}$$
$$CA = 134 \text{ mm}$$

The following example illustrates the 'ambiguous case' referred to previously.

Example

Figure 4.71 shows the elements of a crank and connecting rod mechanism. The crank OA is of length 75 mm and rotates about O. The connecting rod AB is of length 200 mm. Calculate the crank angle BOA so that the angle of obliquity of the connecting rod (angle B) is 17°. (Restrict the values to range zero to 180°.)

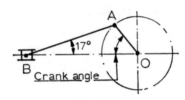

Fig. 4.71

$$\frac{OA}{\sin B} = \frac{AB}{\sin O}$$

$$\therefore \sin O = \frac{AB \sin B}{OA}$$

$$\sin O = \frac{200 \times \sin 17°}{75} = \frac{8 \times 0.292\,4}{3}$$

$$= 0.779\,7$$
$$O = \arcsin 0.779\,7$$

sin is positive in the first and second quadrants
Principal value = $\arcsin 0.779\,7 = 51° \ 14'$
First value = 51° 14′
Second value = 180° − 51° 14′ = 128° 46′

Answers: Crank angle is 51° 14′ or 128° 46′

The above ambiguous case is illustrated in Figure 4.72.

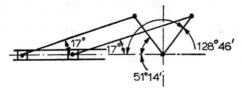

Fɪɢ. 4.72

4.6.2 ᴛʜᴇ ᴄᴏsɪɴᴇ ʀᴜʟᴇ

It is possible to deduce another formula to assist the solving of triangles which helps to avoid the ambiguity regarding the value of an angle. The cosine of an angle is positive for angles between zero and 90°, and negative for those between 90° and 180°. Hence if a value is obtained for the cosine of an angle, there can be one angle only between 0 and 180° which is applicable.

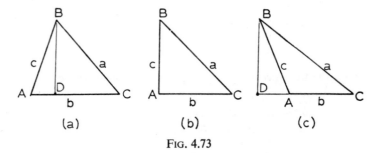

Fɪɢ. 4.73

Referring to Figure 4.73:

$$BD = a \sin C$$
$$DC = a \cos C$$
$$\therefore AD = AC - DC = b - a \cos C$$

Applying the Theorem of Pythagoras to the triangle ABD:

$$(AB)^2 = (BD)^2 + (AD)^2$$
$$c^2 = (a \sin C)^2 + (b - a \cos C)^2$$
$$= a^2 \sin^2 C + b^2 - 2ab \cos C + a^2 \cos^2 C$$
$$= a^2 (\sin^2 C + \cos^2 C) + b^2 - 2ab \cos C$$
$$\therefore c^2 = a^2 + b^2 - 2ab \cos C \text{ (since } \sin^2 C + \cos^2 C = 1)$$

a relationship we shall prove in the next article.

In a similar manner, the relationships:

$$b^2 = a^2 + c^2 - 2ac \cos B \quad \text{and} \quad a^2 = b^2 + c^2 - 2bc \cos A$$

can be obtained by dropping perpendiculars from A and C on to the opposite sides.

Referring to Figure 4.73(*b*), the relationship:

$$a^2 = b^2 + c^2 - 2bc \cos A$$

is true, since A is a right-angle and $\cos A = 0$,

$$a^2 = b^2 + c^2$$

being the application of the Theorem of Pythagoras.

By dropping a perpendicular from A on to BC, and using a similar manner to a preceding paragraph, the relationships:

$$b^2 = c^2 + a^2 - 2ac \cos B \quad \text{or} \quad c^2 = a^2 + b^2 - 2ab \cos C$$

can be deduced.

In Figure 4.73(*c*):

$$BD = c \sin A$$
$$DA = c \cos (180° - A) = -c \cos A$$
$$DC = AC + AD = b - c \cos A$$

Applying the Theorem of Pythagoras to triangle BDC:

$$(BC)^2 = (BD)^2 + (CD)^2$$
$$\therefore \ a^2 = (c \sin A)^2 + (b - c \cos A)^2$$
$$\therefore \ a^2 = c^2 \sin^2 A + b^2 - 2bc \cos A + c^2 \cos^2 A$$
$$= c^2 (\sin^2 A + \cos^2 A) + b^2 - 2bc \cos A$$
$$\therefore \ a^2 = b^2 + c^2 - 2bc \cos A$$

The other equations including $\cos B$ and $\cos C$ can be deduced by dropping perpendiculars from A and C.

Thus in any triangle:

$$a^2 = b^2 + c^2 - 2bc \cos A$$
or
$$b^2 = a^2 + c^2 - 2ac \cos B$$
or
$$c^2 = a^2 + b^2 - 2ab \cos C$$

These equations are formulae which state that *in any triangle, whether it be right-angled or not, the square of a particular side is the sum of the squares of the other two sides minus twice the product of the other two sides and the cosine of the angle opposite the particular side.* This is known as the *cosine rule.*

Example

Three holes lie on a pitch circle at chordal distances of 6·472 mm, 6·928 mm and 7·308 mm. Determine the diameter of the pitch circle and the angle subtended at the centre by the chord of 6·472 mm.

Figure 4.74 shows a scale drawing. By measurement the pitch circle diameter is about 8 mm and the angle subtended by the 6·472 chord is about 110°.

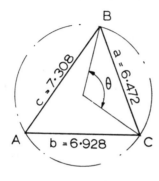

Fɪɢ. 4.74

Since three sides of a triangle are given, the cosine rule must be used. We shall find the smallest angle, which will be opposite the smallest side, in this case angle A.

$$a^2 = b^2 + c^2 - 2bc \cos A, \quad 2bc \cos A = b^2 + c^2 - a^2$$

$$\cos A = \frac{b^2 + c^2 - a^2}{2bc} = \frac{(6 \cdot 928)^2 + (7 \cdot 308)^2 - (6 \cdot 472)^2}{2 \times 6 \cdot 928 \times 7 \cdot 308}$$

No.	Log
2	0·301 0
6·928	0·840 6
7·308	0·863 8
Denom.	2·005 4
59·51	1·774 6
Denom.	2·005 4
cos 54°	$\overline{1}$·769 2

Using tables of squares:

$$\cos A = \frac{48 \cdot 00 + 53 \cdot 40 - 41 \cdot 89}{\text{Denom.}}$$

$$= \frac{59 \cdot 51}{\text{Denom.}}$$

$$\therefore A = 54°$$

Rough check:

$$\frac{60}{2 \times 7 \times 7 \cdot 5} = \frac{60}{105} = \frac{4}{7}$$

$$= \text{about } 0 \cdot 57 = \cos 55° \text{ roughly}$$

ɪ

251

$$D = \frac{a}{\sin A} = \frac{6{\cdot}472}{\sin 54°} = \frac{6{\cdot}472}{0{\cdot}809} = 8{\cdot}000$$

The angle subtended by a chord at the centre of a circle is twice that subtended at the circumference, hence angle subtended = twice 54° = 108°

Answer: Pitch circle diameter = 8·00 mm
Angle subtended = 108°

Example

In the crank and connecting-rod mechanism of a feed mechanism shown in Figure 4.75, the crank rotates at 120 rev/min. For the

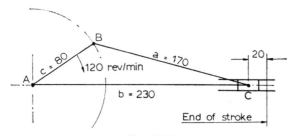

Fig. 4.75

position indicated, i.e. when the crosshead is 20 mm from dead centre, calculate:

(*a*) the crank angle A;
(*b*) the time it will take the crosshead to travel a further 20 mm to reach dead centre.

All three sides of the triangle are known, hence initially the cosine rule will be applied:

$$a^2 = b^2 + c^2 - 2bc \cos A, \quad 2bc \cos A = b^2 + c^2 - a^2$$

Let us work in centimetres to ease the calculations:

$$\cos A = \frac{b^2 + c^2 - a^2}{2bc} = \frac{23^2 + 8^2 - 17^2}{2 \times 8 \times 23} = \frac{529 + 64 - 289}{16 \times 23}$$

$$= \frac{593 - 289}{16 \times 23} = \frac{304}{16 \times 23} = \frac{19}{23} = 0{\cdot}826\,1$$

$$A = 34° \; 18'$$

The crank rotates 1 rev in 0·5 second:

$$\therefore \text{ time to rotate } 34° \, 18' = \frac{34° \, 18'}{360°} \times 0·5$$

$$= \frac{34·3 \times 0·5}{360}$$

$$= \frac{17·15}{360} = 0·047 \, 6 \text{ second}$$

Answer: (a) Crank angle $A = 34° \, 18'$
(b) Time to reach outer dead centre $= 0·047 \, 6$ second

Problems 4.6

1. In a triangle PQR, $q = 10$, $R = 30°$ and $P = 68°$. Find the value of r using the sine rule.

2. In a triangle ABC, side AB is 100 mm long, angle ABC is 135°, and angle ACB is 15°. Calculate the length of side BC.

3. In a triangle ABC, the side AB is 80 mm long. The angles ABC and BAC are 100° and 30° respectively. Calculate the length of side BC.

4. In a triangle ABC, the side AB is 100 mm long, angle CAB is 30° and angle ACB is 45°. Draw the triangle and calculate:

   (a) the length of the side BC;
   (b) the angle ABC;
   (c) the length of the side AC.

5. In Figure 4.76, AB represents an electricity supply, the distance AB being 5 km. C represents the position of a factory, such that $\angle CAB = 32°$ and $\angle ABC = 48°$. Calculate:

   (a) the distance BC;
   (b) the shortest distance from the factory to the supply, i.e. distance CD.

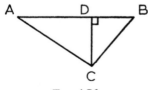

Fig. 4.76

6. Figure 4.77 shows the dimensioning of the centres of three holes, *A*, *B* and *C*, on an instrument panel. Calculate the distance *AB*, and the radius of the circle that passes through the centres of the three holes.

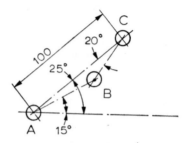

FIG. 4.77

7. Figure 4.78 shows a triangle of forces diagram. Calculate the magnitude of the forces denoted by F_1 and F_2.

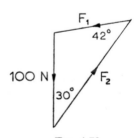

FIG. 4.78

8. Figure 4.79 shows a mechanism which allows the slotted link *OR* to have a limited rotation about pivot *O*. Link *PQ* has a peg 60 mm from *P* which slides in the slot in link *OR*. The slot prevents the angle *ROP* becoming less than 30°. Calculate:

   (*a*) the two values of angle *QPO* when angle *ROP* is 30°;
   (*b*) the corresponding values of distances *x* and *y*;
   (*c*) the maximum possible magnitude of angle *ROP*.

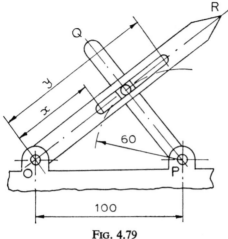

FIG. 4.79

9. In a crank and connecting rod mechanism, the crank radius is 40 mm and the connecting rod is 160 mm long. If θ denotes the angle turned by the crank from outer dead-centre, calculate the distance the slider moves as θ changes from 30° to 120°.

10. *A, B* and *C* represents the centres of three holes which lie on a pitch circle. If *O* represents the centre, angle $AOB = 60°$, angle $BOC = 140°$ and $AB = 100$ mm, calculate:

    (*a*) the pitch circle diameter;
    (*b*) the distances *BC* and *CD*.

11. Figure 4.80 shows one panel of a pin-jointed framework, the panel being in the form of a parallelogram. Calculate the length of the diagonal *BD*.

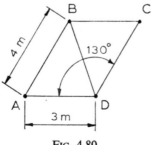

FIG. 4.80

255

12. Figure 4.81 shows diagrammatically a flap *OP* held at 45° to the horizontal by the stay *QR*. If *OQ* = 200 mm and *OR* = 160 mm, calculate the length *QR*.

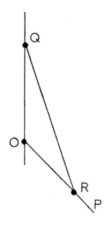

FIG. 4.81

13. In Figure 4.82, *A* and *B* represent the centres of two gears. An idler is to be positioned at *C* so that *AC* = 180 mm and *CB* = 160 mm. Calculate:

   (*a*) the distance *AB*;
   (*b*) the angle *ABO*;
   (*c*) the angle *CBO*.

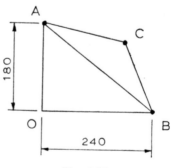

FIG. 4.82

14. In the layout shown in Figure 4.83, $AB = 300$ mm, $BC = 160$ mm and $CA = 400$ mm. Find the co-ordinates x and y of the centre of hole B with reference to the axes shown.

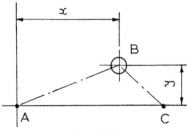

FIG. 4.83

15. Determine the distance between the centres of the holes shown in Figure 4.84.

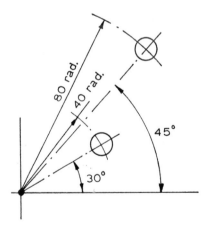

FIG. 4.84

16. In the crank and connecting rod mechanism shown in Figure 4.85, the crank OP has a length of 20 mm and the connecting rod PQ a length of 110 mm. The limits of the stroke of Q are indicated by A and B. Determine the angle θ when Q is at mid-stroke. (For diagram see overleaf.)

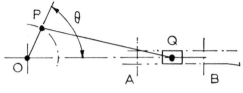

FIG. 4.85

17. (*a*) Write down a formula, usually called the cosine rule, which connects the three sides *a*, *b* and *c* of any triangle with a trigonmetric ratio of angle *A*.

(*b*) Figure 4.86 shows a jig-plate. Calculate:
(i) the checking distance *x* between the centres of the two holes;
(ii) the angle marked *θ*.

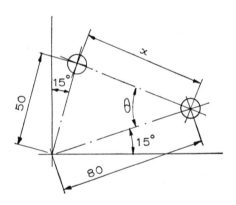

FIG. 4.86

18. In Figure 4.87, *A*, *B* and *C* represents the centres of three gear wheels. Calculate:
(*a*) the angle *BAC*;
(*b*) the co-ordinates *x* and *y*.

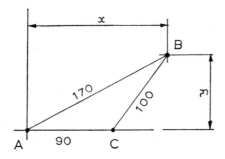

FIG. 4.87

Answers to Problems 4.6

1. 5·05
2. 193 mm
3. 52·2 mm
4. (*a*) 70·7 mm   (*b*) 105°   (*c*) 137 mm
5. (*a*) 2·69 km   (*b*) 2·00 km
6. 68·4 mm, 200 mm
7. $F_1 = 74·8$ N, $F_2 = 142$ N
8. (*a*) 65° 26′ and 123° 34′   (*b*) 53·4 mm and 120 mm
     (*c*) 36° 52′
9. 57·1 mm
10. (*a*) 200 mm   (*b*) $BC = 188$ mm, $CA = 197$ mm
11. 3·09 m
12. 333 mm
13. (*a*) 300 mm   (*b*) 36° 52′   (*c*) 66° 48′
14. $x = 280$ mm, $y = 106$ mm
15. 42·6 mm
16. 84° 47′
17. (*a*) $a^2 = b^2 + c^2 - 2\,bc \cos A$ or $\cos A = \dfrac{b^2 + c^2 - a^2}{2\,bc}$

     (*b*) (i) 70 mm; (ii) 38° 13′
18. (*a*) 28° 4′   (*b*) $x = 150$ mm, $y = 80$ mm

4.7 Identities

Equations are statements true for particular values of the unknown quantity only. The statement $2x = 8$ is true only when $x = 4$, and the statement $x^2 - 4x + 3 = 0$ is true only when $x = 1$ or $x = 3$.

Hence $2x = 8$ and $x^2 - 4x + 3 = 0$ are equations. The statement $\dfrac{\sin \theta}{\cos \theta} = \tan \theta$, on the other hand, is true irrespective of the value of θ, and is termed an *identity*. We shall deduce certain identities based on the right-angled triangle shown in Figure 4.88.

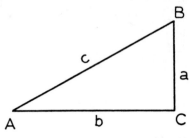

FIG. 4.88

$$\frac{\sin A}{\cos A} = \frac{\dfrac{a}{c}}{\dfrac{b}{c}} = \frac{a}{c} \times \frac{c}{b} = \frac{a}{b} = \tan A$$

$$\therefore \frac{\sin A}{\cos A} = \tan A$$

Applying the Theorem of Pythagoras to the triangle ABC:

$$a^2 + b^2 = c^2$$

We will divide through by a^2, b^2 and c^2 in turn.

$$\frac{a^2}{a^2} + \frac{b^2}{a^2} = \frac{c^2}{a^2}$$

$$1 + \left(\frac{b}{a}\right)^2 = \left(\frac{c}{a}\right)^2$$

$$\therefore 1 + \cot^2 A = \operatorname{cosec}^2 A$$

$$\frac{a^2}{b^2} + \frac{b^2}{b^2} = \frac{c^2}{b^2}$$

$$\left(\frac{a}{b}\right)^2 + 1 = \left(\frac{c}{b}\right)^2$$

$$\therefore \tan^2 A + 1 = \sec^2 A$$

$$\frac{a^2}{c^2} + \frac{b^2}{c^2} = \frac{c^2}{c^2}$$

$$\left(\frac{a}{c}\right)^2 + \left(\frac{b}{c}\right)^2 = 1$$

$$\therefore \sin^2 A + \cos^2 A = 1$$

Recapitulating these results, the following identities should be committed to memory. Note that in order to distinguish an identity from an equation, the equals sign is replaced by the identity sign. The sign $\equiv$ is read as 'is identical to'.

1. $\dfrac{\sin A}{\cos A} \equiv \tan A$ 2. $\sin^2 A + \cos^2 A \equiv 1$

3. $1 + \tan^2 A \equiv \sec^2 A$ 4. $1 + \cot^2 A \equiv \operatorname{cosec}^2 A$

Example

Prove the following identities:

(a) $\sin \theta - \sin^3\theta \equiv \sin \theta \cos^2\theta$

(b) $(\sec \theta + \tan \theta)(\sec \theta - \tan \theta) \equiv 1$

(c) $\dfrac{\cos^2\theta - \cos^4\theta}{1 - \sin^2\theta} \equiv \sin^2\theta$

(d) $\dfrac{\cos^2\theta - \sin^2\theta}{\cos \theta\,(\cos \theta - \sin \theta)} \equiv 1 + \tan \theta$

(a)
$$\sin \theta - \sin^3\theta \equiv \sin \theta\,(1 - \sin^2\theta)$$
$$\equiv \sin \theta \cos^2\theta$$

(b)
$$(\sec \theta + \tan \theta)(\sec \theta - \tan \theta) \equiv \sec^2\theta - \tan^2\theta$$
$$\equiv (1 + \tan^2\theta) - \tan^2\theta$$
$$\equiv 1$$

(c)
$$\frac{\cos^2\theta - \cos^4\theta}{1 - \sin^2\theta} \equiv \frac{\cos^2\theta\,(1 - \cos^2\theta)}{\cos^2\theta}$$
$$\equiv 1 - \cos^2\theta$$
$$\equiv \sin^2\theta$$

(d)
$$\frac{\cos^2\theta - \sin^2\theta}{\cos \theta\,(\cos \theta - \sin \theta)} \equiv \frac{(\cos \theta + \sin \theta)(\cos \theta - \sin \theta)}{(\cos \theta)(\cos \theta - \sin \theta)}$$
$$\equiv \frac{\cos \theta + \sin \theta}{\cos \theta} = 1 + \frac{\sin \theta}{\cos \theta}$$
$$\equiv 1 + \tan \theta \qquad \text{(Q.E.D.)}$$

Example

Simplify the following expressions:

(a) $(\cos A + \sin A)^2 + (\cos A - \sin A)^2$

 (b) $\sin A \cos A (1 + \tan^2 A)$

 (c) $\dfrac{1}{1 + \sin A} + \dfrac{1}{1 - \sin A}$

 (d) $1 - \cos^2 A + \sin^2 A \tan^2 A$

(a) $(\cos A + \sin A)^2 + (\cos A - \sin A)^2$

$$= \cos^2 A + 2 \sin A \cos A + \sin^2 A +$$
$$\cos^2 A - 2 \sin A \cos A + \sin^2 A$$
$$= 2 \cos^2 A + 2 \sin^2 A = 2 (\sin^2 A + \cos^2 A) = 2$$

(b) $\sin A \cos A (1 + \tan^2 A) = \sin A \cos A \sec^2 A$

$$= \frac{\sin A \cos A}{\cos^2 A}$$
$$= \frac{\sin A}{\cos A} = \tan A$$

(c) $\dfrac{1}{1 + \sin A} + \dfrac{1}{1 - \sin A} = \dfrac{1(1 - \sin A) + 1(1 + \sin A)}{(1 + \sin A)(1 - \sin A)}$

$$= \frac{1 - \sin A + 1 + \sin A}{1 - \sin^2 A}$$
$$= \frac{2}{\cos^2 A} = 2 \sec^2 A$$

(d) $1 - \cos^2 A + \sin^2 A \tan^2 A = \sin^2 A + \sin^2 A \tan^2 A$

$$= \sin^2 A (1 + \tan^2 A)$$
$$= \sin^2 A \sec^2 A$$
$$= \frac{\sin^2 A}{\cos^2 A} = \left(\frac{\sin A}{\cos A}\right)^2 = \tan^2 A$$

Answers: (a) 2 (b) $\tan A$ (c) $2 \sec^2 A$ (d) $\tan^2 A$

The identities which introduced this article were obtained by the use of algebraic terms for the trigonometrical ratios in a right-angled triangle. Hence a simple way of proving identities or simplifying trigonometrical expressions is to represent the trigonometrical ratios by algebraic terms, and to apply formal algebraic manipulation, which may include an algebraic statement of the Theorem of Pythagoras. We will illustrate this point with worked examples.

Example

Prove the identity:

$$(\cos A + \sin A)^2 + (\cos A - \sin A)^2 \equiv 2$$

In the triangle ABC shown in Figure 4.88 (page 260):

$$\cos A = \frac{b}{c} \quad \text{and} \quad \sin A = \frac{a}{c}$$

$$\therefore \left(\frac{b}{c} + \frac{a}{c}\right)^2 + \left(\frac{b}{c} - \frac{a}{c}\right)^2 = 2$$

$$\left(\frac{b+a}{c}\right)^2 + \left(\frac{b-a}{c}\right)^2 = 2$$

$$\frac{b^2 + 2ab + a^2}{c^2} + \frac{b^2 - 2ab + a^2}{c^2} = 2$$

$$\frac{2b^2 + 2a^2}{c^2} = 2$$

$$2b^2 + 2a^2 = 2c^2$$

$$b^2 + a^2 = c^2$$

The above is true since it is a statement of Pythagoras' Theorem applied to the triangle ABC; hence the identity is proved.

Example

Simplify $\sin A \cos A (1 + \tan^2 A)$.

Using Figure 4.88:

$$\sin A = \frac{a}{c}, \quad \cos A = \frac{b}{c}, \quad \tan A = \frac{a}{b}$$

$$\sin A \cos A (1 + \tan^2 A) \equiv \left(\frac{a}{c}\right)\left(\frac{b}{c}\right)\left(1 + \frac{a^2}{b^2}\right)$$

$$\equiv \left(\frac{ab}{c^2}\right)\left(\frac{a^2 + b^2}{b^2}\right)$$

$$\equiv \left(\frac{ab}{c^2}\right)\left(\frac{c^2}{b^2}\right)$$

since $a^2 + b^2 = c^2$ (the Theorem of Pythagoras applied to the particular triangle)

$$\equiv \frac{a}{b}$$

$$\equiv \tan A$$

Answer: $\sin A \cos A (1 + \tan^2 A) \equiv \tan A$

Problems 4.7

1. (*a*) What is the difference between an equation and an identity?

263

    (*b*) Show that $\dfrac{\sin \theta}{\cos \theta} \equiv \tan \theta$

    (*c*) Prove the identity $1 + \tan^2\theta \equiv \sec^2\theta$

2. Use the identity $\sin^2\theta + \cos^2\theta \equiv 1$ to establish the following results:

    (*a*) $1 + \tan^2\theta \equiv \sec^2\theta$ (*b*) $\cot^2\theta + 1 \equiv \mathrm{cosec}^2\theta$

3. Simplify $\sin A \cos A + \sin^2 A \tan A$.

4. Simplify $(1 + \tan^2\theta) \cos^2\theta$.

5. Given that $\sin^2\theta + \cos^2\theta \equiv 1$ and $\tan \theta \equiv \dfrac{\sin \theta}{\cos \theta}$, prove that:

$$\tan \theta + \frac{1}{\tan \theta} \equiv \frac{1}{\sin \theta \cos \theta}$$

and find the value on either side of this identity when $\sin \theta = \dfrac{\sqrt{3}}{2}$.

6. Show that for all values of ϕ:

$$(\cos \phi + \sin \phi)^2 \equiv 1 + 2 \sin \phi \cos \phi$$

7. Prove that $\dfrac{1}{1 - \sin \theta} - \dfrac{1}{1 + \sin \theta} \equiv \dfrac{2 \tan \theta}{\cos \theta}$.

8. Prove that $\dfrac{\sin^2\theta}{1 + \tan^2\theta} \equiv (\sin \theta \cos \theta)^2$.

9. Show that for all values of θ:

$$\frac{\sin \theta}{1 + \cos \theta} + \frac{1 + \cos \theta}{\sin \theta} \equiv \frac{2}{\sin \theta}$$

Answers to Problems 4.7

    Only three problems require numerical answers.

    3. $\tan A$

    4. 1

    5. 2·31

Chapter Five

Mensuration

5.1 The Length of a Line

Mensuration is the branch of mathematics which gives us the rules for finding the lengths of lines, the areas of plane figures and the volumes of solids. We will proceed with our studies in that order.

5.1.1 THE LENGTH OF A STRAIGHT LINE

If we have two points on a graphical field, P_1 and P_2, indicated by the values (x_1, y_1) and (x_2, y_2), as shown in Figure 5.1, then the distance between vertical lines drawn through the points is $(x_2 - x_1)$ and the distance between horizontal lines drawn through the points is $(y_2 - y_1)$.

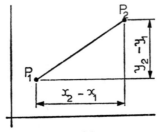

FIG. 5.1

Using the theorem of Pythagoras:
$$(P_1P_2)^2 = (x_2 - x_1)^2 + (y_2 - y_1)^2$$
hence
$$P_1P_2 = \sqrt{\{(x_2 - x_1)^2 + (y_2 - y_1)^2\}}$$

Example

Calculate the distance between the points $(5, 3)$ and $(-1, -5)$.
$$\text{Distance} = \sqrt{[\{5 - (-1)\}^2 + \{3 - (-5)\}^2]}$$
$$= \sqrt{(6^2 + 8^2)} = \sqrt{(36 + 64)}$$
$$= \sqrt{100} = 10 \text{ units}$$

Answer: Distance = 10 units

5.1.2 THE CIRCUMFERENCE OF A CIRCLE

The ratio of the circumference of a circle to the diameter is represented by π. The value cannot be expressed precisely either as a vulgar fraction or in denary notation. The value we use for π depends upon the accuracy we desire in an answer. To ten significant figures:

$$\pi = 3 \cdot 141\ 592\ 654$$

The reader has probably wondered how the value of π can be established to any degree of accuracy. Mathematicians have developed several series which can be used to determine π. Every single one of those series is unending and hence, as previously stated, π cannot be expressed precisely either as a vulgar fraction or a denary number.

It can be proved in a branch of higher mathematics that

$$\frac{\pi}{4} = 1 - \frac{1}{3} + \frac{1}{5} - \frac{1}{7} + \frac{1}{9} - \frac{1}{11} + \frac{1}{13} \cdots$$

The use of this series (or a similar series) can be used to determine π to any degree of accuracy. The calculations become very tedious by formal processes but a suitable computer can easily establish the value to fifty decimal places in less than a minute.

Unless we are informed to the contrary, at our present stage of studies we can use the approximate value of $\frac{22}{7}$. The error of the approximation is only about one part in twenty-five hundred, i.e. about 0·04%.

If C is the circumference of a circle and d is the diameter, then:

$$\frac{C}{d} = \pi \text{ or } C = \pi d$$

The diameter d is twice the radius r, hence:

$$C = \pi d = 2\pi r$$

5.1.3 THE LENGTH OF A CIRCULAR ARC

In a previous article dealing with the circular measure of angles, we have seen that if the ends of an arc of length L and radius r subtend an angle of θ, then:

$$\frac{L}{r} = \theta, (\theta \text{ being expressed in radians,})$$

hence $\qquad L = r\theta$

(The symbol L is used for length instead of l to avoid confusion with unity.)

If θ is expressed in degrees, we know that we can convert degrees to radians by dividing by $\frac{2\pi}{360}$. Hence:

$$L = r\left(\theta \times \frac{2\pi}{360}\right), \theta \text{ now being expressed in degrees}$$

$$= \frac{\theta}{360}(2\pi r)$$

To summarize, if an arc of length L and radius r subtends an angle of θ:

$$L = r\theta, \text{ if } \theta \text{ is expressed in radians}$$

or $\qquad L = \dfrac{\theta}{360}(2\pi r)$, if θ is expressed in degrees

Example

Find the angle subtended at the centre of a circle of radius 12 mm by an arc of length 15 mm, giving the answer in radians and degrees.

$$L = r\theta$$
$$\therefore \theta = \frac{L}{r} = \frac{15 \text{ mm}}{12 \text{ mm}} = 1.25 \text{ radians}$$

From tables: 1·249 7 radians = 71° 36′
    0·000 3 radians = $\qquad$ 1′
    1·250 0 radians = 71° 37′

Answer: Angle subtended = 1·25 radians = 71° 37′

Example

A circle of radius 8 mm contains a chord of length 10 mm. Calculate:

(*a*) the angle subtended at the centre of the circle by the chord, giving the answer both to the nearest minute and in circular measure;

(*b*) the length of the shortest arc between the ends of the chord.

267

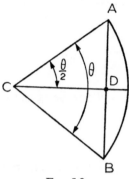

FIG. 5.2

(a) The chord and arc are shown in Figure 5.2. *D* is the mid-point of *AB*.

$$\frac{\theta}{2} = \arcsin \frac{AD}{AC} = \arcsin \frac{5}{8}$$
$$= \arcsin 0{\cdot}625 = 38° \ 41'$$
$$\theta = 2(38° \ 41') = 77° \ 22'$$

From tables: $77° \ 22' = 1{\cdot}350 \ 3$ radians

(b) $L = r\theta$, θ being expressed in radians
        $= 8(1{\cdot}350 \ 3) = 10{\cdot}802 \ 4$ mm

Answers: (a) Angle subtended $= 77° \ 22' = 1{\cdot}35$ radians
     (b) Length of arc $= 10{\cdot}8$ mm

Example

Figure 5.3 shows the cross-section of a strengthening bracket for an instrument panel. Neglecting the thickness of material, calculate the length between the two ends when the section is opened out flat.

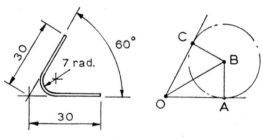

FIG. 5.3

Referring to Figure 5.3:
$$OA = 7 \cot 30° = 7 \times 1·732\ 1 = 12·124\ 7$$
Length of flat of each leg $= 30 - 12·124\ 7 = 17·875\ 3$

$$\text{Angle } BOA = \frac{60°}{2} = 30°$$

Angle $ABO = 90° - 30° = 60°$

Angle ABC = twice angle $ABO = 2 \times 60° = 120°$

$$\text{Length of arc} = \frac{\theta}{360°}(2\pi r) = \frac{120°}{360°}\left(\frac{2 \times 22 \times 7}{7}\right)$$

$$= \frac{44}{3} = 14·666\ 7$$

Developed length $= 2(17·875\ 3) + 14·666\ 7$
$$= 35·750\ 6 + 14·666\ 7$$
$$= 50·417\ 3$$

Answer: Developed length $= 50·4$ mm

Example

Calculate the length of the belt of an open belt drive connecting pulleys of diameter 100 mm and 240 mm spaced at a centre distance of 250 mm.

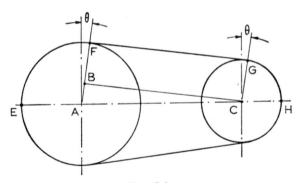

Fig. 5.4

Working throughout in centimetres, in triangle ABC (Figure 5.4):

$$AC = 25$$
$$AB = 12 - 5 = 7$$
$$\sin \angle ACB = \frac{AB}{AC} = \frac{7}{25} = 0·28$$

269

$$\angle ACB = 16° \, 16'$$
Length of belt $= 2(\text{arc } EF + FG + \text{arc } GH)$

The angles θ are equal to $\angle ACB = 16° \, 16'$.

$$\text{Arc } EF = r\theta = 12(90° + 16° \, 16'), \text{ when the}$$
angle is expressed in radians
$$= 12(1·570 \, 8 + 0·283 \, 9)$$
$$= 12(1·854 \, 7)$$
$$= 22·256 \, 4$$
$$FG = BC = \sqrt{\{(AC)^2 - (AB)^2\}} = \sqrt{\{25^2 - 7^2\}}$$
$$= \sqrt{\{625 - 49\}} = \sqrt{576} = 24$$
$$\text{Arc } GH = r\theta = 5(90° - 16° \, 16'), \text{ when the}$$
angle is expressed in radians
$$= 5(1·570 \, 8 - 0·283 \, 9)$$
$$= 5(1·286 \, 9)$$
$$= 6·434 \, 5$$
$$\therefore \text{ length of belt } = 2(22·256 \, 4 + 24 + 6·434 \, 5)$$
$$= 2(52·690 \, 9)$$
$$= 105·381 \, 8 \text{ cm } = 1 \, 053·818 \text{ mm}$$

Answer: Length of belt $= 1 \, 050$ mm

Example

Calculate the length of the belt of a crossed belt drive connecting pulleys of diameter 300 mm and 180 mm spaced at a centre distance of 400 mm.

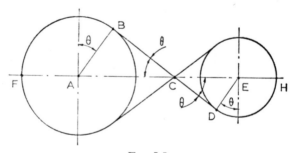

FIG. 5.5

Referring to Figure 5.5 and working throughout in centimetres:
Triangles ABC and CDE are similar. Let $AC = x$, then $CE = 40 - x$.

$$\frac{AB}{AC} = \frac{DE}{CE}$$

$$\therefore \frac{15}{x} = \frac{9}{40-x}$$
$$\therefore 15(40-x) = 9x$$
$$600 - 15x = 9x$$
$$600 = 24x$$
$$x = 25$$

In Figure 5.5, the four angles θ are equal. In triangle ACB:

$$\sin C = \frac{15}{25} = 0.6$$
$$C = 36° 52'$$

i.e.
$$\theta = 36° 52'$$

Length of belt $= 2(\text{arc } FB + BC + CD + \text{arc } DH)$

Arc $FB = r\theta = 15(90° + 36° 52')$, when the

angle is expressed in radians

$$= 15(1.570\ 8 + 0.643\ 5)$$
$$= 15(2.214\ 3)$$
$$= 33.214\ 5$$

$$BC = \sqrt{\{(AC)^2 - (AB)^2\}} = \sqrt{\{25^2 - 15^2\}}$$
$$= \sqrt{\{625 - 225\}} = \sqrt{400} = 20$$

$$CD = \sqrt{\{(CE)^2 - (DE)^2\}} = \sqrt{\{15^2 - 9^2\}}$$
$$= \sqrt{\{225 - 81\}} = \sqrt{144} = 12$$

Arc $DH = 9(90° + 36° 52')$, when the

angle is expressed in radians

$$= 9(2.214\ 3)$$
$$= 19.928\ 7$$

Length of belt $= 2(33.214\ 5 + 20 + 12 + 19.928\ 7)$
$$= 2(85.143\ 2)$$
$$= 170.286\ 4 \text{ cm} = 1\ 702.864 \text{ mm}$$

Answer: Length of belt $= 1\ 700$ mm

5.1.4 THE PERIMETER OF AN ELLIPSE

There is no precise formula which can be easily applied to find the perimeter of an ellipse. We can use approximations; the more accurate the approximation, the more involved becomes the formula. The accuracy of an approximation usually depends on the ratio of the length of the major axis a to the length of the minor axis b.

A very rough approximation is $\frac{\pi}{2}(a+b)$.

A more accurate approximation is $\pi\sqrt{\dfrac{a^2+b^2}{2}}$.

An even more accurate approximation, suitable for this stage of studies is:

$$\pi \sqrt{\left\{ \frac{a^2 + b^2}{2} - \frac{(a - b)^2}{8 \cdot 8} \right\}}$$

There is no point in remembering these formulae; they are given for interest only. If a candidate in an examination has to determine the perimeter of an ellipse, the method of determination should be given.

5.1.5 PERIPHERAL SPEED

Let us consider any point on the circumference of a wheel. If that wheel rotates about its centre, the velocity of that point and similar points on the periphery is called the *peripheral speed*.

If d is the diameter of the circle, the length of the circumference is πd. If the wheel rotates once, the point travels a distance equal to πd. If the wheel makes n revolutions, the point travels a distance equal to $\pi d n$. If the n revolutions are made in unit time, then the point moves with a speed of $\pi d n$. Hence:

if
v = the peripheral speed
d = the wheel diameter
n = the rotational speed

then
$v = \pi d n$

The unit of v depends upon the units given to d and to n. Using basic SI units, a speed is given in metres per second and a diameter in metres. Consequently the rotational speed to give a peripheral speed in m/s when the diameter is quoted in metres should be stated in revolutions per second.

It must be accepted that for some time to come strict SI usage cannot be expected in everyday life, and many rotational speeds will be quoted in rev/min. Just for a moment let us return to the formula $v = \pi d n$. Let us presume that the symbol n represents revolutions per second. Let us introduce another symbol ω (the small Greek letter omega), where ω represents the rotational speed in radians per second. There are 2π radians in a complete revolution, hence:

$$\omega = 2\pi n \qquad \text{and} \qquad n = \frac{\omega}{2\pi}$$

Substituting this value for n in $v = \pi d n$, we obtain:

$$v = \pi \times d \times \frac{\omega}{2\pi}$$

$$= d \times \frac{\omega}{2}$$

Now $\dfrac{d}{2}$ is the radius r, hence:

$$v = \omega r$$

This relationship is quite fundamental, and should be considered the preferred usage. A rotational speed, where necessary, should be converted to radians per second. If the rotational speed is quoted as N rev/min, this is equal to $2\pi N$ radians per minute, which itself is equal to $\dfrac{2\pi N}{60} = \dfrac{\pi}{30} \times N$ radians per second. Hence to convert rev/min to rad/s we have to multiply by $\dfrac{\pi}{30}$.

It should be noted from the definition of the radian that it is obtained from dividing a length by a length, and as far as the manipulation of units is concerned the magnitude of an angle in radians is a numerical value only. For example, in unit manipulation:

$$30 \text{ rad/s}^2 \text{ is regarded as } \dfrac{30}{s^2}$$

The reader is strongly recommended to avoid usages such as $v = \pi dn$ or $v = \dfrac{\pi dN}{60}$. These could cause complications in later studies. The recommended usage as a first order of preference is:

$$v = \omega r$$

Example

A drill has a diameter of 10 mm. Calculate the cutting speed at the periphery, in m/min, when the drill rotates at 210 rev/min.

$$r = \dfrac{d}{2} = \dfrac{10 \text{ mm}}{2} = 5 \text{ mm} = 0{\cdot}05 \text{ m}$$

$$\omega = 210 \text{ rev/min} = 210 \times \dfrac{\pi}{30} \text{ rad/s} = \dfrac{210 \times 22}{7 \times 30} = 22 \text{ rad/s}$$

$$v = \omega r = 22 \times 0{\cdot}05 \dfrac{1}{s} \times \text{m}$$

$$= 1{\cdot}1 \text{ m/s}$$
$$= 1{\cdot}1 \times 60 \text{ m/min} = 66 \text{ m/min}$$

Answer: Cutting speed $= 66$ m/min

Example

The safe peripheral speed of a particular grinding wheel is stated by the manufacturers to be 1 650 m/min. Calculate the maximum angular velocity, in rev/min, of a wheel of diameter 175 mm.

$$v = 1\ 650 \text{ m/min} = \frac{1\ 650}{60} \text{ m/s}$$

$$r = \frac{d}{2} = \frac{175 \text{ mm}}{2} = 87 \cdot 5 \text{ mm} = 0 \cdot 087\ 5 \text{ m}$$

$$v = \omega r$$

$$\therefore \omega = \frac{v}{r}$$

$$= \frac{1\ 650}{60 \times 0 \cdot 087\ 5} \text{ rad/s}$$

To convert rad/s to rev/min we multiply by $\dfrac{30}{\pi}$.

$$\omega = \frac{1\ 650 \times 30 \times 7}{60 \times 0 \cdot 087\ 5 \times 22} = 3\ 000 \text{ rev/min}$$

Answer: Maximum speed = 3 000 rev/min

Let us review these solutions, because the reader, quite understandably, may feel we have made very heavy weather of what seem to be fairly simple tasks. If v is required in m/sec when d is given in millimetres and N is given in revolutions per minute, then a suitable formula is:

$$v = \frac{\pi d N}{60\ 000}$$

The use of this formula would certainly have eased the calculations in the two previous examples. While, however, the formula is true for the units used in these particular cases, for any other case where the units are different we shall require a different formula. What we really require is one single formula as an overall strategy. It is pointless to burden one's mind with a cumbersome collection of special formulae for special cases. Diameters are not necessarily quoted in millimetres, neither are speeds necessarily quoted in rev/min. It is repeated that the reader is well advised to use as the basic relationship between linear and rotational speeds the fundamental relationship:

$$v = \omega r$$

Problems 5.1

1. Calculate the distances between the following points:
   (*a*) the origin and (5, 12);   (*b*) (2,3) and (17, 11);
   (*c*) (−7, −2) and (2, 38).

2. A straight line is plotted to the law $y = \dfrac{3x}{4} - 2$. Calculate the length of the line between the points representing values of x of 9 and 17.

3. A straight line is plotted to the law $4x - 3y + 5 = 0$. Find the length of the line between the points representing the values $x = 1$ and $x = 4$.

4. On a receiver chassis, two terminals occupy the positions indicated by the co-ordinates, in millimetres (80, 100) and (116, 148). An eyeletted connector piece connects the two terminals in a straight line. Calculate the distance between the centres of the two eyelets.

5. On an instrument panel, the centres of two rotating dials are indicated by the co-ordinates, in millimetres (47, 53) and (167, 117). The diameters of the two dials are 96 mm and 120 mm respectively. Calculate the smallest distance between the peripheries of the two dials.

6. An instrument dial has to have 50 equal divisions around its periphery. The peripheral distance between adjacent divisions is to be 2·2 mm. Determine the diameter of the dial.

7. A circular arc of radius 105 mm subtends an angle of 75°. Calculate:
   (a) the length of the arc;
   (b) the chordal distance between the ends of the arc.

8. Cable is wrapped around a drum at an effective diameter of 2·1 m. Through what angle (in degrees) does the drum rotate when a portion of cable of length 4·95 m is unwound from the drum?

9. A belt wraps round a motor pulley of diameter 210 mm with a contact angle of 150°.
   (a) Calculate the length of belt in contact with the pulley.
   (b) Calculate the belt velocity, in m/s, when the pulley revolves at 720 rev/min.

10. Calculate the length of the periphery of the shape shown in Figure 5.6 overleaf.

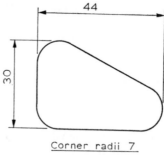

Corner radii 7

FIG. 5.6

11. Cable is being unwound from a drum and rewound on to a spool. At a particular instant, cable is unwinding from the drum at an effective radius of 350 mm, the drum rotating at 60 rev/min. The cable is being wound on to the spool at an effective radius of 70 mm. Calculate:

   (a) the linear velocity of the cable, in m/min;
   (b) the rotational speed of the spool.

12. A thin-walled tube of diameter 30 mm is made from material of width 100 mm.

   (a) What is the amount of overlap?
   (b) If the strip were joined by butt welding, what would then be the diameter of the tube? (Take π as 3·142.)

13. An oxy-cutting machine is cutting out a circular disc of diameter 2·4 m by means of a rotating arm. The flame travels around the circle at the rate of 250 mm per minute.

   (a) Through what angle, to the nearest degree, does the arm turn in one minute?
   (b) How long does the arm take to turn a full circle? (Take π as $\frac{22}{7}$.)

14. The heating surface in a heat-exchanger consists of the outer surface of sixty tubes each of outside diameter 100 mm and length 2·5 m. Calculate the magnitude of the heating surface in square metres. (Take π as 3·142.)

15. What should be the spindle speed of a lathe to provide a cutting speed of 66 m/min with a workpiece of diameter 280 mm? (Take π as $\frac{22}{7}$.)

16. Calculate the length of wire in the paper clip shown in Figure 5.7. The dimensions given apply to the centre line and it may be assumed that the length of the wire is identical to the length of the centre line. (Take $\pi = \frac{22}{7}$.)

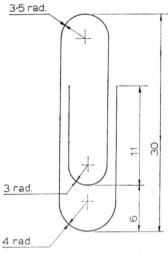

3·5 rad.

3 rad.

4 rad.

11

30

6

FIG. 5.7

17. Figure 5.8 represents the front plate of a guard used to enclose a gear train completely. Determine:

(a) the angle θ;
(b) the distance around the periphery, i.e. the distance around *ABCDEFA*.

Give the answer to three significant figures, taking π as 3·142.

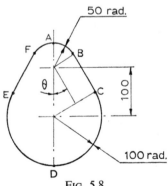

50 rad.

A

F

B

E

θ

C

100

100 rad.

D

FIG. 5.8

18. Calculate the length of the centre line of the wire form shown in Figure 5.9. (There is no straight portion on the centre line.)

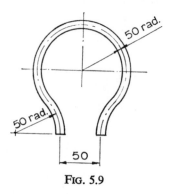

FIG. 5.9

19. Figure 5.10 shows a gusset which is to be cut from mild steel plate by an oxy-acetylene flame which travels round the edge. If it takes 1 minute to burn a starting hole through the plate, and then the flame moves round the form at the rate of 160 mm/min, how long altogether will it take to cut the gusset from the plate? The width of the cut may be neglected.

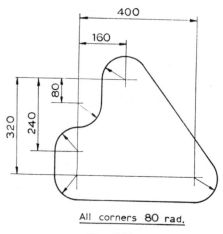

All corners 80 rad.

FIG. 5.10

20. Neglecting the thickness of the material, calculate the developed lengths of the brackets shown in Figures 5.11(*a*), 5.11(*b*) and 5.11(*c*). Take $\pi = \frac{22}{7}$.

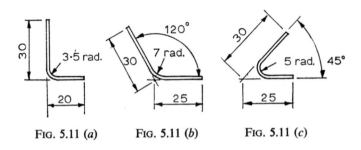

FIG. 5.11 (*a*)   FIG. 5.11 (*b*)   FIG. 5.11 (*c*)

21. Calculate the developed length of the cable clamp shown in Figure 5.12. Assume that the developed length is the length along the centre line.

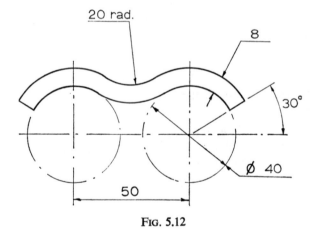

FIG. 5.12

22. Calculate the length of an open belt drive connecting pulleys of diameter 360 mm and 180 mm at a centre distance of 410 mm.

23. Calculate the length of the belt of a crossed belt drive connecting pulleys of diameter 160 mm and 320 mm at a centre distance of 510 mm.

279

Answers to Problems 5.1

1. (*a*) 13   (*b*) 17   (*c*) 41
2. 10
3. 5
4. 60 mm
5. 28 mm
6. 35 mm
7. (*a*) 137 mm   (*b*) 128 mm
8. 270°
9. (*a*) 275 mm   (*b*) 7·92 m/s
10. 124 mm
11. (*a*) 132 m/min   (*b*) 300 rev/min
12. (*a*) 5·74 mm   (*b*) 31·8 mm
13. (*a*) 12°   (*b*) 30·2 min
14. 47·1 m²
15. 75 rev/min
16. 94·0 mm
17. (*a*) 30°   (*b*) 697
18. 302 mm
19. 11·7 min
20. (*a*) 48·5 mm   (*b*) 54·3 mm   (*c*) 42·6 mm
21. 103 mm
22. 1 690 mm
23. 1 890 mm

5.2 The Area of Plane Figures

5.2.1 POLYGONS

A *polygon* is any plane figure bounded by straight sides. If the number of sides exceed three, it is assumed that no straight lines cross, otherwise there would be more than one plane figure. Names are given to polygons according to the number of sides; some of the more common polygons are given in the following list:

Number of sides	Name
Three	Triangle
Four	Quadrilateral
Five	Pentagon
Six	Hexagon
Seven	Heptagon
Eight	Octagon
Ten	Decagon
Twelve	Dodecagon

5.2.2 THE AREA OF A TRIANGLE

Triangles can be conveniently classified into three types. We have already introduced in this volume the equilateral triangle, with three equal sides and three equal angles. We have also discussed an isosceles triangle, in which two sides are equal and the angles opposite the equal sides are also equal. The remaining type is the scalene triangle, a triangle having unequal sides and unequal angles.

A rather special kind of triangle is one containing a right angle, which, for obvious reasons, we call a right-angled triangle. A right-angled triangle cannot possibly be equilateral. It could, however, be isosceles, in which case the two shorter sides which contain the right angle are equal in length and the two smaller angles are each of 45°. With a scalene right-angled triangle, the two smaller angles are of different magnitude but add up to 90°, i.e. they are complementary angles.

The accepted mathematical convention for representing the area of a triangle **is to** use the symbol $\triangle$. The most commonly known formula for the area of a triangle is:

$$\triangle = \frac{\text{base} \times \text{perpendicular height}}{2}$$

This very simply formula includes a dimension of a triangle which is rarely specified, that of the perpendicular height. There are many other formulae we can use for the area of a triangle, each one being particularly suitable for a specific set of dimensions.

If the three sides of a triangle are a, b and c, then the perimeter is $a + b + c$. Let us represent the semi-perimeter by s, so that $s = \dfrac{a + b + c}{2}$. The reader can accept without proof that:

$$\triangle = \sqrt{\{s(s - a)(s - b)(s - c)\}}$$

This formula can be applied when the three sides are known. Let us proceed to a suitable formula for two sides and the included angle between those two sides.

Figures 5.13(*a*) and 5.13(*b*) show two triangles. In Figure 5.13(*a*), the angle A is acute, in Figure 5.13(*b*), the angle A is obtuse. In both cases b is the base and BD the perpendicular height (diagrams overleaf).

In Figure 5.13(*a*):

$$BD = c \sin A$$

hence $\qquad \triangle = \dfrac{\text{base} \times \text{perpendicular height}}{2} = \dfrac{bc \sin A}{2}$

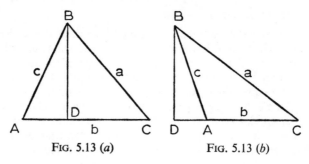

FIG. 5.13 (*a*)   FIG. 5.13 (*b*)

In Fig. 5.13(*b*):

$$BD = c \sin (180° - A) = c \sin A$$

since $$\sin (180° - A) = \sin A$$

Once more $$\Delta = \frac{bc \sin A}{2}$$

Hence the area of a triangle is given by one half of the product of any two sides and the sine of the included angle.

We have considered thus far in this article suitable formulae when three or two sides are known. We will conclude with a formula which can be used if one side is known. To specify such a triangle completely, in addition we should require to know two angles (the third would be 180° minus the sum of the two known angles).

We have already established that:

$$\Delta = \frac{bc \sin A}{2}$$

and from the sine rule $\dfrac{a}{\sin A} = \dfrac{b}{\sin B} = \dfrac{c}{\sin C}$

we can obtain $$b = \frac{a \sin B}{\sin A} \text{ and } c = \frac{a \sin C}{\sin A}$$

By substitution $$\Delta = \left(\frac{a \sin B}{\sin A} \right) \left(\frac{a \sin C}{\sin A} \right) \left(\frac{\sin A}{2} \right)$$

or $$\Delta = \frac{a^2 \sin B \sin C}{2 \sin A}$$

We now have four different formulae we can use to find the area of a triangle. The reader should note that these formulae are not the only formulae; many more can be developed, the four quoted are the most convenient. The formula which should be used to determine the area of a particular triangle depends upon the dimensions supplied. Let us summarize the formulae:

$$\triangle = \frac{\text{base} \times \text{perpendicular height}}{2}$$

$$\triangle = \sqrt{\{s(s-a)(s-b)(s-c)\}} \text{ where } s = \frac{a+b+c}{2}$$

$$\triangle = \tfrac{1}{2} ab \sin C (\text{or} \tfrac{1}{2} bc \sin A \text{ or } \tfrac{1}{2} ac \sin B)$$

$$\triangle = \frac{a^2 \sin B \sin C}{2 \sin A} \left(\text{or } \frac{b^2 \sin A \sin C}{2 \sin B} \text{ or } \frac{c^2 \sin B \sin A}{2 \sin C} \right)$$

Example

A triangle has sides of length 5 mm, 12 mm and 13 mm.

(*a*) Prove that the triangle is right-angled.

(*b*) Determine its area:

    (i) from $\triangle = \dfrac{bh}{2}$

    (ii) from $\triangle = \sqrt{\{s(s-a)(s-b)(s-c)\}}$

(*a*) If the triangle is right-angled, then:

$$(\text{longest side})^2 = \text{sum of squares of other two sides}$$
$$13^2 = 12^2 + 5^2$$
$$169 = 144 + 25$$
$$169 = 169$$

The triangle is right-angled since the sizes satisfy the Theorem of Pythagoras.

(*b*) The sides containing the right-angle are perpendicular to each other, hence:

(i) $\triangle = \dfrac{bh}{2} = \dfrac{5 \times 12}{2} = \dfrac{60}{2} = 30 \text{ mm}$

(ii) $a = 5, \quad b = 12, \quad c = 13 \qquad s = \dfrac{a+b+c}{2} = \dfrac{30}{2} = 15$

$\triangle = \sqrt{\{s(s-a)(s-b)(s-c)\}} = \sqrt{\{15(15-5)(15-12)(15-13)\}}$
$= \sqrt{\{15 \times 10 \times 3 \times 2\}} \quad = \sqrt{900} = 30 \text{ mm}$

Answer: Area of triangle = 30 mm (by either method)

5.2.3 THE AREA OF A QUADRILATERAL

A *quadrilateral* is any plane figure having four straight sides. If two, and only two, of the sides are parallel, the figure becomes a *trapezium*. If both pairs of opposing sides are parallel, the figure is a *parallelogram.* A special case occurs when the parallelogram has adjacent sides at right angles; this figure is more commonly referred to as a *rectangle.* A further special case of a parallelogram occurs when all four sides are of equal length, the figure being known as a *rhombus.* A *square,* in fact, is a rhombus where adjacent sides are at right angles. Let us review these statements with some definitions, and include in the definitions some reference to the length of sides:

A quadrilateral is *any* plane figure bounded by four straight sides.
A trapezium is a plane figure bounded by four straight sides, two of which are parallel (but which are unequal in length).
A parallelogram is a plane figure bounded by four straight sides, opposite pairs of sides being parallel (and equal in length).
A rhombus is a plane figure bounded by four straight sides all of equal length (opposite sides being parallel).

The area of any polygon can be found by dividing that polygon into triangles and summating the area of individual triangles. Let us apply this principle to special quadrilaterals.

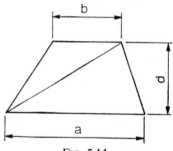

FIG. 5.14

Figure 5.14 shows a trapezium, the parallel sides being of lengths *a* and *b* and their distance apart being *d*. Two triangles have been formed by drawing a line between opposite corners.

$$\text{Area of a triangle} = \frac{\text{base} \times \text{perpendicular height}}{2}$$

$$\text{Area of trapezium} = \text{sum of areas of two triangles}$$

$$= \frac{ad}{2} + \frac{bd}{2} = \frac{(a + b)}{2} d$$

i.e. mean length of parallel sides multiplied by the distance between them.

If we extend this reasoning to a parallelogram, since opposing sides are of equal length, the area of a parallelogram is the product of the length of a side and the distance between that side and its parallel side. In Figure 5.15, the area of the parallelogram is either *ad* or *bh*.

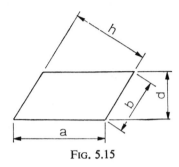

FIG. 5.15

It should be noted that since:

$$ad = bh$$

then

$$\frac{a}{b} = \frac{h}{d}$$

Figure 5.16(*a*) shows a rhombus with a line drawn between opposite corners, this line being termed a *diagonal*.

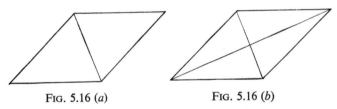

FIG. 5.16 (*a*)　　　　　FIG. 5.16 (*b*)

Since the sides of a rhombus are of equal length, the diagonal divides the rhombus into two congruent isosceles triangles. In Figure 5.16(*b*) the second diagonal has been added, again dividing the triangle into congruent isosceles triangles. These diagonals bisect the angles they join. Since the bisector of the vertex of an isosceles triangle is at right-angles to the base, the diagonals of a rhombus intersect at right angles, and bisect each other. The diagonals of a rhombus produce four congruent right-angled triangles. The area of a rhombus is the sum of the areas of these four triangles; hence the area of a rhombus can also be obtained from half the product of the diagonals.

Example

Calculate the area of a rhombus with side 7·2 mm and the longer diagonal 10·5 mm.

First method:

The area consists of the sum of the areas of two triangles having sides 7·2, 7·2 and 10·5 mm long (Figure 5.17).

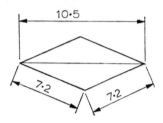

Fɪɢ. 5.17

$$a = 7·2 \qquad b = 7·2 \qquad c = 10·5$$
$$s = \frac{a + b + c}{2} = \frac{7·2 + 7·2 + 10·5}{2} = \frac{24·9}{2} = 12·45$$
$$s - a = 12·45 - 7·2 = 5·25 \qquad s - b = 12·45 - 7·2 = 5·25$$
$$s - c = 12·45 - 10·5 = 1·95$$

$$\text{Area} = \sqrt{\{s(s - a)(s - b)(s - c)\}} = \sqrt{\{(12·45)(5·25)(5·25)(1·95)\}}$$
$$= 25·87$$

$$\text{Area of rhombus} = 2 \times 25·87$$
$$= 51·74 = 51·7 \text{ mm}^2 \text{ (to 3 sig. figs)}$$

Rough check:
$$12 \times 5 \times 5 \times 2 = 600$$
$$\sqrt{600} = \text{about } 25$$

No.		Log
12·45		1·095 2
5·25		0·720 2
5·25		0·720 2
1·95		0·290 0
Root	2	2·825 6
25·87		1·412 8

Second method:

Diagonals *AD* and *CB* bisect each other at right angles, hence *ABE* is a right-angled triangle (Figure 5.18).

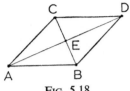

Fig. 5.18

$$AB = 7·2 \qquad AE = \frac{10·5}{2} = 5·25$$
$$(AB)^2 = (EB)^2 + (AE)^2$$
$$7·2^2 = (EB)^2 + 5·25^2$$
$$51·84 = (EB)^2 + 27·56$$
$$(EB)^2 = 51·84 - 27·56 = 24·28$$
$$EB = \sqrt{24·28} = 4·927$$
$$\text{Diagonal } BC = 2(EB) = 2 \times 4·927 = 9·854$$
$$\text{Area of rhombus} = \frac{\text{product of diagonals}}{2}$$
$$= \frac{10·5 \times 9·854}{2} = 51·733\ 5$$

Answer: Area of rhombus $= 51·7$ mm^2

5.2.4 THE AREA OF ANY REGULAR POLYGON

Consider any regular polygon whose side has a length of L, the polygon having n sides. If lines are drawn from adjacent corners to the centre of the polygon, we shall obtain an isosceles triangle. A polygon of n sides with lines drawn to the centre from every corner will produce n congruent isosceles triangles. The area of the polygon will be n times the area of a single isosceles triangle. The total of the apex angles of all n congruent triangles is $360°$, hence the apex angle of a single triangle is $\frac{360°}{n}$. One such triangle is in Figure 5.19 (a).

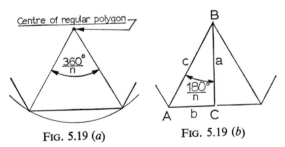

Fig. 5.19 (a)　　　Fig. 5.19 (b)

If we bisect the apex angle of an isosceles triangle, the bisector is at right angles to the base. Hence in Figure 5.19(b), *ABC* is a right-angled triangle and angle *B* is half of $\frac{360°}{n}$, i.e. $\frac{180°}{n}$.

Side *b* is half the length of side *L*, or $b = \frac{L}{2}$.

Perpendicular height of triangle *ABC* = *a*. In the right-angled triangle *ABC*:

$$a = \frac{L}{2} \cot \frac{180°}{n}$$

Area of large triangle = $\frac{1}{2}$ base × perpendicular height
$$= ba$$
$$= \frac{L}{2} \times \frac{L}{2} \cot \frac{180°}{n}$$

Area of polygon having *n* sides = total area of *n* congruent triangles as Fig. 5.19 (a)
$$= n \left\{ \frac{L}{2} \times \frac{L}{2} \cot \frac{180°}{n} \right\}$$
$$= \frac{nL^2}{4} \cot \frac{180°}{n}$$

For a square: $n = 4$

Hence   area $= \frac{4L^2}{4} \cot \frac{180°}{4}$
$$= L^2 \cot 45° = L^2 \times 1$$
$$= L^2, \text{ as we would expect}$$

For a pentagon: $n = 5$

Hence   area $= \frac{5L^2}{4} \cot \frac{180°}{5}$
$$= 1 \cdot 25 \, L^2 \cot 36°$$
$$= \mathbf{1} \cdot 25 \, L^2 \times 1 \cdot 376 \, 4$$
$$= 1 \cdot 720 \, L^2$$

For a hexagon: $n = 6$

Hence   area $= \frac{6L^2}{4} \cot \frac{180°}{6}$
$$= 1 \cdot 5 \, L^2 \cot 30°$$
$$= 1 \cdot 5 \, L^2 \times 1 \cdot 732 \, 1$$
$$= 2 \cdot 598 \, L^2$$

For an octagon: $n = 8$

Hence
$$\text{area} = \frac{8L^2}{4} \cot \frac{180°}{8}$$
$$= 2L^2 \cot 22° \, 30'$$
$$= 2L^2 \times 2.414 \, 2$$
$$= 4.828 \, L^2$$

If the polygon has an even number of sides, opposing sides are parallel. A convenient way of indicating the size of a regular polygon with an even number of sides is to state the distance between opposing sides. In engineering this is known as the *distance across flats*.

Let us use a method similar to the previous method to obtain area of any regular polygon having an even number of sides when the distance across flats is W.

Referring back to Figure 5.19(*b*), the distance a will be $\frac{W}{2}$ and the angle $B = \frac{180°}{n}$. Hence:

$$b = a \tan B = \frac{W}{2} \tan \frac{180°}{n}$$
$$\text{Area of one triangle} = \frac{\text{base} \times \text{vertical height}}{2}$$
$$= \frac{W}{2} \tan \frac{180°}{n} \times \frac{W}{2}$$
$$= \frac{W^2}{4} \tan \frac{180°}{n}$$
$$\text{Area of } n \text{ congruent triangles} = \frac{nW^2}{4} \tan \frac{180°}{n}$$

Hence the area of any regular polygon having an even number of sides n and measuring W across the flats is given by:
$$\frac{nW^2}{4} \tan \frac{180°}{n}$$

For a square: $n = 4$

Hence
$$\text{area} = \frac{4W^2}{4} \tan \frac{180°}{n} = W^2 \tan 45°$$
$$= W^2, \text{ as we would expect}$$

For a hexagon: $n = 6$

Hence
$$\text{area} = \frac{6W^2}{4} \tan \frac{180°}{6} = \frac{6W^2 \tan 30°}{4}$$
$$= \frac{6W^2 \times 0.577 \, 4}{4} = 0.866 \, W^2$$

For an octagon, $n = 8$

Hence $$\text{area} = \frac{8W^2}{4} \tan \frac{180°}{8} = \frac{8W^2 \tan 22\frac{1}{2}°}{4}$$
$$= 2W^2 \times 0.414\,2 = 0.828\ W^2$$

Example

Find the area of a regular octagon whose distance across flats is 5 mm.

$$\text{Area} = \frac{nW^2}{4} \tan \frac{180°}{n}$$
$$= \frac{8(5^2)}{4} \tan \frac{180°}{8} = 50 \tan 22° \ 30'$$
$$= 50 \times 0.414\,2 = 20.71 \text{ mm}^2$$

Answer: Area of octagon $= 20.7$ mm^2

5.2.5 THE AREA OF A CIRCLE, AN ANNULUS AND AN ELLIPSE

For the time being, the reader must accept without proof that the area A of a circle of radius r is given by the formula $A = \pi r^2$, or in terms of the diameter, $A = \frac{\pi d^2}{4}$. The reader is reminded that Castle's *Four-figure Mathematical Tables* can be used to find areas of circles and used in reverse to find the diameter if the area is known.

If C is the circumference of a circle:

$$C = \pi d, \text{ hence } d = \frac{C}{\pi} \text{ and } \pi = \frac{C}{d}$$

Hence, if $$A = \frac{\pi d^2}{4}$$

substituting for d gives $A = \frac{\pi}{4}\left(\frac{C}{\pi}\right)^2 = \frac{C^2}{4\pi}$

and $$A = \frac{d^2}{4} \times \frac{C}{d} = \frac{Cd}{4}$$

Here we have another example of different formulae for the area of a plane figure. The formula we use for a particular circumstance depends upon the dimensions we are given. As is our custom, we will summarize the results.

If d is the diameter of a circle, and C the circumference, then the area A is given by the formulae:

$$A = \frac{\pi d^2}{4}, \text{ or } A = \frac{C^2}{4\pi}, \text{ or } A = \frac{Cd}{4}$$

An *annulus* is the area which lies between two concentric circles. Once more we remind the reader that areas of circles can be found from tables. On the occasions that a formula has to be used, if D is the diameter of the larger circle and d is the diameter of the smaller circle, the area A of the annulus is given by the difference in the areas of the two circles. Hence:

$$A = \frac{\pi D^2}{4} - \frac{\pi d^2}{4}$$

$$= \frac{\pi}{4}(D^2 - d^2) = \frac{\pi}{4}(D + d)(D - d)$$

An *ellipse* is usually specified by quoting the length of the major axis a and the length of the minor axis b. The area A is then given by the formula:

$$A = \frac{\pi ab}{4}$$

Example

Discs of steel of diameter 9 mm are stamped out from strip 38·5 mm wide so that the smallest distance between each hole or a hole and the strip edge is 0·5 mm. What percentage of the strip is waste if:

(*a*) the discs are punched out in rows of four;
(*b*) the discs are punched out in alternate rows of four and three?

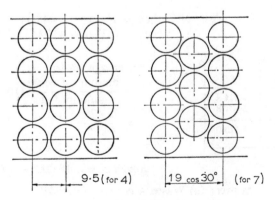

9·5 (for 4)   19 cos 30°   (for 7)

Fig. 5.20

Figure 5.20 shows the different patterns.
In the first case, a progression of 9·5 produces 4 discs.

$$\text{Area fed for 4 discs} = 38\cdot5 \times 9\cdot5 = 365\cdot75$$
Area of a circle 9 mm in diameter, from tables $= 63\cdot62$
Area of 4 discs $= 4(63\cdot62) = 254\cdot48$
Waste $= 365\cdot75 - 254\cdot48 = 111\cdot27$

$$\text{Percentage waste} = \frac{\text{amount of waste}}{\text{amount fed}}\,(100\%)$$

No.	Log
11 127 365·75	4·046 4 2·563 2
30·42	1·483 2

$$= \frac{11\ 127}{365\cdot75} = 30\cdot42\%$$

Rough check:
$$\frac{110}{4}\% = 27\tfrac{1}{2}\%$$

In the second case, lines joining the centres of discs form equilateral triangles; hence a progression of $2(9\cdot5 \cos 30°)$ produces 7 discs.

No.	Log
38·5 19 cos 30°	1·585 5 1·278 8 $\bar{1}$·937 5
633·6	2·801 8

Area fed for 7 discs
$$= 38\cdot5 \times 19 \cos 30°$$
$$= 633\cdot6$$

Rough check:
$$40 \times 20 \times 0\cdot8 = 640$$

Area of 7 discs $= 7(63\cdot62) = 445\cdot34$
Waste $= (633\cdot6 - 445\cdot34) = 188\cdot26$

No.	Log
18 826 633·6	4·274 8 2·801 8
29·72	1·473 0

Percentage waste
$$= \frac{\text{amount of waste}}{\text{amount fed}}\,(100\%)$$
$$= \frac{18\ 826}{633\cdot6}$$
$$= 29\cdot72\%$$

Rough check: $18\ 000 \div 600 = 30$

Answer: (*a*) Waste, 4 per row $= 30\cdot4\%$
(*b*) Waste, alternate rows $= 29\cdot7\%$

5.2.6 THE AREAS OF SECTORS AND OF SEGMENTS OF A CIRCLE

A *sector* is an area bounded by a circular arc and two radii. Inserting two radii into a circle divides that circle into two sectors. If the radii are not in line the sectors are unequal in area, and we can refer to them as the major sector (the larger in area) and the minor sector (the smaller in area). Unless we are specifically instructed to the contrary we shall consider a sector to be the minor sector, i.e. the smallest area bounded by a circular arc and two radii.

A sector can be completely defined by the radius of the circular arc r and the included angle θ between the two radii, as shown in Figure 5.21. The area of the complete circle of which the sector forms

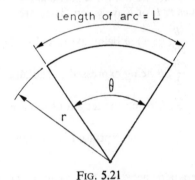

Length of arc = L

FIG. 5.21

part is given by πr^2. We can imagine the circle to be constructed of 360 identical narrow sectors each having an included angle of one degree. The area of each of these narrow sectors is given by $\frac{\pi r^2}{360}$. If the included angle of a particular sector is $\theta°$, there are θ of these narrow sectors and hence the area of a sector A is given by the formula:

$$A = \frac{\theta}{360}(\pi r^2),\ \theta \text{ being in degrees}$$

To convert an angle in radians to an angle in degrees, we multiply by $\frac{360}{2\pi}$. Hence if the included angle θ is expressed in radians:

$$A = \frac{\theta}{360} \times \frac{360}{2\pi}(\pi r^2)$$
$$= \frac{r^2\theta}{2},\ \theta \text{ now being in radians}$$

293

If θ is expressed in radians, the length of the circular arc is $r\theta$. Let us represent this by L:

$$A = \frac{r^2\theta}{2} = \frac{r \times r\theta}{2} = \frac{rL}{2}$$

(note the similarity with the area of a triangle)

In a similar manner: if $L = r\theta$, then $r = \dfrac{L}{\theta}$

$$A = \frac{rL}{2} = \frac{L}{\theta} \times \frac{L}{2} = \frac{L^2}{2\theta}$$

We therefore have four different formulae we can use for the area of a sector; the formula we use for a particular sector depends upon which of the values r, L or θ are given. They are:

$$A = \frac{\theta}{360}(\pi r^2), \theta \text{ being expressed in degrees}$$

$$A = \frac{r^2\theta}{2}, \theta \text{ being expressed in radians}$$

$$A = \frac{rL}{2}, L \text{ being the length of the arc}$$

$$A = \frac{L^2}{2\theta}, \theta \text{ being expressed in radians}$$

Example

Taking $\pi = \frac{22}{7}$ where necessary, calculate the areas of the following sectors:

    (*a*) radius 7 mm, included angle 60°;
    (*b*) length of arc 8 mm, radius = 6 mm;
    (*c*) length of arc 10 mm, included angle 45°.

(*a*) $A = \dfrac{\theta}{360}(\pi r^2) = \dfrac{60}{360} \times \dfrac{22}{7} \times \dfrac{7}{1} \times \dfrac{7}{1}$

            $= \dfrac{77}{3} = 25{\cdot}7 \text{ mm}^2$

(*b*) $A = \dfrac{rL}{2} = \dfrac{6 \times 8}{2} = 24 \text{ mm}^2$

(*c*) $A = \dfrac{L^2}{2\theta}$, and $45° = \dfrac{\pi}{4}$ radians

            $A = \dfrac{10 \times 10 \times 4}{\pi \times 2} = \dfrac{200 \times 7}{22} = \dfrac{700}{11} = 63{\cdot}6 \text{ mm}^2$

Answers: (*a*) 25·7 mm²   (*b*) 24 mm²   (*c*) 63·6 mm²

Example

An annulus is formed by two concentric circles of radii 6 mm and 5 mm. Calculate the area of that part of the annulus which lies between two radii inclined at 54° to one another.

From tables: area of a circle of diameter 12 mm = 113·1 mm²
area of a circle of diameter 10 mm = 78·54 mm²

By subtraction: area of complete annulus = 34·56 mm²

$$\text{Area of annular sector} = \frac{54}{360} \times 34\cdot56 = \frac{3 \times 34\cdot56}{20}$$

$$= \frac{103\cdot68}{20} = 5\cdot184 \text{ mm}^2$$

Answer: Area of annular sector = 5·18 mm²

A *segment* is the area contained by an arc of a circle and a chord. A chord divides a circle into two areas. Unless that chord is a diameter, one area is greater than the other. We can differentiate between the two segments by nominating the major segment to be the segment of greater area. The smaller of the two segments can be referred to as the minor segment. Unless we are specifically informed to the contrary, we shall consider the area of a segment contained by a chord and a circular arc to be that of the minor segment.

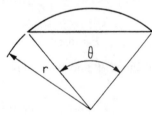

Fig. 5.22

In Figure 5.22, we have a segment of a circle of radius r. The radii drawn to the ends of the segment contain an angle of θ.

Area of segment = area of sector − area of triangle

Area of sector $= \dfrac{r^2\theta}{2}$

Area of triangle = half product of two sides and the sine of the included angle

$$= \tfrac{1}{2}(r)(r) \sin \theta$$

$$= \frac{r^2 \sin \theta}{2}$$

$$\text{Area of segment} = \frac{r^2\theta}{2} - \frac{r^2 \sin \theta}{2}$$
$$= \frac{r^2}{2} (\theta - \sin \theta)$$

Since no unit is quoted for θ, it is implied that the angle is in radians. The formula requires the knowledge of the angle before a determination of the area can be made. It would be most unusual to find a segment to be dimensioned in such a way that it is quoted directly. In many cases θ has to be established from other dimensions. In Figure 5.23, the more usual information is illustrated.

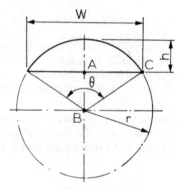

Fig. 5.23

If the length of the chord W and the radius r are known, then:

$$\frac{\frac{W}{2}}{r} = \sin \frac{\theta}{2} \text{ whence } \frac{\theta}{2} = \arcsin \frac{W}{2r}$$

from which θ can be established.

If two of the variables h, L and r are known, the third can be determined.

In the right-angled triangle ABC:

$$AB = r - h \quad AC = \frac{W}{2} \quad BC = r$$

According to Pythagoras:

$$(AB)^2 + (AC)^2 = (BC)^2$$
$$(r - h)^2 + \left(\frac{W}{2}\right)^2 = r^2$$

$$r^2 - 2rh + h^2 + \frac{W^2}{4} = r^2$$

$$2rh = h^2 + \frac{W^2}{4}$$

and
$$r = \frac{W^2}{8h} + \frac{h}{2}$$

This formula is easy to apply if r or L have to be determined. If the unknown is h, manipulation of the equation produces a quadratic equation in terms of h, usually with most awkward values. If h is required, it is advisable to revert to a simple application of the Theorem of Pythagoras.

Example

A circular bar has a diameter of 34 mm. A flat of width 16 mm is machined along the whole length of the bar. Calculate:

    (a) the depth of cut;
    (b) the cross-sectional area of metal removed, in mm².

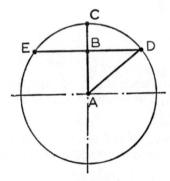

FIG. 5.24

Referring to Figure 5.24:

$$AD = \frac{\text{diameter}}{2} = 17 \text{ mm}$$
$$BD = \text{half width of flat} = 8 \text{ mm}$$
$$(AD)^2 = (BA)^2 + (BD)^2$$
$$(BA)^2 = (AD)^2 - (BD)^2$$
$$= 17^2 - 8^2 = 289 - 64$$
$$= 225$$
$$BA = \sqrt{225} = 15$$

$$\text{Depth of cut} = CB = \text{radius } CA - BA$$
$$= 17 - 15 = 2 \text{ mm}$$

In the triangle ABD:

$$\text{Angle } A = \text{arccosec } \tfrac{17}{8} = \text{arccosec } 2.125 = 28° \, 5'$$
$$\text{Angle } \theta \text{ of segment} = \text{angle } EAD = 2(28° \, 5')$$
$$= 56° \, 10'$$
$$56° \, 10' = 0.980 \, 3 \text{ radians}$$
$$\sin 56° \, 10' = 0.830 \, 6$$
$$\text{Area of segment} = \frac{r^2}{2}(\theta - \sin \theta)$$
$$= \frac{17 \times 17}{2}(0.980 \, 3 - 0.830 \, 6)$$
$$= \frac{289 \times 0.149 \, 7}{2} = 21.63 \text{ mm}^2$$

No.	Log
289 0·149 7	2·460 9 $\bar{1}$·175 2
2	1·636 1 0·301 0
21·63	1·335 1

Rough check: $\dfrac{280 \times 0.14}{2} = 19.6$

Answers: Depth of cut = 2 mm
Cross-sectional area = 21·6 mm²

Example

Calculate the cross-sectional area of a tunnel whose dimensions are that of the major segment formed by a circle of 1 m radius and a chord of length 1·6 m.

Figure 5.25 shows the cross-section of the tunnel.

$$\sin A = 0.8/1 = 0.8$$
$$\therefore A = 53° \, 8'$$
$$\theta = 360° - 2(53° \, 8') = 360° - 106° \, 16'$$
$$= 253° \, 44'$$
$$\text{Area of segment} = \frac{r^2}{2}(\theta - \sin \theta)$$

$$
\begin{array}{rl}
180° & = 3.141 \, 6 \text{ radians} \\
73° \, 44' & = 1.286 \, 9 \text{ radians} \\
\hline
253° \, 44' & = 4.428 \, 5 \text{ radians}
\end{array}
$$

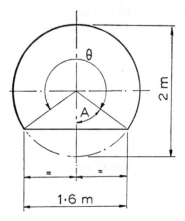

Fig. 5.25

253° 44' lies in the third quadrant:

$$\sin 253° 44' = -\sin 73° 44' = -0.960\ 0$$

$$\text{Area} = \frac{r^2}{2}\ (\theta - \sin \theta) = \frac{1}{2}\ \{4.428\ 5 - (-0.960\ 0)\}$$

$$= 0.5\ \{4.428\ 5 + 0.960\ 0\}$$

$$= 0.5\{5.388\ 5\}$$

$$= 2.694\ 25\ \text{m}^2$$

Answer: Area of cross-section $= 2.69\ \text{m}^2$

5.2.7 DEVELOPMENT OF CURVED SURFACES

If we position a cylinder of radius r and length L with its curved surface on a plane, there is a line of contact of length L between the cylinder and the plane. If we imagine the line of contact to be drawn on the cylinder, and then rotate the cylinder until the line contacts the plane once more, as in Figure 5.26, we observe that if the curved surface of the cylinder was developed into a flat surface, it would form a rectangle with sides of length $2\pi r$ and L. Hence the curved surface of a cylinder of radius r and length L has an area of $2\pi rL$.

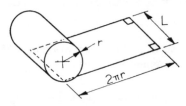

Fig. 5.26

We can develop the curved surface of a cone in exactly the same manner. If the cone has a slant height of L, the development is a sector of a circle of radius L, as shown in Figure 5.27. The length of the arc of the sector is equal to the circumference of the base of the cone.

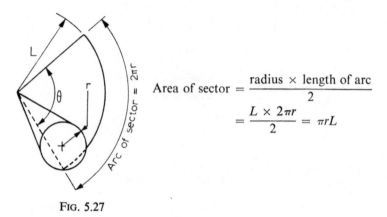

$$\text{Area of sector} = \frac{\text{radius} \times \text{length of arc}}{2}$$

$$= \frac{L \times 2\pi r}{2} = \pi r L$$

FIG. 5.27

The included angle θ of the sector, in radians, is found by dividing the length of the arc by the radius:

$$\theta \text{ (radians)} = \frac{2\pi r}{L}$$

To convert an angle in radians to degrees we multiply by $\dfrac{360}{2\pi}$.

Hence

$$\theta \text{ (degrees)} = \frac{2\pi r}{L} \times \frac{360}{2\pi} = \frac{360r}{L}$$

A *frustum* of a cone is that portion of a cone contained between two parallel planes, the planes being at right-angles to the vertical axis. A frustum can be visualized as a large cone minus a small cone. The development of the curved surface is thus the sector of a large circle minus the sector of a small circle, i.e. a sector of an annulus.

Example

The total curved surface of a cylinder of length 15 mm is 968 mm². Taking π as $\frac{22}{7}$, determine the radius.

    Let radius $= r$
    Total area $=$ area of two ends $+$ area of curved surface
$$A = 2\pi r^2 + 2\pi r L$$

Substituting $A = 968$, $2\pi = \dfrac{44}{7}$ and $L = 15$:

$$968 = \frac{44r^2}{7} + \frac{44r \times 15}{7}$$

Dividing through by 44: $22 = \dfrac{r^2}{7} + \dfrac{15r}{7}$

Multiplying through by 7:

$$154 = r^2 + 15r$$
$$r^2 + 15r - 154 = 0$$
$$(r + 22)(r - 7) = 0$$

A negative root is illogical, hence:

$$r - 7 = 0 \text{ and } r = 7$$

Check: Area of ends $= \dfrac{2}{1} \times \dfrac{22}{7} \times \dfrac{7}{1} \times \dfrac{7}{1} = 308$

Area of curved surface $= \dfrac{2}{1} \times \dfrac{22}{7} \times \dfrac{7}{1} \times \dfrac{15}{1} = 660$

Total $= 308 + 660 = 968$

Answer: Radius $= 7$ mm

Example

A sector of a circle has a radius of 15 mm and an included angle of 216°. The sector is formed into the curved surface of a cone, the two radii abutting without lap. Calculate:

    (*a*) the base radius of the cone;
    (*b*) the vertical height;
    (*c*) the apex angle. (Take π as $\frac{22}{7}$.)

(*a*) Sector angle in degrees $= \dfrac{360r}{L}$. The radius of the sector is the slant height of the cone.

$$L = 15 \text{ mm}$$
$$216° = \frac{360° \times r}{L}$$
$$r = \frac{216L}{360} = \frac{216 \times 15}{360} = 9 \text{ mm}$$

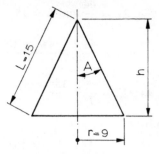

FIG. 5.28

(*b*) Referring to Figure 5.28:

$$L^2 = r^2 + h^2$$
$$h^2 = L^2 - r^2, h = \sqrt{(L^2 - r^2)}$$
$$h = \sqrt{(225 - 81)} = \sqrt{144} = 12 \text{ mm}$$

(*c*) From Figure 5.28, $A = \arcsin \dfrac{r}{L} = \arcsin \dfrac{9}{15} = \arcsin 0\cdot6$

$$A = 36° 52'$$
$$\text{Apex angle} = 2A = 2(36° 52') = 73° 44'$$

Answers: (*a*) Base radius = 9 mm
(*b*) Vertical height = 12 mm
(*c*) Apex angle = 73° 44'

Example

Find the area of the curved surface of a frustum of a cone. The frustum is of height 8 mm and the radii of the top surface and the base are 6 mm and 12 mm respectively.

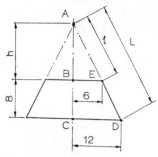

FIG. 5.29

Figure 5.29 shows the dimensions of the frustum, which will be considered as a difference between two similar cones. Triangles *ABE* and *ACD* are similar:

$$\therefore \frac{AB}{AC} = \frac{BE}{CD} \qquad \therefore \frac{h}{h+8} = \frac{6}{12}$$
$$\therefore 12h = 6(h+8), \qquad 12h = 6h + 48$$
$$12h - 6h = 48, \qquad 6h = 48, \qquad h = 8$$
$$l = \sqrt{(6^2 + 8^2)} = \sqrt{(36+64)} = \sqrt{100} = 10$$
$$L = \sqrt{(12^2 + 16^2)} = \sqrt{(144+256)} = \sqrt{400} = 20$$

$$\begin{aligned}
\text{Area of sector of annulus} &= \pi RL - \pi rl \\
&= \pi(RL - rl) \\
&= \pi(12 \times 20 - 6 \times 10) \\
&= \pi(240 - 60) \\
&= 180\pi \\
&= 565{\cdot}56 \text{ mm}^2
\end{aligned}$$

Answer: Area of curved surface $= 566$ mm^2

5.2.8 THE SURFACE AREA OF A SPHERE, OF A SPHERICAL CAP, AND OF A SPHERICAL ZONE

A logical development of the formulae connected with the surface area of a sphere, and of parts of the surface area of a sphere, is outside the scope of this book. The formulae must be accepted without proof. The surface area A of a sphere is given by the formula:

$$A = 4\pi r^2$$

or, in terms of the diameter d:

$$A = \pi d^2$$

If a sphere is cut by a plane, the smaller portion is called a *spherical cap*. If this cap rests on its circular face, the maximum distance from that face to the curved surface is referred to as the height h of the spherical cap. The curved spherical surface area A of a spherical cap is given by the formula:

$$A = 2\pi rh$$

If a sphere is cut by two parallel planes, the portion lying between those planes is called a *zone* of the sphere. If the cutting planes lie at a distance h apart, the curved spherical surface area A is given by:

$$A = 2\pi rh$$

(an identical formula to that for the curved spherical surface area of a spherical cap).

303

Example

A hot-water storage tank consists of a cylinder surmounted by a hemisphere. The common radius is 400 mm and the overall height is 900 mm. Find the area, in square metres, required to cover the entire tank with lagging material.

$$400 \text{ mm} = 0.4 \text{ m}, \qquad 900 \text{ mm} = 0.9 \text{ m}$$
$$\text{Height of cylinder} = 0.9 \text{ m} - 0.4 \text{ m} = 0.5 \text{ m}$$

Total surface area
= area of a circle + area of the curved surface of a cylinder + surface area of a hemisphere

$$= \pi r^2 + \pi r^2 h + \frac{4\pi r^2}{2}$$
$$= \pi r^2 + \pi r^2 h + 2\pi r^2$$
$$= \pi r^2 (1 + h + 2)$$
$$= \pi r^2 (3 + h)$$
$$= \pi r^2 (3 + 0.5)$$
$$= \frac{22 \times 0.4 \times 0.4 \times 3.5}{7} = 1.76 \text{ m}^2$$

Answer: Area of lagging material = 1.76 m^2

5.2.9 THE AREA OF SIMILAR PLANE FIGURES

If a rectangle is similar in shape to another rectangle, so that the length of a second rectangle is n times the length of the first, and the breadth of the second rectangle is n times the breadth of the first then:

$$\text{Area of first rectangle} = LB$$
and $$\text{area of second rectangle} = nL \times nB = n^2LB$$
in which case $$\frac{\text{area of second rectangle}}{\text{area of first rectangle}} = \frac{n^2LB}{LB} = n^2$$

If the diameter of a second circle is n times the area of first circle, then:

$$\frac{\text{Area of second circle}}{\text{Area of first circle}} = \frac{\pi(nd)^2}{4} \div \frac{4}{\pi d^2} = \frac{4\pi n^2 d^2}{4\pi d^2} = n^2$$

We could continue in the same manner for all plane figures. We should find that if a second figure has all linear dimensions n times the corresponding linear dimensions of a first figure, then:

$$\frac{\text{Area of second figure}}{\text{Area of first figure}} = n^2$$

Example

Find the area of a circle of diameter 0·82 mm.
From tables, area of circle of diameter 8·2 mm is 52·81 mm².

$$\frac{\text{Area of circle of diameter 0·82 mm}}{\text{Area of circle of diameter 8·2 mm}} = \left(\frac{0·82}{8·2}\right)^2 = \left(\frac{1}{10}\right)^2 = \frac{1}{100}$$

$\therefore$ area of circle of diameter 0·82 mm $= \dfrac{1}{100} \times 52·81 = 0·528\,1$

Answer: Area $= 0·528$ mm²

Problems 5.2

1. Calculate the area of a triangle with sides of length 8 mm, 11 mm and 15 mm.

2. Calculate the area of a triangle having sides of length 7·8 mm, 15·3 mm and 16·5 mm.

3. Calculate the area of a triangle with sides 3·12, 4·78 and 5·26 mm long.

4. Two circles, of diameter 78 mm and 50 mm respectively, intersect at A and B. If their common chord AB has a length of 30 mm, C being the centre of the larger circle, calculate:
   (a) the distance between their centres, C and D;
   (b) the area of triangle CAD;
   (c) the angle CAD.

5. In a triangle ABC, the side AB is 10 mm long, angle CAB is 30° and angle ACB is 45°. Draw the triangle and calculate;
   (a) the length of the side BC;
   (b) the angle ABC;
   (c) the length of side AC;
   (d) the area of the triangle.

6. Calculate the area of a triangle ABC, where:

   $$a = 15 \text{ mm}, B = 54° \text{ and } C = 66°$$

7. Calculate the area of a regular polygon having 20 sides, the distance across flats being 16 mm.

8. Find the area of a regular octagon:
   (*a*) 10 mm across flats;
   (*b*) with side of length 5 mm.

9. Calculate the area of a regular hexagon:
   (*a*) with width across flats 5 mm;
   (*b*) with length of side 3 mm.

10. Calculate the area of the trapezium shown in Figure 5.30.

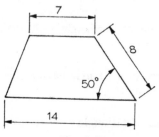

FIG. 5.30

11. In the trapezium *ABCD* shown in Figure 5.31, the line *EF* divides the trapezium into two equal areas. Calculate the distance *x*.

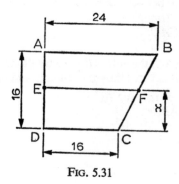

FIG. 5.31

12. A rhombus has sides of length 5 mm, one of the acute angles of the rhombus being 45°. Calculate the area of the rhombus and the length of both diagonals.

13. A parallelogram has two adjacent sides of length 5 mm and 8 mm, the angle between these sides being 40°. Calculate:

    (*a*) the area;
    (*b*) the distances between parallel sides;
    (*c*) the lengths of the diagonals.

14. Calculate the area of the quadrilateral shown in Figure 5.32.

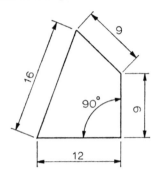

FIG. 5.32

15. What percentage of metal is removed when a cut of depth 1·5 mm is taken in turning the outside diameter of a bar of diameter 20 mm?

16. A pipe is used as a strut, and originally the outside diameter is 30 mm and the wall thickness is 2·5 mm. Calculate the percentage reduction in area when corrosion takes 0·1 mm off the external radius and increases the internal radius by the same amount.

17. It is known that in order to carry a particular load, a tubular strut must have a cross-sectional area of 550 mm². If the outside and inside diameters are to be in the proportion of 4:3, determine the outside diameter. (Take $\pi = \frac{22}{7}$.)

18. A four-way pipe junction has three inlet pipes of diameters 20 mm, 30 mm and 60 mm. Determine the diameter of the outlet pipe if its cross-sectional area is equal to the total cross-sectional area of the inlet pipes. (Take $\pi = \frac{22}{7}$ if required.)

19. An annulus has an area of 2 200 mm², the larger radius being 10 mm greater than the smaller radius. Take π as $\frac{22}{7}$ and calculate the radii.

20. Figure 5.33 shows a right-angled bend in a road with $AB = BC$ $= a$ m (the radius of a circle with centre O). The road is to be modified as shown by the dotted lines to remove the sharp corner. If the width of the road is x m, show that the saving in road surface area of the modification is given by:

$$\left(1 - \frac{\pi}{4}\right)(2ax - x^2) \text{ m}^2$$

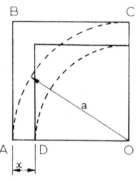

FIG. 5.33

21. An ellipse has axes which differ in length by 3 mm. If the area of the ellipse is 22 mm², take π as $\frac{22}{7}$ and determine the length of the minor axis.

22. (a) The arc of a sector of a circle of radius 5 mm subtends an angle of $\frac{2\pi}{3}$ radians at the centre. Calculate the sector area.

   (b) Find the included angle of the sector of a circle whose radius is 8 mm and whose area is 50 mm².

23. A segment is less than a semicircle and is bounded by a circular arc of radius 30 mm and a straight line of length 40 mm. Find the area to within 1 mm².

24. A bar of steel has a diameter of 20 mm. A flat is machined on the bar of width 10 mm. By what percentage has the cross-sectional area of the bar been reduced?

25. An open channel is semicircular in cross-section, the radius being 5 m. At a certain instant the depth of water at the centre of the

channel is 2 m. Determine the cross-sectional area of the water flow.

26. A semicircle of radius 100 mm is formed into the curved surface of a cone. Calculate the radius and vertical height of the cone.

27. Calculate the area of the smaller segment of a circle of radius 5 mm cut off by a chord of length 8 mm.

28. The end section of a shaft of a motor is in the form of the major arc of a circle of radius 40 mm cut off by a chord of length 40 mm. Calculate the area of the section.

29. A blade of an electric fan is a sector of a circle of radius 100 mm and has an area of 3 600 mm².
    (*a*) Calculate the angle of the sector in degrees and minutes.
    (*b*) Determine the speed of the fan in m/s of a point on the arc of the blade of the fan when the fan is rotating at 200 rev/min.

30. A sector of a circle radius *r* contains an angle θ radians at the centre of the circle. If the total perimeter of the sector is 12 mm, find a formula connecting *r* and θ and show that the area *A* of the sector is given by $A = 6r - r^2$. Find with the aid of a graph the maximum value of *A* and the values of *r* and θ corresponding to this maximum.

31. The radius of the arc of a circular segment is 6 mm and the angle subtended by it at the centre is 35°. Calculate, taking π as $\frac{22}{7}$:
    (*a*) the area of the segment;
    (*b*) the length of the chord;
    (*c*) the distance of the chord from the centre of the circle.

32. A chord is drawn through a circle of diameter 8 mm in such a manner that it bisects the radius which is perpendicular to it.
    (*a*) Calculate the angle which the chord subtends at the centre of the circle. Express this angle in both degrees and radians.
    (*b*) Calculate the areas of the segments of the circle cut off by the chord.

33. Calculate the area of the template shown in Figure 5.34 overleaf.

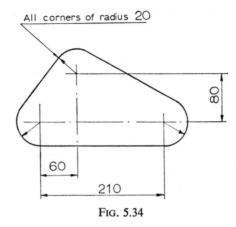

All corners of radius 20

80

60

210

FIG. 5.34

34. Calculate the area of the template shown in Figure 5.35.

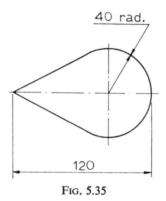

40 rad.

120

FIG. 5.35

35. A circular bar, of diameter 50 mm, is machined so that the uniform cross-section becomes a regular hexagon of the greatest possible area.

   (*a*) Calculate the area of this hexagon.
   (*b*) What percentage of the original bar is machined away?

36. A cone and a cylinder both have a radius of 50 mm and a height of 120 mm. Find the ratio:

$$\frac{\text{area of curved surface of cone}}{\text{area of curved surface of cylinder}}$$

Answers to Problems 5.2

1. 42·8 mm²
2. 59·4 mm²
3. 7·36 mm²
4. (*a*) 56·0 mm   (*b*) 420 mm²   (*c*) 120° 31′
5. (*a*) 7·07 mm   (*b*) 105°   (*c*) 13·7 mm   (*d*) 34·2 mm²
6. 96·0 mm²
7. 203 mm²
8. (*a*) 82·8 mm²   (*b*) 121 mm²
9. (*a*) 21·6 mm²   (*b*) 23·4 mm²
10. 64·3 mm²
11. 8·80 mm
12. 17·7 mm²; 3·83 mm and 9·24 mm
13. (*a*) 25·7 mm²   (*b*) 3·21 mm and 5·14 mm
    (*c*) 5·25 mm and 12·3 mm
14. 120 mm²
15. 27·8%
16. 8%
17. 40 mm
18. 70 mm
19. 40 mm and 30 mm
21. 4 mm
22. (*a*) 26·2 mm²   (*b*) 89° 31′
23. 210 mm²
24. 2·88%
25. 11·2 m²
26. 50 mm, 86·6 mm
27. 11·2 mm
28. 4 880 mm²
29. (*a*) 41° 15′   (*b*) 2·09 m/s
30. $A = 9$ mm², $r = 3$ mm, $\theta = 2$ rad $= 114°$ 36′
31. (*a*) 0·671 mm²   (*b*) 3·61 mm   (*c*) 5·72 mm
32. (*a*) $120° = \dfrac{2\pi}{3}$ rad $= 2·094\ 4$ rad

    (*b*) 9·83 mm² and 40·4 mm²
33. 19 300 mm²
34. 6 120 mm²
35. (*a*) 1 620 mm²   (*b*) 17·3%
36. 13/24

5.3 The Area of Irregular Plane Figures

5.3.1 THE TRAPEZOIDAL RULE

If a plane figure is bounded by straight lines, or combinations of straight lines and geometrical curves, although the calculations may be very lengthy, the area of that plane figure can be determined very accurately. There are occasions when a precise determination is unnecessary, and rapidity of obtaining an approximate value of reasonable accuracy is of more importance. On other occasions, the perimeter of the figure may include portions of randomly curved lines which follow no regular geometrical pattern.

In these two latter cases the area of the irregularly shaped figure is determined approximately. There are a great many methods of determining approximately the area of an irregular figure. The simpler methods tend to be less accurate and, as greater accuracy is desired, the method adopted tends to become more complex. In our present studies we have to learn two methods, both being based on the area of a trapezium.

The irregular plane figure is divided into strips by parallel lines, called ordinates. It is conventional practice, to ease a subsequent calculation, for the strips to be of equal width. Figure 5.36 shows an irregular plane figure divided into strips of equal width by ordinates. The area of the figure is the sum of the areas of the individual strips.

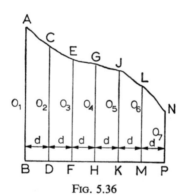

Fig. 5.36

Consider the particular strip $ABCD$. Its area is approximately equal to a trapezium of sides O_1 and O_2, whose distance apart is d.

$$\text{Area of strip } ABCD \simeq \left(\frac{O_1 + O_2}{2}\right)d$$

The sign $\simeq$ is read as 'is approximately equal to'.

The strip *CDEF* has an area approximately equal to a trapezium of sides O_2 and O_3 whose distance apart is d.

$$\text{Area of strip } CDEF \simeq \left(\frac{O_2 + O_3}{2}\right)d$$

We proceed across the figure in the same manner, the area of next strip being approximately equal to $\left(\frac{O_3 + O_4}{2}\right)d$.

The area of the figure is the sum of the areas of individual strips.

$$\text{Total area} \simeq \left(\frac{O_1 + O_2}{2}\right)d + \left(\frac{O_2 + O_3}{2}\right)d + \left(\frac{O_3 + O_4}{2}\right)d \text{ etc.}$$

$$\simeq d\left(\frac{O_1 + O_2 + O_2 + O_3 + O_3 + O_4 + O_4}{2} \ldots\right)$$

$$\simeq \frac{d}{2}(O_1 + 2O_2 + 2O_3 + 2O_4 \ldots O_L)$$

where O_L is the length of the last ordinate

$$\simeq d\left(\frac{O_1 + O_L}{2} + O_2 + O_3 + O_4 \ldots\right)$$

Hence the area is given approximately by the width of a strip multiplied by sum of the mean of the first and last ordinates and the remaining ordinates. It is usually stated as:

$$\text{Area} \simeq \text{width of strip}\left\{\frac{\text{first} + \text{last}}{2} + (\text{sum of other ordinates})\right\}$$

Example

Sketch the graph of $y = 9 - x^2$ between $x = -3$ and $x = +3$. Shade the area which is bounded by the curve and the x-axis. Determine this area by the trapezoidal rule:

    (*a*) with six vertical strips of equal width;
    (*b*) with twelve vertical strips of equal width.
    (*c*) The area is precisely 36 units of area. Hence show that the trapezoidal rule tends to be more accurate if a greater number of strips is used.

The area is in Figures 5.37(*a*) and 5.37(*b*) overleaf. Figure 5.37(*a*) shows six vertical strips and Figure 5.37(*b*) twelve vertical strips.

(a) Six vertical strips:
Ordinates are 0, 5, 8, 9, 8, 5 and 0.

$$\text{Area} = \text{width of strip} \left\{ \frac{\text{first + last}}{2} + (\text{sum of others}) \right\}$$

$$= 1 \left\{ \frac{0 + 0}{2} + (5 + 8 + 9 + 8 + 5) \right\} = 1\{35\}$$

$$= 35 \text{ units of area}$$

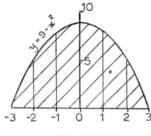

FIG. 5.37 (*a*)

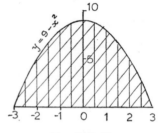

FIG. 5.37 (*b*)

(*b*) *Twelve vertical strips:*

Ordinates are 0, 2·75, 5, 6·75, 8, 8·75, 9, 8·75, 8, 6·75, 5, 2·75, 0.

$$\text{Area} = \text{width of strip} \left\{ \frac{\text{first + last}}{2} + (\text{sum of others}) \right\}$$

$$= \frac{1}{2} \left\{ \frac{0 + 0}{2} + 71\cdot5 \right\}$$

$$= \frac{71\cdot5}{2}$$

$$= 35\cdot75 \text{ units of area}$$

(*c*)   Error of six strips = 1 unit of area

               Error of twelve strips = 0·25 unit of area

Use of twelve strips produces a more accurate result.

Answer: (*a*) 35 units of area

           (*b*) 35·75 units of area

           (*c*) Using a greater number of strips gives smaller error, and hence is more accurate.

5.3.2 THE MID-ORDINATE RULE

The trapezoidal rule is the easiest method to apply of all the methods for determining approximately the area of an irregular figure. It is reasonably accurate provided at least one end of the figure is a straight line. If the ends of the figure are curved, then both

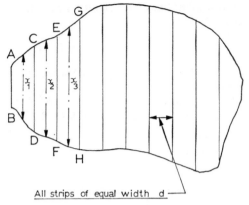

All strips of equal width d

FIG. 5.38

the first and last ordinates are zero. This means that the first and last strips are approximated to triangles.

In most cases where the ends of the figure are curved, a closer approximation is obtained if the areas of strips are approximated to trapezia whose mean length of side is the length of another ordinate drawn midway between the existing ordinates.

Referring to Figure 5.38, we see that chain-dotted lines have been erected to indicate lengths of lines positioned midway between the ordinates.

$$\text{Area of strip } ABCD \simeq x_1 \times d$$
$$\text{that of } CDEF \simeq x_2 \times d$$
$$\text{that of } EFGH \simeq x_3 \times d$$

and so on.

$$\text{Total area} \simeq \text{the sum of the areas of separate strips}$$
$$\simeq x_1 d + x_2 d + x_3 d + x_4 d, \text{ etc.}$$
$$\simeq d \text{ (the sum of the mid-ordinates)}$$

This formula is generally known as the *mid-ordinate rule*. We divide the irregular figure into strips of equal width by erecting ordinates. We measure the width of the figure in the centres of strips, and call these the mid-ordinates. The area of the figure is given by the product of the sum of the mid-ordinates and the width of one strip.

The reader should appreciate that the accuracy of either the trapezoidal rule or the mid-ordinate rule depends on the number of strips. As the strips become narrower, so the profiles of their ends become nearer to straight lines. The greater the number of strips, the greater the accuracy.

Example

Use the mid-ordinate rule with six vertical strips to find the shaded area in the previous example.

Mid-ordinates occur at $x = -2.5$, -1.5, -0.5, 0.5, 1.5 and 2.5.
Lengths of mid-ordinates are 2.75, 6.75, 8.75, 8.75, 6.75 and 2.75.

$$\text{Area} = \text{width of one strip} \times \text{sum of mid-ordinates}$$
$$= 1 \times 36.5$$
$$= 36.5 \text{ units of area}$$

Answer: 36·5 units of area

Whether the trapezoidal rule or the mid-ordinate rule (using the same number of strips) produces the more accurate result depends on the profile of the figure. If the profile shows no violent changes and has curves at each end, the use of the mid-ordinate rule tends to provide the more accurate answer. It should be noted, however, that on occasions the use of the trapezoidal rule with a large number of strips can produce a more accurate result than that provided by the mid-ordinate rule with a small number of strips.

Problems 5.3

1. On squared paper, draw accurately a semicircle on a diameter of 60 mm. Using twelve strips each of width 5 mm, so as to produce thirteen ordinates, find the length of each of the ordinates to the nearest 0·1 mm and find the area of the semicircle using the trapezoidal rule.

2. Use the information from the previous question to find the area by the mid-ordinate rule, using nominally six strips each of width 10 mm.

3. Sketch the area contained by the curve $y = x^2$, the x-axis and the line $x = 10$. Find the area using the mid-ordinate rule and five strips of width 2 units.

4. Draw an arc of a circle of radius 50 mm. Set your compasses to 60 mm, and with the point on the circle mark off and draw a chord of length 60 mm. You now have an area bounded by a circular arc of radius 50 mm and a chord of length 60 mm. Treat the

chord as a base and erect ordinates to divide the figure into ten strips of width 6 mm. Obtain the area of the figure by means of the mid-ordinate rule.

5. Plot the curve, in the first quadrant, $xy = 100$. Shade the area contained by:

      (i) the x-axis   (ii) the y-axis   (iii) the line $y = 20$
      (iv) the curve $xy = 100$ (v) the line $x = 25$

(*a*) Using vertical strips each of width 5 units, find the area of the shaded figure by the trapezoidal rule.

(*b*) Repeat the exercise with horizontal strips of height 4 units.

6. The following table gives the depth below ground level of a cable. Plot a graph of *d* against *l*.

Horizontal distance *d* m	0	50	100	150	200	250	300	350	400
Depth of cable *l* m	1·8	2·5	3·0	3·3	3·5	3·8	3·5	2·7	1·7

Use the mid-ordinate rule to find the area under the horizontal base line and hence calculate the volume of earth, in cubic metres, to be removed in order to uncover the whole length of the cable if the trench is 1·5 m wide. Give the answer to the nearest whole number.

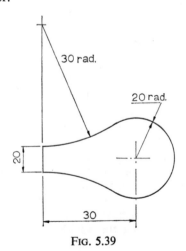

Fig. 5.39

7. Use a scale drawing and the mid-ordinate rule with 5 strips of equal width to find the area of the template shown in Figure 5.39.

8. Sketch the curve $y = 16 - x^2$. Shade the area which lies between the x-axis and the curve. Divide the area into 8 strips of equal width, calculate the mid-ordinates, and hence determine the shaded area with the aid of the mid-ordinate rule. If it is known that the area is $85\frac{1}{3}$ units, what is the percentage error, to 2 significant figures, caused by the adoption of the mid-ordinate rule?

Answers to Problems 5.3

1. Ordinates are 0, 16·6, 22·4, 26·0, 28·3, 29·6, 30·0, 29·6, 28·3, 26·0, 22·4, 16·6 and 0. These give an area of 1 380 mm².

    (The actual area is 1 414, and the error when the extremes of the figure are points producing zero ordinates should be noticed.)

2. Mid-ordinates are 16·6, 26·0, 29·6, 29·6, 26·0 and 16·6. These give an area of 1 440 mm².

3. Mid-ordinates are 1, 9, 25, 49 and 81. These give an area of 330 square units.

4. Mid-ordinates are 2·1, 5·4, 7·7, 9·2, 9·9, 9·9, 9·2, 7·7, 5·4 and 2·1. These give an area of 412 mm².

5. (a) Ordinates are 20, 20, 10, $6\frac{2}{3}$, 5 and 4. These given a area of $268\frac{1}{3}$ square units.

    (b) Ordinates are (from top to bottom) 5, $6\frac{1}{4}$, $8\frac{1}{3}$, $12\frac{1}{2}$, 25 and 25. These give an area of $268\frac{1}{3}$ square units.

6. 1 800 m³

7. 1 530 mm²

8. 86 square units, 0·78%

5.4   The Volumes of Solids

5.4.1   PRISMS, CYLINDERS AND PIPES

A *prism* is a solid of constant cross-section. Unless it is specifically stated to the contrary, a prism is assumed to be a *right prism*, where the ends, having the shape of a regular polygon, lie at right angles to the axis which passes through the centres of the ends. Prisms are described by the shape of the constant cross-section, such as a triangular prism, a hexagonal prism, and so on. A square prism whose length is the same as the length of the side of the square cross-section is usually called a *cube*. A right solid of constant circular cross-section is known as a *cylinder*, while the solid has a constant annular cross-section called a *pipe*.

The volume of any right prism, or solid corresponding to a right prism, is the product of the area of the constant cross-section and the distance between the ends. A prism is usually visualized as standing on an end, when the distance between the ends is normally known as the height.

If a rectangular prism has overall dimensions L, B and H, the volume V is given by the formula:

$$V = LBH$$

(In a cube B and H are both equal to L and $V = L^3$.)

If a cylinder has a radius r and a height h, the volume is given by:

$$V = \pi r^2 h$$

or, in terms of the diameter d:

$$V = \frac{\pi d^2 h}{4}$$

If a pipe has an outside diameter D, an inside diameter d, and a height h, the volume V is given by:

$$V = \frac{\pi}{4}(D^2 - d^2)h$$

In the case of a pipe, it is more usual to have the distance between the ends much greater than a diameter, and we generally refer to the 'length' of a pipe and use the formula:

$$V = \frac{\pi}{4}(D^2 - d^2)L$$

Example

Assuming that there is no reduction in volume during the processing, what length of wire of diameter 2·5 mm can be manufactured from a piece of material in the form of a cylinder of diameter 20 mm and length 150 mm?

> Volume of wire = volume of initial cylinder
> Let the length of wire be x.

Working in millimetres:

$$\frac{\pi}{4}(2\cdot5)^2 \times x = \frac{\pi}{4}(20)^2 \times 150$$

Mathematics for Mechanical Technicians 1

Divide all through by $\frac{\pi}{4}$:

$$(2 \cdot 5)^2 \times x = (20)^2 \times 150$$
$$6 \cdot 25 \times x = 400 \times 150$$
$$x = \frac{400 \times 150}{6 \cdot 25}$$
$$\therefore x = 9\ 600$$

Answer: Length of wire $= 9\ 600$ mm $= 9 \cdot 6$ m

Example

A solid roller of diameter 4 mm has a length of 20 mm. In order to reduce the mass of the roller a co-axial flat-bottomed hole is drilled in the roller of diameter 2 mm and depth 16 mm. Calculate the percentage reduction in mass.

Mass is proportional to volume, so the problem can be worked through on volumes. Working in millimetre units:

$$\text{Volume of original roller} = \frac{\pi d^2 h}{4}$$
$$= \pi(4)^2 \times 20 \div 4$$
$$= 4\pi \times 20$$
$$= 80\pi$$
$$\text{Volume of metal removed} = \pi(2^2) \times 16 \div 4$$
$$= \pi \times 16$$
$$= 16\pi$$
$$\text{Percentage reduction in volume} = \frac{\text{volume removed}}{\text{original volume}} \times 100\%$$
$$= \frac{16\pi}{80\pi} \times 100\%$$
$$= \tfrac{1}{5} \times 100\%$$
$$= 20\%$$

Answer: Reduction in mass $= 20\%$

(The reader should note that since all volumes are multiples of π it was decided not to evaluate actual volumes.)

Example

A cylindrical open-topped canister is to be pressed from sheet metal so that its diameter is equal to its height. The capacity of the canister is to be one litre ($= 10^6$ mm^3). Determine its diameter.

Let the diameter $= d$ mm

Volume of canister V = area of cross-section × height

$$V = \frac{\pi d^2}{4} \times d = \frac{\pi d^3}{4}$$

$$\frac{\pi d^3}{4} = 10^6$$

$$d^3 = \frac{4 \times 10^6}{\pi}$$

$$d = \sqrt[3]{\left(\frac{4 \times 10^6}{\pi}\right)} = 109 \cdot 2 \text{ mm}$$

Rough check:
$$\sqrt[3]{1} \times \sqrt[3]{10^6} = 1 \times 10^2$$
$$= 100$$

No.		Log
4		0·602 1
10^6		6·000 0
Num.		6·602 1
π		0·497 2
Root	3	6·104 9
109·2		2·038 3

Answer: Diameter = 109 mm

5.4.2 PYRAMIDS AND CONES

A *pyramid* is a solid which tapers uniformly from a plane figure to a point. Unless it is specifically stated to the contrary, a pyramid is assumed to be a *right pyramid*, in which a regular polygon known as the base lies at right angles to the axis joining the point to the centre of the base. A section of any pyramid taken at right angles to the base and cutting through the axis reveals a triangle. Pyramids are described by the polygon which forms the base, such as a square pyramid, a rectangular pyramid, and so on. The solid which tapers uniformly from a circular base to a point is called a *cone*.

A pyramid is usually visualized in its most stable position, standing on its base. Bearing in mind that when we say pyramids, without qualification, we are referring to right pyramids, the height of a pyramid is the distance from the point to the centre of the base. The same definition can apply to a cone.

We cannot reason formulae for the volumes of pyramids as we can with prisms. The reader must accept for the time being, although it will be proved in a later stage of the course, that the volume of any solid of pyramid form is one third of the product of the area of the base and the height.

Hence if a square pyramid has a base in the form of a square whose side has a length L, the height of the pyramid being H, then the volume V is given by:

$$V = \frac{L^2 H}{3}$$

Similarly, if a cone has a base of radius r and a height h, the volume V is given by the formula:

$$V = \frac{\pi r^2 h}{3}$$

or, in terms of the diameter d:

$$V = \frac{\pi d^2 h}{12}$$

A frustum of a pyramid is a portion cut off by two parallel planes. We shall only be concerned with frustums produced by cutting planes of *right* pyramids, that is, pyramids whose centre lines are at right angles to their bases, and also where the cutting planes are parallel to the base.

If h is the height of the frustum, A the area revealed by one cutting plane, and B the area revealed by the other cutting plane:

$$\text{volume of the frustum} = \frac{h}{3}\left\{A + \sqrt{(AB)} + B\right\}$$

With the particular case of the frustum of a cone, if the cutting planes reveal circles of diameters R and r:

$$A = \pi R^2, \quad B = \pi r^2$$
$$\sqrt{(AB)} = \sqrt{\{(\pi R^2)(\pi r^2)\}} = \sqrt{\{\pi^2 R^2 r^2\}} = \pi R r$$

$\therefore$ volume of a frustum of a cone $= \dfrac{h}{3}\left\{A + \sqrt{(AB)} + B\right\}$

$$= \frac{h}{3}\left\{\pi R^2 + \pi R r + \pi r^2\right\}$$

Volume of a frustum of a cone $= \dfrac{\pi h}{3}\left\{R^2 + R r + r^2\right\}$

Example

Figure 5.40 shows a countersunk head rivet. The rivets are made by cutting off blanks from bar of diameter 5 mm and then forging the head. At what length should the blanks be cut off?

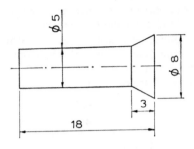

FIG. 5.40

The head is the frustum of a cone:

$$\text{Volume} = \frac{\pi h}{3} (R^2 + Rr + r^2)$$
$$= \frac{3\pi}{3} (4^2 + 4 \times 2\cdot5 + 2\cdot5^2)$$
$$= \pi (16 + 10 + 6\cdot25)$$
$$= 32\cdot25\pi$$

This is to be forged from a cylinder of diameter 5 mm. Let length of cylinder be L:

$$\pi(5)^2 L = 32\cdot25\pi$$
$$L = \frac{32\cdot25\pi}{6\cdot25\pi}$$
$$= 5\cdot16 \text{ mm}$$

Increased length required $= 5\cdot16 - 3 = 2\cdot16$
∴ Length of blank $= 18 + 2\cdot16 = 20\cdot16$

Answer: Length of blank $= 20\cdot2$ mm

5.4.3 THE VOLUME OF A SPHERE, A SPHERICAL CAP AND A SPHERICAL ZONE

A *sphere* is a solid where any point on its surface is equidistant from a point within that sphere known as the *centre*. The distance between the centre of the sphere and its surface is called the *radius* of the sphere. If a sphere is cut by any plane, a circular plane is revealed. If the cutting plane passes through the centre the section revealed is a circle whose radius is equal to that of the sphere. The sphere would be divided into two *hemispheres*.

If a single cutting plane does not pass through the centre of the sphere, it divides the sphere into two portions of unequal volumes.

The smaller of these portions is called a *spherical cap*. A *zone* of a sphere is that portion of a sphere which lies between two parallel cutting planes. At present our knowledge of mathematics is insufficient to deduce formulae connected with a sphere logically, and these must be accepted without proof.

The volume V of a sphere of radius r is given by the formula:

$$V = \frac{4\pi r^3}{3}$$

or, in terms of the diameter d:

$$V = \frac{\pi d^3}{6}$$

The volume V of a spherical cap cut from a sphere of radius r, the height of the cap being h, is given by:

$$V = \pi h^2 \left(r - \frac{h}{3} \right)$$

The volume V of a spherical zone of height h, the radii of the two circles revealed by the cutting planes being r_1 and r_2 is given by the formula:

$$V = \frac{\pi h}{6} \{3(r_1{}^2 + r_2{}^2) + h^2\}$$

Example

A hot-water tank has the form of a vertical cylinder surmounted by a hemisphere, the cylinder and hemisphere having the same diameter. If the diameter of the cylinder is 500 mm and the capacity of the tank is 200 litres, find the overall height of the tank.

$$1 \text{ m}^3 \text{ contains } 1\,000 \text{ litres, hence } V = \frac{200}{1\,000} = 0 \cdot 2 \text{ m}^3$$

$$500 \text{ mm} = 0 \cdot 5 \text{ m}$$

Let the common diameter be d and the height of the cylinder be h.

$$\text{Capacity} = \text{volume of cylinder} + \text{volume of hemisphere}$$

$$= \frac{\pi d^2 h}{4} + \frac{\pi d^3}{12}$$

$$= \frac{\pi d^2}{12}(3h + d)$$

$$0 \cdot 2 = \frac{\pi}{2 \times 2 \times 12}(3h + 0 \cdot 5)$$

$$3h + 0 \cdot 5 = \frac{0 \cdot 2 \times 2 \times 2 \times 12}{\pi} = \frac{9 \cdot 6}{\pi} = 3 \cdot 056$$

$$3h = 3 \cdot 056 - 0 \cdot 5 = 2 \cdot 556$$

$$h = \frac{2 \cdot 556}{3} = 0 \cdot 852$$

Overall height $= h + r = 0 \cdot 852 + 0 \cdot 25 = 1 \cdot 102$

Answer: Overall height $= 1 \cdot 10$ m

Example

Figure 5.41 shows the proportions of a storage vessel having a cylindrical portion between two hemispherical ends.

   (*a*) Taking π as $\frac{22}{7}$, deduce the simplest formula for its volume V in terms of R.

   (*b*) Find the capacity, in litres, when R is 500 mm.

   (*c*) Find the value of R, in millimetres, to give a capacity of 500 litres.

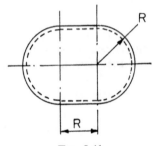

FIG. 5.41

(*a*) $V =$ volume of a sphere of radius R + volume of a cylinder of radius R and length R

$$= \frac{4 \pi R^3}{3} + \pi R^2 \times R = \frac{4 \pi R^3}{3} + \pi R^3$$

$$= \frac{4 \pi R^3 + 3 \pi R^3}{3} = \frac{7 \pi R^3}{3} = \frac{7 \times 22 \times R^3}{7 \times 3} = \frac{22 R^3}{3}$$

(*b*) 500 mm $= 0 \cdot 5$ m

$$V = \frac{22 R^3}{3} = \frac{22 \times 0 \cdot 5 \times 0 \cdot 5 \times 0 \cdot 5 \text{ m}^3}{3} = \frac{11}{12} \text{ m}^3$$

$$1 \text{ m}^3 = 1\,000 \text{ litres}$$

$$\text{Capacity} = \frac{11 \times 1\,000}{12} \text{ litres} = 916\cdot7 \text{ litres}$$

(c) $500 \text{ litres} = 0\cdot5 \text{ m}^3$

$$\frac{22R^3}{3} = 0\cdot5, \ R^3 = \frac{3 \times 0\cdot5}{22} = \frac{1\cdot5}{22} = 0\cdot068\ 2$$

$$R = \sqrt[3]{0\cdot068\ 2} = 0\cdot408\ 6 \text{ m} = 408\cdot6 \text{ mm}$$

Rough check: $0\cdot4^3 = 0\cdot064$

> **Answer:** (a) Volume $= \dfrac{22R^3}{3}$
> (b) Capacity $= 917$ litres
> (c) Radius $= 409$ mm

Example

A dowel has a diameter of 6 mm and an overall length of 15 mm. The dowel has ends which have spherical radii of 5 mm. One estimator in calculating the volume neglects the effect of the spherical caps on the ends of the dowels and considers them to be cylinders of diameter 6 mm and length 15 mm. A second estimator works precisely. What is the percentage error of the inaccurate estimator?

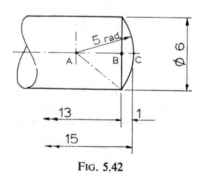

Fig. 5.42

Figure 5.42 shows the end of the dowel, with important dimensions deduced as follows: Using the 3, 4, 5 rule for a right-angled triangle, $AB = 4$ mm, $BC = 1$ mm.

A dowel consists of a cylinder of radius 3 mm and length 13 mm, with two spherical caps of radius 5 mm and height 1 mm.

Accurate method:

Volume of dowel = volume of cylinder
$$+ 2(\text{volume of spherical cap})$$
$$= \pi(3^2)13 + 2\{\pi(1)^2(5 - \tfrac{1}{3})\}$$
$$= 117\pi + 9\tfrac{1}{3}\pi$$
$$= 126\tfrac{1}{3}\pi \text{ mm}^3$$

Inaccurate method:

Volume of dowel = volume of cylinder of radius
$$\qquad\qquad 3 \text{ mm and height 15 mm}$$
$$= \pi(3^2)15$$
$$= 135\pi$$

Amount of error $= (135\pi - 126\tfrac{1}{3})\text{mm}^3$
$$= 8\tfrac{2}{3}\pi \text{ mm}^3$$

Percentage inaccuracy $= \dfrac{\text{amount of error}}{\text{correct volume}} \times 100\%$

No.	Log
2 600 379	3·415 0 2·578 6
6·861	0·83ᴏ 4

$$= \frac{8\tfrac{2}{3} \text{ mm}^3}{126\tfrac{1}{3} \text{ mm}^3} \times 100\%$$

$$= \left(\frac{26}{3} \times \frac{3}{379}\right) 100\%$$

$$= \frac{2\,600}{379}\% = 6.861\%$$

Rough check: $\qquad \dfrac{9}{125} = \dfrac{72}{1\,000} = \dfrac{7.2}{100} = 7.2\%$

Answer: Inaccuracy $= 6.86\%$

5.4.4 THE VOLUME OF SIMILAR SOLIDS

If a first sphere has a diameter d, and a second sphere has a diameter n times larger, so that the diameter of the second sphere is nd, then:

$$\frac{\text{volume of second sphere}}{\text{volume of first sphere}} = \frac{\pi(nd)^3}{6} \times \frac{6}{\pi d^3}$$

$$= \frac{6\pi n^3 d^3}{6\pi d^3} = n^3$$

In a similar manner, if the linear dimensions of a second cone are each n times the linear dimensions of a first cone, i.e.

radius of first cone $= r$ height of first cone $= h$
radius of second cone $= nr$ height of second cone $= nh$

327

then $\dfrac{\text{volume of second cone}}{\text{volume of first cone}} = \dfrac{\pi(nr)^2(nh)}{3} \times \dfrac{3}{\pi r^2 h}$

$$= \dfrac{3\pi n^3 r^2 h}{3\pi r^2 h} = n^3$$

We could proceed in a similar manner for all solids. We should find that if a second solid has all linear dimensions n times the corresponding linear dimensions of a first solid, then:

$$\dfrac{\text{volume of second solid}}{\text{volume of first solid}} = n^3$$

5.4.5 THE THEOREMS OF PAPPUS (OR GULDINUS)

If a right-angled triangle is rotated about one of the sides containing the right angle for one complete revolution, the *solid of revolution* swept out in space will be a cone. Similarly, the solid of revolution known as a sphere can be generated by rotating a semicircle for one complete revolution about a diameter.

If in rotating the right-angled triangle we consider the line which forms the hypotenuse, one revolution generates a *surface of revolution* which is the curved surface of the cone. The base of the triangle generates a circle.

Two very useful theorems, due to Pappus (or Guldinus), allow us to calculate the area of surfaces of revolution and the volumes of solids of revolution:

Theorem 1: *If a curve does not cut an axis, and rotates about that axis, it generates a surface whose area is the length of the curve multiplied by the distance travelled by its centroid.* (Note that a straight line can be considered as an arc of infinite radius.)

Theorem 2: *If an area does not cut an axis, and rotates about that axis, it generates a solid whose volume is the area multiplied by the distance travelled by its centroid.*

If there is one complete revolution about the axis, the theorems can be expressed as simple formulae.

For surfaces:

if L = length of curve
$\bar{x}$ = distance from centroid of curve to axis of rotation
A = surface area generated
then $A = 2\pi L\bar{x}$

For volumes:

if A = area being rotated

         $\bar{x}$ = distance from centroid to axis of rotation

         V = volume generated

then $V = 2\pi A\bar{x}$

Example

Find the volume of a cone of radius r and vertical height h. The cone is generated by rotating a right-angled triangle of base r and vertical height h about the vertical side. (See Figure 5.43.)

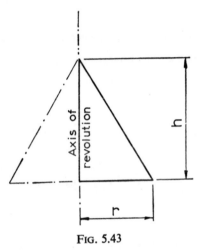

FIG. 5.43

The centroid of the triangle is $\dfrac{r}{3}$ from the axis of revolution.

$$V = 2\pi A\bar{x}$$
$$= 2\pi \times \frac{rh}{2} \times \frac{r}{3}$$
$$\therefore V = \frac{\pi r^2 h}{3}$$

Answer: Volume of cone $= \dfrac{\pi r^2 h}{3}$

Example

Find the volume of a circular anchor ring of mean diameter D made from material having a circular cross-section of diameter d.

329

$$V = 2\pi A\bar{x}$$

$$= 2\pi \times \frac{\pi d^2}{4} \times \frac{D}{2}$$

$$\therefore V = \frac{\pi^2 d^2 D}{4}$$

Answer: Volume of anchor ring $= \dfrac{\pi^2 d^2 D}{4}$

The theorem can be used in reverse to find the position of the centroid of plane figures, as in the following two examples.

Example

How far from the diameter is the centroid of a semicircle?

Rotating the semicircle about a diameter generates a sphere:

$$V = 2\pi A\bar{x}$$

$$\therefore \bar{x} = \frac{V}{2\pi A} = \frac{\dfrac{4\pi r^3}{3}}{2\pi\left(\dfrac{\pi r^2}{2}\right)}$$

$$= \frac{4\pi r^3}{3} \times \frac{1}{2\pi} \times \frac{2}{\pi r^2}$$

$$= \frac{4r}{3\pi}$$

Answer: The centroid of a semicircle is at $\dfrac{4r}{3\pi}$ from the diameter

Example

Show that the distance y to the centroid of the shaded area in Figure 5.44 is approximately equal to $\dfrac{2r}{9}$.

If the shaded area be rotated about the line AA, it will generate a solid whose volume is that of a cylinder of radius r and height r minus the volume of a hemisphere of radius r.

$$V = 2\pi A\bar{x}$$
$$= (\pi r^2 \times r) - \tfrac{1}{2}(\tfrac{4}{3}\pi r^3)$$
$$= \pi r^3 - \tfrac{2}{3}\pi r^3 = \frac{\pi r^3}{3}$$

$$A = r^2 - \frac{\pi r^2}{4} = r^2 \left(1 - \frac{\pi}{4} \right)$$

$$\bar{x} = \frac{V}{2\pi A} = \frac{\dfrac{\pi r^3}{3}}{2\pi r^2 \left(1 - \dfrac{\pi}{4} \right)}$$

$$= \frac{\pi r^3}{6\pi r^2 \left(1 - \dfrac{\pi}{4} \right)} = \frac{r}{6 \left(1 - \dfrac{\pi}{4} \right)} = \frac{r}{6(1 - 0.785\,4)}$$

$$= \frac{r}{6(0.214\,6)} = \frac{r}{1.287\,6} = 0.776\,6\,r$$

$$y = r - 0.776\,6\,r = 0.223\,4\,r = \text{approximately } \frac{2r}{9}$$

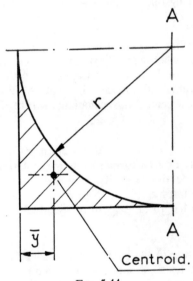

FIG. 5.44

Problems 5.4

1. A length of 250 mm is cut off from a bar of rectangular section 120 mm × 40 mm. The block is subsequently machined to a rectangular prism 117 mm × 36 mm × 240 mm. What percentage of the bar is removed by machining?

2. A component consists of a bar of steel of 40 mm × 5 mm rectangular section and length 120 mm. In a large face, four holes of diameter 20 mm are bored straight through the 5 mm thickness. What percentage of metal is removed by the boring process?

3. The blank for a hexagon-head bolt consists of a hexagonal prism 22 mm across flats and 9 mm long together with a circular prism of diameter 14 mm and length 40 mm. Presuming the blanks are cold-headed from circular bar of diameter 14 mm without loss of volume, calculate the length of bar required per blank.

4. In an impact extrusion process, a cylindrical slug has a diameter of 20 mm and a length of 30 mm. A punch of hexagonal cross-section 14 mm across flats enters one end; the diameter remains at 20 mm, and when the slug is removed from the die the hexagonal hole is flat-bottomed and of depth 10 mm. Presuming that the ends of the slug remain flat, by how much has its length been increased?

5. A duct has a flat bottom of width 240 mm. The sides slope outwards so that when water flows in the duct, the cross-sectional area of flow is in the form of a trapezium. If the width of flow at the water level is 400 mm and the depth of flow is 125 mm, the velocity of flow being 2 m/s, calculate the rate of flow in litres per hour.

6. A strip of steel, of rectangular section 20 mm × 0·25 mm is wound tightly on to a former of diameter 450 mm to produce a coil of outside diameter 600 mm and thickness 20 mm. By equating volumes of the strip in its coiled and uncoiled form, calculate the length of strip, in metres, that has been wound on the former.

7. A rough casting in the form of a short length of piping has an outside diameter of 80 mm, an inside diameter of 60 mm and a length of 125 mm. During machining, 2·5 mm is removed from every surface. Taking π as $\frac{22}{7}$, determine the percentage of the original volume removed by machining.

8. Assuming no loss of volume in the process, what length of section shown in Figure 5.45 can be extruded from a solid billet of diameter 35 mm and length 80 mm?

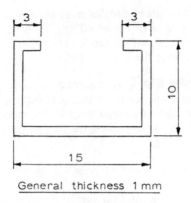

General thickness 1 mm

Fig. 5.45

9. Calculate the capacity, in litres, of a cylindrical storage tank whose internal dimensions are a diameter of 700 mm and a length of 1 200 mm.

10. A metal billet of diameter 30 mm and length 80 mm is eventually processed into discs of diameter 10 mm and thickness 1 mm. Assuming no loss of metal, calculate the number of discs produced.

11. A vertical section on the axis of a right circular cone reveals an isosceles triangle with one side of length 100 mm and two sides of length 130 mm. Calculate, taking π as $\frac{22}{7}$, the vertical height and the volume of the cone.

12. The base radius R, the top radius r and the height h of the frustum of a cone are in the proportion of 7 : 4 : 7 respectively. If the volume is 5 456 mm³, take π as $\frac{22}{7}$ and determine the height of the frustum.

13. A pan-head rivet of diameter 15 mm has a head in the form of the frustum of a cone. The diameters of the frustum are 28 mm and 20 mm, the height being 6 mm. If the length under the head of the rivet is 40 mm, calculate the volume of material in a single rivet.

14. A vessel with a constant circular cross-section of diameter 50 mm contains water to a depth of 60 mm. If a sphere of diameter 40 mm is completely submerged in the water, how much higher does the water level rise in the vessel?

15. The volume of a hollow sphere made of thin material is often taken as the external surface area multiplied by the thickness of material. Find the percentage error if this method is used for a hollow sphere of outside diameter 50 mm and inside diameter 48 mm.

16. The head of a snap rivet of nominal diameter 10 mm can be assumed to be the cap of a sphere of radius 8 mm and height 6 mm. Calculate the total volume of a 10 mm snap rivet which holds together plates of total thickness 20 mm, i.e. that of two spherical caps and a cylindrical portion. (Take π as $\frac{22}{7}$.)

17. A sphere has a radius of 15 mm. Parallel planes cut the sphere between the centre and the outside, at distances of 9 mm and 12 mm from the centre. Calculate the volume of the zone of the sphere between the cutting planes. (Take π as $\frac{22}{7}$.)

18. By considering a pipe to be a solid of revolution obtained by rotating a rectangular area about a centre line, obtain a formula for the volume of a pipe of outside diameter D, inside diameter d and length L.

19. (a) Obtain a formula for the volume of a circular chain ring of mean diameter D made from material of circular cross-section of diameter d.
    (b) Obtain the volume of such a ring when $D = 35$ mm and $d = 4$ mm.
    (c) Obtain the volume of a similar ring whose dimensions are twice those given in (b).

Answers to Problems 5.4

1. 15·8%
2. 26·2%
3. 64·5 mm
4. 35·4 mm
5. 4 800
6. 495 m

7. 52%
8. 2 080 mm
9. 462 litres
10. 720
11. 120 mm, 314 000 mm²
12. 14 mm
13. 4 900 mm³
14. 17·1 mm
15. 4·11%
16. 2 930 mm³
17. 1 080 mm³
18. $V = \dfrac{\pi(D^2 - d^2)L}{4}$

19. (a) $V = \dfrac{\pi^2 d^2 D}{4}$ (b) 1 380 mm³   (c) 11 100 mm³

5.5 Mass Calculation from Drawings

5.5.1 DENSITY AND RELATIVE DENSITY

The mass of an object composed of one substance only can be accurately estimated from a drawing of that object by determining its volume, and then multiplying that volume by the mass per unit volume of the substance from which the object is made.

The mass per unit volume of a substance is known as the *density* of that substance. The basic SI unit of mass is the kilogramme. The basic SI unit of volume is derived from the basic unit of length, and will therefore be the metre cubed, or cubic metre. Hence the basic unit of density is the kilogramme per cubic metre, the abbreviation for which is kg/m³.

When metric units were first being formulated, about the time of the French Revolution, one gramme was taken as the mass of a cubic centimetre of water. This was a reasonable basis for use at that time but, unfortunately for very precise work, water has a variable density. The variation of the density of water depends mainly upon temperature, but it also depends upon the amount of dissolved gases, this latter amount itself depending upon pressure. However, the variation in the density of water is not significantly large in terms of the accuracy required in our present studies. We can therefore assume, for the purposes of our studies, that:

$$\text{density of water} = 1 \text{ g/cm}^3$$

We are using SI units as a first order of preference, and:

$$1 \text{ g} = 10^{-3} \text{ kg} \qquad \text{while} \qquad 1 \text{ cm}^3 = 10^{-6} \text{ m}^3$$

$$\text{then density of water} = \frac{10^{-3} \text{ kg}}{10^{-6} \text{ m}^3} = 10^3 \text{ kg/m}^3$$

$$= 1\,000 \text{ kg/m}^3$$

It is interesting to note that a further convenient practical value for the density of water, since there are 1 000 litres in a cubic metre, is one kilogramme per litre.

The symbol for density is the small Greek letter rho (ρ). Sometimes we find it convenient to compare the density of a given substance with the density of water. The *relative density* of a substance (symbol d) is the ratio:

$$\frac{\text{density of that substance}}{\text{density of water}}$$

As a typical example, the relative density of aluminium is about 2·70. Hence for aluminium:

$$d = \frac{\rho}{1\,000 \text{ kg/m}^3}$$

and $\qquad \rho = d \times 1\,000 \text{ kg/m}^3 = \text{about } 2{\cdot}7 \times 1\,000 \text{ kg/m}^3$
$$= \text{about } 2\,700 \text{ kg/m}^3$$

The following tables give some approximate relative densities of materials commonly used in engineering:

Magnesium	1·74	Brass (60 Cu/40 Zn)	8·36
Aluminium	2·70	Brass (70 Cu/30 Zn)	8·44
Zinc	7·10	Brass (90 Cu/10 Sn)	8·78
Tin	7·30	Nickel	8·80
Cast iron	7·00–7·80	Copper	8·89
Carbon steel	7·84	Lead	11·30

5.5.2 SPECIFIC GRAVITY

At a later stage in technician studies we shall be introduced to weight. The *weight* of a body is the gravitational force exerted on the mass of that body. The SI unit of force is the newton, and hence, theoretically speaking, a weight should be expressed in newtons. In everyday life, we shall often hear people refer to a 'weight of one kilogramme'. Such a statement is theoretically incorrect, but it is tolerated, somewhat reluctantly by the purist, in everyday life.

The specific weight of a substance is the weight of unit volume. The *specific gravity* of a substance is the ratio:

$$\frac{\text{specific weight of that substance}}{\text{specific weight of water}}$$

We shall see eventually that the weight of a body is directly proportional to its mass, and hence the specific gravity of a substance has precisely the same numerical value as its relative density. It seems, therefore, that it is irrelevant which expression is employed, but as a first order of preference, since we are dealing with masses, the expression relative density should be used.

5.5.3 MANIPULATION OF UNITS

The conventional unit of length used on engineering drawings is the millimetre. The calculation of volumes using the millimetre invariably results in very large numbers. It may therefore seem advisable to use a larger unit of length. The next larger preferred unit of length is the metre. However, for general usage this is usually too large. It may therefore be suggested that a unit between the millimetre and the metre will prove satisfactory. The centimetre is immediately brought to mind, particularly since a material having a relative density of d has a density of d g/cm^3.

However, let us not proceed hastily. If the centimetre is used, this means that every linear dimension not in centimetres has to be converted to centimetres, and it is easy to make an error. Errors are even more likely in the conversion of areas and volumes. As a general rule, the reader is advised to compute a volume in terms of the units used for the particular item under consideration, then to convert this volume into cubic metres as a single step. A density should be established in kg/m^3, and the final computation gives the mass in kilogrammes when the volume in m^3 is multiplied by the density in kg/m^3. On the rare occasions when there is a combination of different units in the original data, one of these units should be selected, choice falling on the one which results in the least number of conversions. To a reader whose previous education has included the use of metric quantities this may seem a little unwieldy, especially if he is accustomed to working in a centimetre-gramme-second system. However, let him be assured that in later studies there is much to say for converting all values into basic SI units before applying them to a formula. It is therefore suggested that this principle should be firmly established before studies progress too far.

To facilitate computation, the reader should note:

$$1 \text{ mm}^3 = 10^{-9} \text{ m}^3$$

and
$$1 \text{ cm}^3 = 10^{-6} \text{ m}^3$$

Even quite complicated geometrical configurations can be divided into simpler geometrical shapes for which there are standard formulae for evaluating volumes. The arithmetical work involved can be considerably eased by the use of tabulated data. It is pointless to compute areas if they are readily available in works of reference, unless it is advantageous for the particular purposes of a solution to leave an area as a multiple of π. Many reference works provide excellent tables of items such as the mass per metre run of circular steel bars, the mass per metre run of flat copper bars, and so on.

Example

A factory orders 2 metric tonnes of rectangular steel sheets 1·6 m × 1·2 m of nominal thickness 1·6 mm. If the tolerance on the thickness is 1·60 mm to 1·70 mm, what is:

    (*a*) the greatest number,   (*b*) the least number

of complete sheets that can be expected? (1 metric tonne = 1 000 kg and take the relative density of steel to be 7·85.)

Let all the sheets be piled into a slab 1·6 m × 1·2 m and thickness t m.

$$\rho = 1\,000\, d \text{ kg/m}^3 = 7\,850 \text{ kg/m}^3$$

$$\rho = \frac{m}{V} \quad \therefore V = \frac{m}{\rho} = \frac{2 \times 1\,000}{7\,850} \frac{\text{kg} \times \text{m}^3}{\text{kg}}$$

$$= \frac{1\,000}{3\,925} \text{ m}^3 = 0\cdot254\,8 \text{ m}^3$$

$$V = LBt, \; t = \frac{V}{LB} = \frac{0\cdot254\,8 \text{ m}^3}{1\cdot6 \text{ m} \times 1\cdot2 \text{ m}} = 0\cdot132\,7 \text{ m}$$

$$1\cdot6 \text{ mm} = 0\cdot001\,6 \text{ m}, \qquad 1\cdot7 \text{ mm} = 0\cdot001\,7 \text{ m}$$

(*a*) Greatest number of sheets $= \dfrac{t}{\text{smallest thickness}} = \dfrac{0\cdot132\,7 \text{ m}}{0\cdot001\,6 \text{ m}}$

$$= 82\cdot94, \text{ i.e. } 82 \text{ complete sheets}$$

(*b*) Smallest number of sheets $= \dfrac{t}{\text{largest thickness}} = \dfrac{0\cdot132\,7 \text{ m}}{0\cdot00\,17 \text{ m}}$

$$= 78\cdot65, \text{ i.e. } 78 \text{ complete sheets}$$

    Answers: (*a*) Greatest number of sheets = 82
                 (*b*) Least number of sheets = 78

Example

From an engineer's reference book it is found that a metre length of steel of diameter 20 mm has a mass of 2·47 kg, and that a metre length of flat steel bar 40 mm × 10 mm has a mass of 3·14 kg. Use this information to find the mass of the lever shown in Figure 5.46.

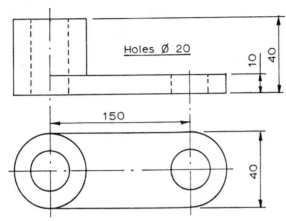

Fig. 5.46

The lever can be analysed into:

    (*a*) a cylinder of diameter 40 mm and length 40 mm,
        PLUS
    (*b*) the equivalent of a length of 150 mm of 40 mm × 10 mm flat bar,
        LESS
    (*c*) the holes, both of diameter 20 mm, totalling 50 mm in length.

The masses per metre run are proportional to the squares of their diameter.

$$\frac{\text{Mass per metre run of 40 mm bar}}{\text{Mass per metre run of 20 mm bar}} = \left(\frac{40}{20}\right)^2 = 4$$

Mass per metre run of 40 mm bar $= 4 \times 2\cdot47 = 9\cdot88$ kg

$$\text{Total mass} = \left(9\cdot88 \times \frac{40}{1\,000}\right) + \left(3\cdot14 \times \frac{150}{1\,000}\right) - \left(2\cdot47 \times \frac{50}{1\,000}\right)$$

$$= 0\cdot395\,2 \text{ kg} + 0\cdot471 \text{ kg} - 0\cdot123\,5 \text{ kg}$$
$$= 0\cdot866\,2 \text{ kg} - 0\cdot123\,5 \text{ kg}$$
$$= 0\cdot742\,7 \text{ kg}$$

Answer: Mass of lever $= 0\cdot743$ kg

Example

Calculate the mass of the light alloy vee-pulley shown in Figure 5.47. Take the density of the light alloy as 2 750 kg/m³ and π as $\frac{22}{7}$. Depth of the vee-groove is 22·5 mm.

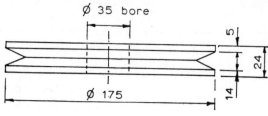

Fig. 5.47

The volume can be analysed into the volume of a cylindrical disc minus the volume of the hole minus the volume of the vee-groove.

Volume of cylinder of $\phi175$ and thickness 24

$$= \frac{\pi d^2 h}{4} = \frac{22 \times 175 \times 175 \times 24}{7 \times 4} = 577\,500 \text{ mm}^3$$

Volume of hole of $\phi35$ and length 24

$$= \frac{\pi d^2 h}{4} = \frac{22 \times 35 \times 35 \times 24}{7 \times 4} = 23\,100 \text{ mm}^3$$

Volume of groove $= 2\pi A\bar{x}$

$$= \frac{44}{7} \left(\frac{14 \times 22\cdot5}{2} \right) \left(87\cdot5 - \frac{22\cdot5}{3} \right) = \frac{44 \times 157\cdot5 \times 80}{7}$$

$$= 79\,200 \text{ mm}^3$$

Volume of pulley $= \begin{pmatrix} \text{volume of} \\ \text{cylinder} \end{pmatrix} - \begin{pmatrix} \text{volume of} \\ \text{hole} \end{pmatrix} - \begin{pmatrix} \text{volume of} \\ \text{groove} \end{pmatrix}$

$$= 577\,500 - 23\,100 - 79\,200$$
$$= 577\,500 - 102\,300 = 475\,200 \text{ mm}^3$$

$$1 \text{ mm}^3 = 10^{-9} \text{ m}^3$$
$$V = 475\,200 \times 10^{-9} \text{ m}^3$$
$$\rho = 2\,750 \text{ kg/m}^3$$

$$\rho = \frac{m}{V}, \qquad m = V\rho$$

Mass of pulley $= 2\,750 \times 475\,200 \times 10^{-9} \dfrac{\text{m}^3 \times \text{kg}}{\text{m}^3}$

$$= 1\cdot307 \text{ kg}$$

No.	Log
2 750	3·439 3
475 200	5·676 9
10^{-9}	$\bar{9}$·000 0
1·307	0·116 2

Rough check:

$3 \times 10^{-3} \times 5 \times 10^5 \times 10^{-9}$

$= 15 \times 10^{-1} = \dfrac{15}{10} = 1.5$

Answer: Mass of pulley = 1·31 kg

Problems 5.5

1. A circular bar of a particular aluminium alloy with a diameter of 50 mm and a length of 200 mm has a mass of 1·1 kg. Calculate:
   - (*a*) the density of the alloy, in kg/m^3;
   - (*b*) the relative density of the alloy.

2. (*a*) If copper has a relative density of 8·89, calculate its density in kg/m^3.
   - (*b*) Calculate the mass, in kilogrammes, of a copper bus-bar of rectangular section 50 mm × 16 mm and length 7·5 m.

3. Taking the density of 70 Cu/30 Zn brass as 8 440 kg/m^3, construct a table that will give the mass, in kilogrammes per square metre, of 70 Cu/30 Zn brass sheets of thickness 1, 1·6, 2·5 and 4 mm.

4. Taking the relative density of steel to be 7·84, and where necessary π as $\frac{22}{7}$, calculate the mass, in kilogrammes per metre run, of:
   - (*a*) circular bar of diameter 50 mm;
   - (*b*) flat bar of 50 mm × 16 mm section;
   - (*c*) pipe of outside diameter 80 mm and wall thickness 10 mm.

5. Taking the density of steel to be 7 840 kg/m^3, calculate the mass, in kilogrammes, of 1 000 steel washers of outside diameter 40 mm, inside diameter 20 mm and thickness 3·2 mm.

6. Find the mass, in kilogrammes, of a triangular gusset plate with sides of length 180 mm, 200 mm and 260 mm, the thickness of the plate being 16 mm and the density of the material 7 840 kg/m^3.

7. A hollow float, closed at both ends, has the external appearance of a cylinder. The outside dimensions are a diameter of 200 mm and a depth of 100 mm. The constant metal thickness is 5 mm. Calculate its mass, in kilogrammes, if it is made of a material having a density of 8 400 kg/m^3.

8. Taking the density of steel to be 7 840 kg/m^3, what length (in metres) of steel pipe of outside diameter 40 mm and wall thickness

3 mm can be expected from one metric tonne (= 1 000 kg) of such piping?

9. A rivet can be considered to be a hemisphere of radius 20 mm, together with a cylinder of diameter 25 mm and length 70 mm. Taking the density of the rivet material to be 7 840 kg/m³, calculate the mass, in kilogrammes, of 100 rivets.

10. A sector of sheet metal is manipulated to form a cone of radius 50 mm and vertical height 120 mm. Assuming no allowance for seaming, and that a reference work states that the sheet metal has a mass of 0·9 kg/m², determine the mass of the sector, in grammes.

11. Calculate the mass, in kilogrammes, of a 400 mm length of shaft whose section is the larger segment of a circle of radius 50 mm, cut off by a chord of length 40 mm. The density of the material is 7 840 kg/m³.

12. An impurity in a casting can be assumed to take the form of a spherical bubble of air. The loss in mass due to the presence of the bubble is 20 g. The casting material has a relative density of 7·84. Calculate the diameter of the bubble, in millimetres.

13. Given that a metre length of steel of diameter 20 mm has a mass of 2·46 kg, construct a table that will give the mass per hundred of steel dowels 40 mm long, the diameters ranging from 5 mm to 25 mm in increments of 5 mm.

14. Calculate the mass, in kilogrammes, of a right-angled bend of cast iron pipe of outside diameter 190 mm and inside diameter 160 mm, the mean radius of the bend being 600 mm. The density of the particular grade of cast iron is 7 280 kg/m³, and π can be taken as $\frac{22}{7}$.

15. With the aid of the Theorem of Pappus, or otherwise, calculate the mass of the aluminium alloy sleeve shown in Figure 5.48. The density of the alloy is 2 800 kg/m³, and π can be taken as $\frac{22}{7}$.

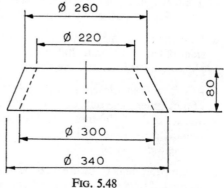

FIG. 5.48

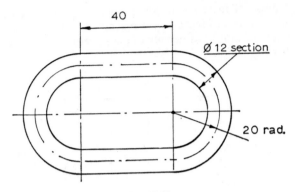

FIG. 5.49

16. Taking the mass of a metre length of steel of diameter 12 mm to be 0·9 kg, calculate the mass of 100 chain links of the kind shown in Figure 5.49.

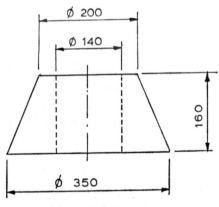

FIG. 5.50

17. Calculate the mass of the conveyor roller shown in Figure 5.50. The relative density of the material is 7·2 and π can be taken as $\frac{22}{7}$.

18. Calculate the mass, in kilogrammes, of steel removed when a semicircular groove of radius 16·5 mm is machined around a steel shaft of diameter 160 mm. The density of the steel is 7 840 kg/m³ and the centroid of a semicircle lies at $\frac{4r}{3\pi}$ from the diameter; π can be taken as $\frac{22}{7}$.

343

19. What mass of material, in kilogrammes, is removed when the chamfer shown in Figure 5.51 is machined on the end of a bar of diameter 160 mm? The density of the material is 7 840 kg/m³ and π can be taken as $\frac{22}{7}$.

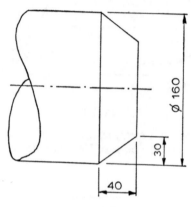

Fig. 5.51

20. Figure 5.52 shows the dimensions of an ingot cast in an alloy of relative density 2·8, the shape being that of the frustum of a rectangular pyramid. Calculate the number of ingots that can be made from one metric tonne ($= 1\,000$ kg) of the alloy.

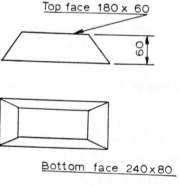

Top face 180 × 60

Bottom face 240×80

Fig. 5.52

21. Find the mass, in grammes, of the die casting shown in Figure 5.53, the material having a relative density of 2·80. Rectangular portion is 20 mm thick.

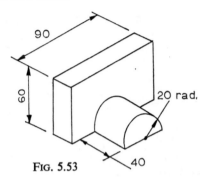

90

60

20 rad.

40

FIG. 5.53

22. Find the mass, in kilogrammes, of the casting shown in Figure 5.54, the material being a grey cast iron of density 7 200 kg/m³.

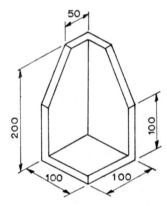

50

200

100

100   100

General thickness 10.

FIG. 5.54

23. (a) Wire of diameter 2 mm is passed through a drawing die to reduce its diameter by 20%. If the wire enters the die at a speed of 1·6 m/s, at what speed does the wire leave the die?

(b) After leaving the die, the wire is coiled around a rotating drum. At what speed is the drum rotating, in rev/min, at the instant the wire is coiling at an effective diameter of 700 mm?

(c) What mass of wire, in kilogrammes, is processed per hour? Take the density of the wire to be 8 750 kg/m³.

24. Castings are to be made to the design shown in Figure 5.55.

(a) If the material is an aluminium alloy of relative density 2·80, calculate:

(i) the mass of a single casting, in grammes;
(ii) the number of complete castings that can be obtained from one metric tonne (= 1 000 kg) of the alloy. (Neglect scrap.)

(b) If a cast iron of relative density 7·28 were substituted for the aluminium alloy and the cast iron castings cost, by mass, one quarter the price of the aluminium alloy, calculate:

(i) the percentage increase in mass;
(ii) the percentage saving at cost.

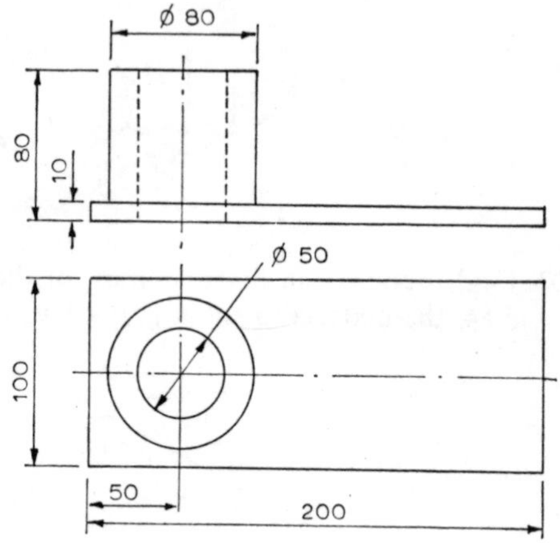

FIG. 5.55

Answers to Problems 5.5

1. (a) 2 800 kg/m³   (b) 2·8
2. (a) 8 890 kg/m³   (b) 53·3 kg
3. 8·44, 13·5, 21·1 and 33·8 kg
4. (a) 15·4 kg   (b) 6·27 kg   (c) 17·2 kg
5. 23·6 kg   7. 4·96 kg   9. 40·1 kg   11. 24·3 kg
6. 2·25 kg   8. 3 666 m   10. 18·4 g   12. 16·8 mm
13. 0·615, 2·46, 5·64, 9·84 and 15·4 kg
14. 56·6 kg   17. 52·4 kg   20. 402
15. 7·88 kg   18. 1·54 kg   21. 373 g
16. 18·5 kg   19. 2·07 kg   22. 2·96 kg
23. (a) 2·5 m/s   (b) 68·2 rev/min   (c) 158 kg
24. (a) (i) 1 100 g; (ii) 909   (b) (i) 160%; (ii) 35%